The experts praise *The Intimate Ape*

"An extraordinary book that adds to our understanding
of the animal world."

—**Jeffrey Moussaieff Masson,** author of *When Elephants Weep*

"Heartfelt, humanistic . . . makes a compelling case
for why we should save the orangutans and how we can do that
by protecting their natural habitat—the rain forest."

—**Tensie Whelan,** president, The Rainforest Alliance

"A grippng eco-travelogue."

—**Peter Fairley,** member of the board of the
Society of Environmental Journalists

"A fantastic read! Thompson's insightful portrayal of orangutans
connects us with ourselves and with our humanity."

—**Leif Cocks,** president of the Australian Orangutan Project

"An excellent book . . . vivid, unforgettable, rich, and readable."

—**Bernard E. Rollin,** author of *Animal Rights and Human Morality*

"A thrilling and intimate journey into the heart of the orangutan's
jungle world . . . unforgettable."

—**Osha Gray Davidson,** author of *Fire in the Turtle House*

"A wondrous adventure story laying bare a fight for good
in the face of tremendous odds."

—**Gisela Kaplan,** author of *The Orangutans:
Their Evolution, Behavior, and Future*

The Intimate Ape

Orangutans and the Secret Life of a Vanishing Species

Shawn Thompson

Foreword by Jeffrey Moussaieff Masson

CITADEL PRESS
Kensington Publishing Corp.
www.kensingtonbooks.com

CITADEL PRESS BOOKS are published by

Kensington Publishing Corp.
119 West 40th Street
New York, NY 10018

All Kensington titles, imprints, and distributed lines are available at special quantity discounts for bulk purchases for sales promotions, premiums, fund-raising, educational, or institutional use. Special book excerpts or customized printings can also be created to fit specific needs. For details, write or phone the office of the Kensington special sales manager: Kensington Publishing Corp., 119 West 40th Street, New York, NY 10018, attn: Special Sales Department; phone 1-800-221-2647.

CITADEL PRESS and the Citadel logo are Reg. U.S. Pat. & TM Off.

Text design by Christopher Grassi

First printing: March 2010

10   9   8   7   6   5   4   3   2   1

Printed in the United States of America

Library of Congress Control Number: 2009937070

ISBN-13: 978-0-8065-3133-5
ISBN-10: 0-8065-3133-9

To Caitlin and Pearce, my human offspring

Contents

Foreword: Orangutans, Us, and a Common Planet
by Jeffrey Moussaieff Masson

For those of us with a deep interest in animals these are fascinating times indeed. We no longer live in a time when scientists can simply ignore the complex emotional lives of animals. When my book *When Elephants Weep* came out in 1995 the time was long overdue to recognize that animals have as rich an emotional life as we do. But now a groundswell among a new generation of scientists has begun chipping away at the traditional taboo that denies the internal world of animals. Some of that new generation of scientists make appearances in this book, *The Intimate Ape.*

Like many of the people in *The Intimate Ape*, I have always had animals as part of my life. Growing up, I had pet lizards and horned toads, built frog ponds in my backyard, and had pet ducks that followed me to school and swam with me in our pool. Once, while we were on vacation, the neighbors ate the ducks. I felt awful. I was raised a vegetarian.

I was at Harvard University for a year in 1999 and spent a lot of time with the American zoologist Donald Griffin, who published books on thinking and consciousness in animals. I had already decided to write about animal emotions—nobody had done so since Darwin. Donald Griffin was amazing. He took me to beaver lodges. In his late eighties at the time, he was diving down into the lodges and inserting tiny video cameras so that he could see what the beavers did at night. He was interested in absolutely all matters about animals, completely open to everything while retaining his scientific credibility. (This was the man who discovered bat sonar.)

Griffin loved the fact that I was investigating animal emotions. He completely believed that such an investigation was essential, that it was the next step, but one he could not take because he had already been the target of so much flack for his relatively harmless comment that animals have consciousness. He showed me some of the letters he had received, and the reviews—they were horrendous. That they could attack such a gentle, kindly, great man utterly confused me. What was going on? Well, something was, but I am still not certain why scientists felt so deeply challenged by his ideas.

We need books like *The Intimate Ape* to connect us to the internal life of the animals who live on the planet with us. When I read this book, what got to me the most were the descriptions of orangutans reaching out to a human being. Something about this is riveting: touching hands, handing over the baby, allowing the person to sit close; all these things speak volumes for something wonderful going on in the mind of orangutans with respect to us. It is humbling. It is marvelous.

Now almost every day a new and wonderful book like this appears about animals, telling us things we never suspected—that animals have a sense of justice or morality, that they can be empathic with members of their own species and even of other species, that they can express gratitude.

The Intimate Ape adds to our understanding of the animal world, and particularly about orangutans, which have been neglected by other writers. Far more books have been written for a popular audience about gorillas and chimpanzees. This book rectifies that omission with an intimate portrait of so many different people involved in orangutan research, all seen through the unique prism of the author, who comes across as a real personality in his own right. It is a book that will speak to anyone interested in these amazing beings as they face extinction.

The Intimate Ape is different from other books about our animal cousins because it is about people and apes together, and the lives they share. We learn about human nature and ape nature in a single book, until we suddenly realize that we and apes really are the same. That, surely, is one of the main lessons of this book: orangutans and humans are so very much alike.

This explains why there are people (and you will meet the most fascinating among them in this book) who devote their lives to orangutans. It is another way of learning about ourselves. After all, these primates are, along with chimpanzees, bonobos, and gorillas—the great apes—our closest animal relatives. We share at least 97 percent of our DNA with orangutans and there are many ways in which we resemble one another.

Both of us need creature comforts and can be creative in finding them. One of my heroes is the University of Zurich's Carel van Schaik (you will meet him in this book). He discovered, for example, that orangutans make what appears to be a leaf doll that they take to bed with them, just as a human being would. They also decorate their nests with a row of neatly arranged twigs. These examples and others in *The Intimate Ape* suggest that orangutans have more in common with human beings than any other creature.

There are many other ways in which our two species resemble one another. Like the best human mothers, the best mother orangutans never hit, bite, or chastise their infants. They are indulgent, patient, and compassionate. In ideal conditions, the relation between a female orangutan and her infant is among the most intense in the natural world. The average interval between births is eight years, and the young will often stay with their mother even after a sibling is born. A female orangutan breast-feeds her infant for a long time. They are not weaned until age seven, as is true of only a few enlightened La Leche moms today. (In a conversation I had with the late Ashley Montagu in 1987, he convinced me that this was the ideal age for humans to wean children.)

Primarily vegetarians, orangutans eat food that, with a few exceptions, human beings can also eat. That is something I can understand as a vegan myself. Although I grew up vegetarian, I gave it up for many years and only came back to it after writing *When Elephants Weep.* Then I did the research about farm animal emotions for *The Pig Who Sang to the Moon,* and that turned me into a vegan. So I appreciate the rule of thumb in the Sumatran and Bornean forests that humans can usually eat whatever an orangutan has eaten—not true for other animal species. Here, too, they surpass us: orangutans have been known to eat more than four hundred different food types, for which they know obscure facts of botany, including details about trees that bear fruit only once in eight years.

Orangutans depend on forests in another way. Unlike us, they live in the trees and do everything an orangutan needs to do in the branches, rarely descending from them. It is safer up there. But it may not be safer for long. In an era of climate change we should take all this as a reminder from orangutans that their forests are our forests, and everything in them needs to be preserved for all our sakes.

We still have a lot to learn from orangutans. A good beginning is to read this extraordinary book. I hope others will write books as intimate as this one to extend our knowledge of all the other creatures with whom we share both emotions and a common planet.

JEFFREY MOUSSAIEFF MASSON is the author of *When Elephants Weep, The Pig Who Sang to the Moon,* and *The Face on Your Plate.* He lives in Auckland, New Zealand.

CHAPTER 1

Jungle Confidential

I KNOW MORE about orangutans than any normal human being should have to know and apparently not enough about human nature, at least not in 2001, the year that I was turning fifty and went up a muddy brown river called the Sekonyer into the jungles of southern Kalimantan, on the island of Borneo. Over the years I would come back again and again to this jungle, growing older with a hunger that would never be satisfied, that always wanted more. I would go into the jungle wanting to see orangutans as they really are, to know them the way they deserve to be known. I would come out wishing there were things that I hadn't learned, particularly about human beings, my own species, my biological kin. But you can't always make the choices in your life that you want. And once you start a thing like this you have to finish it. You can't live with yourself if you don't. It's just the way things are.

I started my foray into the jungle from the town of Pangkalan Bun, in southern Kalimantan, where there is a small airport with a goat that nibbles the sweet grass along the edge of the runway as a way of blessing the place. The first time I landed in Pangkalan Bun I imagined the goat would run in front of the airplane and make a personal sacrifice of itself. But the goat wasn't that theatrical. It was a survivor. Pangkalan Bun had one above-average hotel, where I stayed for a while before I realized it was also a brothel for business travelers. If you dialed 7 on the phone you received very personal room service. I never dialed 7, although I was curious. The rooms in the hotel were clean and the food good.

From Pangkalan Bun it's a short drive to the native Dayak village of Pasir Panjang, where there is a clinic for sick and orphan orangutans. I spent hours and hours in this sanctuary and became friends with the Spanish veterinarian there. At the clinic I got closer to orangutans than most people ever do. I kept a paralyzed orangutan company and gazed into the eyes of young orangutans curious about the world outside them. It's a strange feeling to realize for the first time that a creature like this can think and feel like you do. You are different afterward. The world has tilted at a different angle. Because of the clinic, the gateway to the village has a sign with orangutans painted on it. In one of the homes in Pasir Panjang I saw the family spirit jar and heard how it emits a light at times as an omen to the family. It is a connection to the larger forces of the universe. We all want to be connected somehow.

From Pangkalan Bun it's a half-hour drive to the old small port city of Kumai, on a gulf that empties into the Java Sea between Borneo and the island of Java. Kumai has the bustle and sense of self-importance of any small place connected by rivers to other places, with people coming and going in boats. Along the harbor are small iron freighters, maybe a naval vessel painted a naval gray, and ships with peaked bows shaped like half moons, which I imagined were arks from ancient times. At Kumai I would hire the type of slender converted fishing boat called a *klotok* to travel upriver on the Sekonyer, with a captain who didn't speak English, an assistant, and a cook. I couldn't wait for the klotok to leave Kumai for the peace and solitude and cool breezes of the river. Even a small place like Kumai felt crowded, but maybe it was the strangeness of the circumstances for me. There was so much stimulation from new sensations and new experiences that my mind felt crowded. I had to slow down to try to make sense of what was happening.

It is a four-hour trip from Kumai up the Sekonyer by a slow klotok to the orangutans wandering freely on protected park land. The illegal loggers and the poachers ignore the protected status of the land. That's what we human beings do when something isn't convenient for us. One night my klotok was anchored along the river while the captain tried to fix a broken shaft with just a hammer, when a long boom of illegal timber floated past us quietly in the dark. There went the jungle of the orangutan. Floating by in broken pieces. The trips on the Sekonyer gave me the time to think that we don't normally give ourselves. A river will do that. After several trips I got used to the rhythm of travel by klotok, the clatter of the engine, the way it echoed against the jungle, the hot, sensuous, drowsy blur of it all.

On the way upriver I'd be thinking about orangutans like Kusasi and Princess. The presence of Kusasi broods over this patch of jungle like the obscure and long-forgotten deity of a distant lost tribe. Kusasi is a three-hundred-pound male brute who has come to dominate the area around the camp where the orphan orangutans are released. Everyone fears him, orangutan and human alike. He could rip your arms and legs off like daisy petals if he wanted. People see a "steely cold" in his eyes. Princess is one of the orphans and was taught to communicate by sign language by a researcher in the late 1970s. I'd meet her several times, and I listened to the stories others told about her. After a few trips, I'd wonder if I'd see Kusasi or Princess or Siswi this time and what they were doing. Did the other orangutans still fear Kusasi or had he been beaten down yet? Had Princess had another child? Was Siswi still a flirt? Questions like these about orangutans were a way to engage others at the camp in a conversation, no matter how little you knew them. It was like being in a large family with instant relatives. You belonged.

After a while on the klotok, in the languorous equatorial heat, I would enjoy the ride so much that it felt like it didn't matter if we ever found orangutans. It seemed wrong to even think about stopping, as though your heart would stop if the boat stopped. Certainly stopping would make it hotter. The motion of the klotok created a cool breeze that you never wanted to end. When it did cease, you felt startled, like an embrace that ends before you are ready or a dream that fades too soon. I'd watch the feathery Nipa palm trees flow past on the shoreline like a film of someone else's life and couldn't remember what I normally worried about so much in my other existence. Halfway up, the river changed from the saltwater flowing up from the sea, to freshwater flowing down, and I'd wonder where the point of transformation was of one river into another. Where is the place where one thing becomes something else? How do you find that point? Can things like this in life ever be understood fully? Okay, maybe my mind was drifting a little. That happens on a river. I'd have odd arguments with myself, say to myself pointless things like, "It's never going to snow here." I probably thought of snow because of the heat.

At other times on the klotok I'd try to read my battered paperback copy of Conrad's novel of the Congo, *Heart of Darkness,* a story about the madness of Westerners in the jungle. The novel was making more sense after all the things I saw during my trips to Borneo and Sumatra. Reading *Heart of Darkness* would make me drowsy after a few pages, in the way you want to feel drowsy in the tropics. Not many people know that Conrad was in Borneo when he was a young sailor. He knew how to describe a land like this. I spent one afternoon in a small village up-river, drinking hot tea and listening to the shamans talk about ghosts in the trees and magic to keep crocodiles and bad spirits away. It all felt strangely familiar, like how I felt as a child visiting my grandfather in a town so small that even the tedium felt exotic. The bad spirits had been kept away those summers long ago.

I am not a scientist. I am not a conservationist. I am not an activist. I am a writer. Passionate and committed at times, detached at others. Living on the fringe where you look for clarity and meaning. There and not there. Over the years my role in all this jungle travel was to listen and watch and absorb the raw, unfiltered experience. When I had soaked in enough experience and sensation, talked to enough people, asked myself enough if I understood what was happening, then it was time to put words on paper, like I'm doing now in my home in the snowy, untropical mountains of British Columbia. When I told people in the small city where I live that I was writing a book about orangutans they'd pause and reflect on it. The pause and the reflection would be a little too long. Not many people talk a lot about orangutans. Is it normal to do that? Or is it just a bit weird? I don't care. If I think for a moment that there won't be a next time on the river for me, that I will never see the jungle again, that orangutans will only be a faint memory, then it feels like my heart might actually stop. I wonder what happened to me to make me feel that way. Something changed. Something was different. I'm still trying to understand what.

One of the things I struggled with while writing this book was a sense of how little power we have personally. The more I learned about orangutans, the worse I felt, until it seemed that there was little I could do myself. I am just one person. This problem is too big for me alone. The sense of powerlessness and hopelessness was a real obstacle. That would be a low point, I'd say. But I also felt that I was different because I'd seen an orangutan like Kusasi and had felt the individual force of life in him. Kusasi has a spirit that other orangutans don't have. That spirit has to come from somewhere. It has to mean something. And I also felt different because I'd met people who had a spirit in them that other people don't, like Willie Smits, a man with too much intensity in his life who cares for orangutans too much. And then I also met a Spanish veterinarian named Garriga.

It was that year, 2001, the year of my primary foray into the country of orangutans, that I met my first guide to these creatures, Rosa Maria Garriga. It's a musical name if you pronounce it the way that the *r*'s roll in Spanish. Rosa Maria Garriga was thirty-three then, still thin from smoking too many cigarettes, a wildlife veterinarian from the Catalan region of Spain who worked at the orangutan clinic in Pasir Panjang downriver from Kusasi's patch of jungle. The moment was right for me to meet her. I was in a strange, hot place, alone and vulnerable, already battered and betrayed by a series of broken promises for the help I needed to write the book, and here was an honest, dedicated, sincere woman living a solitary existence, one which fit her so naturally.

I didn't understand then why she didn't feel lonely in these circumstances. I'd been there a few days and she'd been there years, and I felt lonely. She wasn't one of those people who deaden themselves inside or become egotistical in order to have the strength to live alone. I made sense of this only later when I met other people like Garriga and realized the different needs they have in their lives. Here's an odd thought. There is a similar combination of solitude and intimacy in the life of an orangutan, since orangutans live spread out in the jungle. They don't cluster in feverish social groups like gorillas and chimpanzees. So is that a similarity between orangutans and us that we could come to understand better?

I thought I'd never see the Catalan again—and yet I did several times, once in Sabah, a Malaysian province in northern Borneo, when she came because she heard I was on my way to the Kinabatangan wilderness. I made a full trip on a klotok on the Sekonyer with her. It was one of those dreamy affairs when you chatter aimlessly, eat the food cooked on the boat, and drift in and out of a warm, drowsy state. She was always thinking about her orangutans, which were her great passion, her commitment, her life. But she also liked pizza and long, sandy beaches like everybody else. That day on the klotok we reached Kumai just around dusk with the water a sluggish, smooth gray and we saw the fin of a dolphin slice the surface of the water in the basin of the Kumai River. Just one dolphin. That's all you need. It makes you feel good inside to see a dolphin.

My new Catalan friend worked in the clinic operated by the U.S.-based Orangutan Foundation International, which also manages the camp in Tanjung Puting National Park where Kusasi and other orphan orangutans live. The clinic is one of a number of sanctuaries operated in Borneo and Sumatra by different independent organizations all working to ease the suffering of orangutans. At the clinic in Pasir Panjang there are between one hundred and two hundred orphan orangutans at any one time who are eventually released to various sites in the jungle. There are also about twenty orangutan regulars, like Kusasi, at the camp upriver, also in the care of Garriga.

It must feel overwhelming at times for her. The orangutans are sick, wounded, burned, suffering inside, suffering outside, abscessed, bleeding, infected, with noses leaking from infection, afflicted with diarrhea. Some will live. Some will die. Sometimes the orangutans came to the clinic with injuries inflicted in the palm oil plantations or from their time as illegal pets in the care of people who couldn't cope with a baby orangutan who grew wilder and stronger as it grew older. They came with slashes from machetes from people protecting their trees and crops. The numbers at the clinic rose and fell from the one-hundred-fifty mark week by week, with one full-time veterinarian for treatment. Every day the Catalan veterinarian ministered to the apes. She gave them a chance to survive when they were born. She autopsied them when they died.

Over several weeks I watched Garriga give shots and medication to orangutans. In an operating room, I saw her perform surgery on a large orangutan, under the cold blue light of a moon-size hospital lamp. It looked like a scene from an alien autopsy film. A big, shaggy, red male orangutan lay sprawled on his back on the operating table. The anesthetic had made him limp. Garriga drained the liquid that was congesting the air sack in his chest, which gives the male the resonance of his voice in the jungle. It is how he increases the power of his voice and the appearance of his size. The long hairy arms of the orangutan lay slumped over the edge of the operating table like the limbs of a drunken man lapsed into sleep. It seemed like long, hot work in the iron clasp of the tropical heat, the heart monitor beeping to keep pace like a clock.

I could see the glint in the dark eyes of the Catalan shining in the gloom over the red body. I wondered where the power and the will to persevere in difficult circumstances come from in a person like this. The veterinarian worked with simple medicine, simple equipment. She said that one time she and the local surgeon amputated the arm of an orangutan using a saw they bought in a hardware store in town.

After the operation on the air sack, Garriga and her assistants took turns sitting on the floor to hold the big orangutan in their arms like a huge stuffed animal. He needed comforting to make the transition from sleep to consciousness. It felt good to know that there are people in the world who do this. The world feels safer and more compassionate with them. I felt an instant affection for people like the Catalan woman. You feel like you want to be part of that. But you can't. And you have to know that. You have to understand what it means to be separate. An orangutan does.

As human beings we think of Kusasi and other apes in terms of power, domination, and survival. It is the language we understand. For years the simple notion of domination preoccupied the male scientists who looked for it in orangutans and in the other great apes—chimpanzees and gorillas. That was before the relatively late discovery of the bonobo or pygmy chimpanzee in the Congo River basin in Africa in 1929 and the slowly evolving realization that bonobo society is organized in a radically different way from the other great apes, with implications for us as primates, too. The bonobo has a peaceful, matriarchal society based on "sexuality, empathy, caring and co-operaton," says the Emory University primatologist Frans de Waal. "Among bonobos," he writes, "there's no deadly warfare, little hunting, no male dominance, and enormous amounts of sex." Not bad.

As for orangutans, there are variations in the degree of the desire to survive and dominate from individual to individual, as there is with human beings. Some orangutans have the will to survive whatever the circumstances. Others grow despondent in captivity and lose the will to exist. I saw an example of an unusually strong will like this in a female orangutan named Kiki at the orangutan clinic. Kiki is paralyzed and held captive in a body that has betrayed her and yet she is indomitable. She has a strong sense of independence.

I met Kiki while I was languishing at the clinic for weeks waiting for the Canadian primatologist Biruté Galdikas to arrive. The only relief in the green and monotonous heat of the tropics was conversation with Garriga and the afternoon tropical storms. One morning Garriga gave me orders in English with a strong Catalan inflection. "Don't let the orangutan slouch," she said, although what it really sounded like was, *"Dahnn' lat dth'awrrrrahnn-yutann ess-louch."* It took a moment to translate in my mind what she meant. The sloucher was a big female orangutan who was leaning against a tile wall, paralyzed from the neck down. Living on the ground like this in a paralyzed state is a painful loss of freedom for an orangutan. Normally an orangutan spends most of its life in the trees, swinging through the branches, sleeping in a nest it makes every night, and even giving birth in a nest high in the trees. Only the older males who have grown heavy are forced to descend from the trees and walk on the ground where orangutans toss their debris.

Kiki had arrived at the clinic when she was two years old, after being confiscated from human beings who had kept her illegally. At six years of age, when she was being prepared for release in the jungle, she was struck with an autoimmune disease that resulted in "soft paralysis." Now she needs around-the-clock care. That day in the clinic the seven-year-old orangutan was propped against a wall, and every time she slid down, she needed to be pulled up. I pulled her up and talked to her while I swatted the flies that buzzed around her face. I can't remember what I said to her, but I talk to all kinds of creatures and assume that the tone of my voice means something to them. It is also a good time to confide your troubles to someone who can keep a secret. Nothing that I have ever said to an orangutan has ever been betrayed.

"She only bites harder when she is angry, nervous, or feels bad," another Catalan, Yvonne Wendelin, told me during a conversation later in Barcelona where Wendelin works as a physiotherapist in a hospital. Wendelin is a volunteer at the orangutan clinic in Borneo. "She spits on men or people she doesn't like or when she is annoyed," Wendelin said. The orangutan's aversion to men likely comes from incidents of brutality she either suffered herself or witnessed. Yet Kiki needs company; she doesn't like to be alone. If she wakes at night, she blows the big flaps of her lips to wake her attendant so that she'll have a companion through the long, dark hours.

"I slept with her," Wendelin said. "I put her to sleep at six p.m., later than the others. She wouldn't fall asleep instantly. We had good nights. When she is deeply asleep she snores."

The orangutan has found ways to express herself and amuse herself even paralyzed. "If there is a cat next to her and she wants the cat to move," Wendelin said, "she spits on him or blows raspberries. She is able to scratch her eyes with her upper lip. She is very good with her mouth. She peels a rambutan fruit alone. Lying on her belly she is able to move a little insect by pushing it with a piece of stiff grass in her mouth. She opens a zipper with her mouth to see what's in the pocket." One time the orangutan used her lips to try to pluck the freckles off Wendelin's face.

"Her eyes tell so much," said Wendelin. "You can see if she is interested by observing how she looks at people or places." She watches soccer matches, with her head turning to follow the action, and Wendelin says, "She was also interested in the sounds or movements when I took her to the forest." Wendelin had to carry the paralyzed orangutan everywhere, like a twenty-kilogram sack of "dead weight." Another volunteer at the clinic, Carol Ritchie, saw "her moving across the floor by turning her head from side to side and dragging her body forward a little with each turn of the head." Now that's determination.

It bothered me the way that this creature survived in a poor, pitiful existence, because I imagined that's how I'd feel. How long could she live like this? Is it even humane to keep a creature alive in this condition? And why spend so much money and effort on a few orangutans when there are larger issues of survival for the thousands of orangutans threatened by wildfires and a shrinking jungle and extinction of the last of their species? The answer from the staff at the clinic was that the president of the organization, Biruté Galdikas, insisted that individual orangutans like this one be kept alive. I put the question to Galdikas later why she wanted this particular paralyzed orangutan to live. Galdikas said, "because she wants to stay alive, so one must grant her her request. I believe in the sanctity of life, having seen so much death." How can you argue against the sanctity of life?

It is a solitary existence for an orangutan and it is a solitary existence for Garriga. Yet it is also a life that you admire in Garriga because she has found a way to use herself fully and selflessly in a good cause. She told me that she was raised in Barcelona and worked as a child in the small vineyard her family owned near the Montsant mountains. A river ran through the valley, and the trees were full of olives, figs, almonds, and hazel nuts. The air was fragrant with thyme, rosemary, and lavender. At twenty she left her home in Barcelona and for eight years studied to be a veterinarian while working as a waitress to support herself. She wanted a master's degree in wildlife medicine from the University of London in Great Britain, but the books were in English. So, for two years before starting the degree, she taught herself English. Now, years later, she was still working hard in the orangutan clinic. She slept in a room at the clinic, with a machete under her pillow for protection because the Dayaks and Madurese were killing each other. The food was bland and tedious. "I cannot eat any more sardines," she told me, and she had to endure a bout of malaria alone. One time she broke her leg. She refused to let that deter her and hobbled around the orangutan clinic in a cast caring for the apes. Later she moved to a house she rented in the village and kept a dog.

One day when I was at the clinic, Garriga allowed herself to take a rare break from the orangutans. We sat outside on the grass, in the shade of a tree, and she spoke in a soft voice about the frustration she felt when an orangutan dies and how it makes her think that the world is unfair, that she might not be a good veterinarian. "They are like babies, humanlike. You get quite attached to them and it's quite sad that they can go."

Then she lowered her voice to a hush as she did when she went deeper into thought. Sometimes, she said, just being with orangutans has a tranquilizing effect. "When I am very stressed and very fed up, I go to where one of the babies are, and I see them and watch them playing and that makes sense of being here. I feel they are very—I don't know the word, *desesperado*. The situation is just so unfair.

"They are like small babies, human babies. If I can do anything for them, if I can improve their lives, take care of their health, I feel good. They like climbing and smiling and playing. When you tickle them, they smile like a baby."

At that moment she stopped to listen to a young orangutan crying somewhere. It was a combination of a shriek and a wail that rose and fell. "It's complaining," she said. "They feel insecure and they need the mother. Some of them are very shy. Some of them are very brave. Some of them are very naughty."

There was the sound of a crack from a tree, like quick, wooden thunder. "The orangutan broke it," she said.

"Big orangutan in a small tree," I said. More naughtiness in the jungle.

She told me how she had arrived in Indonesia from Spain five years earlier unable to speak the language, not knowing what to expect from orangutans. "The first thing I saw was the orangutans in cages and I didn't know if I could touch them or not. They stick the hands out of the cages. Can I touch them? Will they bite me?" she said, and laughed. She had become totally devoted to the orangutans since then and yet she knew that, in a few years, she could be in another part of the world working with other creatures. Wherever she was, she would find the life in herself to tend the sick and injured.

I always spent time with Garriga at the clinic before making the trip upriver. It made everything else seem friendlier and more familiar. I'd think about what I'd seen at the clinic as I watched the same endless trees flow past. It made the forest feel populated even if I couldn't see anything. Then, after several hours on the river, the klotok would turn into the east branch of the Sekoyer and the channel would start to narrow until the long drooping leaves would scratch and rasp against the side of the wooden boat as though trying to feel what it was that was coming into its jungle. The forest seemed to grow deeper and quieter, and then the channel would widen briefly for the long ironwood dock over the swampy land of the camp and there would be a feeling of solace and comfort, like the world had just uttered a big sigh. Sometimes there would be an orangutan standing on the dock thinking about something. If you didn't see an orangutan on the dock when you arrived, the place felt emptier. Alone.

One time I arrived at the camp not by klotok, but in a flotilla of speedboats with soldiers with rifles and the commander of the Indonesian army for Kalimantan. I was sure the day was going to end badly. This was Kusasi's jungle and he was unpredictable. An army commander was touring the jungle and his men were reckless. They didn't understand orangutans and were armed. It seemed that neither the army nor Kusasi would be likely to yield to the other and there would be a clash of primates—human and orangutan.

That day was a particularly bad time to be in Borneo. The Dayaks and the Madurese were slaughtering each other with machetes by the hundreds, after the Indonesian government had moved the Madurese from their islands to land near the Dayaks. The army was dispatched to try to keep the peace with checkpoints, which didn't do much practical good. One day when I was in the office of the local army commander in

Pangkalan Bun, he showed me the photos of the corpses of a man and a woman killed in the conflict a few days earlier in a rice paddy nearby. I'd heard a rumor that their heads had been cut off and the officer showed me the photos to prove that it wasn't true. The tradition is to cut off the head and drink the blood of your enemy, and I'd heard about the preposterous boasts like that in the bars that this was happening again.

Not only was there killing, but the army had been summoned to deal with the plundering of the trees in the tropical forest, even in places like the protected jungle where Kusasi and the other orangutans lived. While I was there the army had just seized several ships full of illegal logs offshore in the sea. I'd spent one afternoon chatting with the loggers forced by circumstances to leave the city they knew and come to log the trees illegally in a jungle they abhorred. Later, in central Kalimantan, I would see the military trying to extort money to allow the illegal logging trucks to pass. In Pangkalan Bun, a local government office had been burned to the ground the year before when the officials accepting the bribes of the poachers had betrayed the poachers. I saw the blackened and charred remains of the building. It is complicated. Different people have different pressures in their lives.

So, between Kusasi, the military, the illegal loggers, and the poachers, that patch of Kusasi's tropical jungle felt like a volatile place to be, and humanity seemed more dangerous and unpredictable than wild orangutans. The day that I was there the Indonesian military commander had decided to tour the protected jungle where Kusasi lived, and I tagged along. It started like a military operation. We were taken in the opposite direction, out to sea, to a staging area, to put together a flotilla of boats with armed soldiers. Then we motored upriver with the speed and importance of an army on the move. It was so out of touch with the jungle that I felt embarrassed. I watched in a glum mood the wake that the speedboats threw against the exposed roots of the trees. It felt insulting, sacrilegious. I hoped the forest didn't see me.

Either Kusasi was in a quiet mood that day or he admired the bravado and swagger of the military, but there was no battle, in spite of some taunting of the large male orangutans that I expected to end in injury. Maybe the orangutans had decided to be charitable that day. Maybe they thought it wasn't worth the effort. The soldiers never seemed to realize the damage that a large male orangutan can do if he wants. On other days when I was there, people were roughed up and badly bitten by orangutans, and I heard about some who were seriously injured trying to thwart the will of an orangutan. That's a mistake. One time a big orangutan bared his teeth at my thirteen-year-old son for touching a vine that trailed near the orangutan. We backed away slowly. Apparently that was his vine and we respected that. Some people thought the bigger orangutans were cute until they found themselves bleeding from a nasty bite.

When the klotok arrived at Camp Leakey, your first thought was to wonder where Kusasi was. You needed to be prepared. And Kusasi required some thought. The other orangutans would be thinking about him, too. He made sure of that. Kusasi is a local celebrity and has been observed and studied most of his life. Gradually I was able to piece together the larger story of his life as seen over the decades through a multitude of eyes. I wondered what had created the essence of what Kusasi had become. Something had transformed this orangutan into the spectacle of power and isolation he was. I wanted to ask the same questions about him that I would about the development of you or me in our lives. Was it chance? Was it inevitable? Was it the result of the force of will? How is it that we change in our lives and become what we become?

According to the story, Kusasi was orphaned at two years of age. He was taken from his mother in the jungle after she was killed, and he was held captive by human beings, at times in a cage or chained. Human beings were larger than him, dominated him in size, and that would have to make an impression on him. A year after his capture he was taken by human beings again, this time confiscated from his captors. It would be an anxious time. He was taken through Kumai and up the Sekonyer River to the camp of a scientist in the jungle where he could be returned to the wild when he was ready, the same place I would find him decades later. That was a better fate for Kusasi than for many orangutans seized by human beings, but it would have still affected him.

At this time, Kusasi, only three years old, needed what other orangutans need, a mother to teach him how to survive in the jungle. In the camp of the scientist there was no orangutan to do that. Kusasi broke out of his cage and disappeared into the trees. The people in camp eventually assumed that he'd been killed by a wild boar. If not, he was too young to know how to survive by himself and would inevitably die. That's life. But that wasn't Kusasi. Eighteen months later he returned to the camp, now five years old. He was bolder by this time and decided that a female orangutan named Siswoyo would be his surrogate mother. She resisted. Kusasi persisted. She reluctantly assumed the role. Even as young as he was, Kusasi was shrewd enough and forceful enough to forge a relationship with the strong-willed and dominant female of the camp. In 1985, his surrogate mother became pregnant again, but by that time, at ten years of age, he was mature enough as an orangutan to be independent. Kusasi was emerging.

Other orangutans became comfortable in camp with the contact with human beings, but not Kusasi. He remained apart. His strength and confidence grew, and he eventually disappeared deep into the forest again. It happened during the period in the life of a sub-adult male when he traditionally learns to be himself and tests how far his power will extend. Kusasi was learning how to be an orangutan. He was gone for so long that nobody expected to see him again.

Following some obscure timetable that only Kusasi could understand, after years of absence, Kusasi returned to the camp by the muddy brown river. He was bolder now. And because he had been exposed to human beings, because he had grown larger and stronger than them, he was no longer afraid of them. He could exert his power over them. One of Kusasi's big, muscular hands could snap the bone in the arm of a human being like a small chicken bone. His massive hand made a human paw look puny by comparison. His teeth looked like the mouth of a lion and could do as much damage as a machete. Orangutans his size have injured people badly and raped women. And Kusasi could see how easily human beings submitted to his supremacy. He knew he had power.

In the early days of his rise, in 1995, when he was twenty, there were challengers and he defeated them methodically one by one. Kusasi had a reputation now in the jungle. He could rely on that. In a few years, his fame even spread through the accounts about him that appeared in print and on film. Documentary film crews came to photograph him. Once he grabbed the movie star Julia Roberts and almost dragged her into the trees after Roberts came to make a documentary about smaller, gentler orangutans. Roberts said she called him "Mr. Kusasi" after that.

Over the years there were a number of romantic liaisons, typical of the male orangutan and the rank of Kusasi in orangutan society. Usually the male stays with the female for two weeks to mate and then returns to his solitary pursuits, particularly in Borneo where the forest has less food for orangutans than in Sumatra and almost no predators dangerous to orangutans. The females would have been attracted to the aura of confidence, power, and dominance in Kusasi.

The females in the camp gave themselves to him, like Unyuk, and Siswi and Princess, although apparently he wasn't interested only in sex. He would play with some of the females. It was said that the big orangutan "protected" the camp and was its "guardian spirit." He sired a number of infants, like Percy with Princess. As the males that Kusasi sired grew older, larger, and more powerful, there was the risk that they would challenge him. But he just took his chances with sex, as we all do, for similar reasons. Besides, Kusasi had a position to maintain, and he knew it. Having romances and children demonstrated his rank.

In time Kusasi could rely on the strength of his reputation to keep power with both orangutans and human beings. He had the fleshy cheek pads at the side of his face that orangutans recognize as the sign that an orangutan is sexually active and the dominant male of the area. He could afford to be diplomatic on occasion, like the time he dragged the Dayak native Umar out of his bed and into the trees while Umar was sleeping. That was a message from Mr. Kusasi that there were consequences to giving him less fruit that day than he thought he was entitled to by rank. It also gave Umar some stature that I admit intrigued even me. I saw Umar in a different way after that. He had been close to Kusasi. I talked with Umar one day about his intimate encounter with Kusasi and he told me that he thought it was a dream at first that he was being dragged into the trees. When he woke and realized what had happened, he was grateful that Kusasi had shown some restraint. That is one of the benefits of the reputation of power—more options. You can rule by what others know you can do. A glance will suffice.

Nevertheless, in the jungle, as elsewhere, a reputation lasts only for so long. The power of an individual waxes and wanes. If the individual is lucky, if he is skillful in deceiving and bluffing, the reputation may remain strong when his actual power is weakening. In Kusasi's case it was inevitable that a new male would emerge to challenge him. There were a number of contenders who wanted to challenge Kusasi, and after a while, one orangutan became more audacious. The two fought. The fights between them grew fiercer. The gashes in Kusasi's forehead were becoming worse and festering. Kusasi was in his early thirties then, about middle age for an orangutan, yet still strong enough and experienced enough to keep his position.

The challenger was a male in his late twenties or early thirties. He had come out of the jungle, bold like Kusasi. And yet he didn't come into the human camp like Kusasi. He tried to lure his rival into the trees, back into the jungle. Even when he was losing to Kusasi, the will of the other orangutan was unbroken. He kept fighting for the prospect of victory.

Kusasi and the orangutan fought one memorable battle high in the trees and fell thirty feet to the ground clutched together in their embrace. It was not clear if there was a victor. Then Kusasi lost a fight. But he didn't surrender. He didn't admit defeat. He knew that he could not betray himself with signs of weakness or doubt. An orangutan knows that he has to control the way that others think about him. He will hide what he is thinking and try to manipulate the impressions of others. It's the basic politics of the jungle and it makes sense, because controlling what others think saves energy and avoids the risk of injury.

"From the beginning, Kusasi was unusually determined and un-usually tough," a scientist who has known him most of his life, Biruté Galdikas, told me. "He wasn't the tallest orangutan. He wasn't neces-sarily the broadest. But he grew into a very large orangutan with a great deal of presence. It was his determination, even as a juvenile and a sub-adult male, that distinguished him from other males. It continues to distinguish him now."

It was "that glint in his eye," the scientist said. "Even in the early pic-tures of him as a juvenile, you can see that glint in his eye, the strange light. That indicated his determination, his strength and tenacity, his abil-ity to absorb punishment. And, when I say tenacity, I mean that he would go into the forest and come back with enormous wounds, badly ripped up, but he would come back. He seemed to be able to take a great deal of pun-ishment. He never lost his tenaciousness. He knew that that tenaciousness would be rewarded with him becoming the dominant male."

"How many years of dominance should he have left?" I asked her one day in her camp in the jungle.

"It depends. If you are going to be a dominant male orangutan, you have to be a risk taker, you have to be audacious, but, you see, he's smart. Kusasi has street smarts."

After a while you couldn't stop thinking about Kusasi. You wondered what he was doing, whether he was about to emerge out of the trees or down a path like a meteor plowing its way through the cosmos. When would he come? I remember one night in his jungle. I heard that haunting cry of his somewhere high in the trees in the dark. I knew the cry was meant to be shared and understood by all those within its range. We were his audience and he knew it. During the day we all kept a respectful distance, but at night we could wander knowing he was asleep in a big nest in the tropical forest.

The night that Kusasi called, I was in the cabin of Galdikas, who had spent most of her life with orangutans. My son, then thirteen, was a few hundred feet away, asleep down by the river on the deck of our klotok. The thought of my son reminded me of the life that kept me attached elsewhere. I found it difficult to be away from my son for long, although male to male that is something we wouldn't discuss between us. Sometimes our feelings are so strong it is difficult to express them with those closest to us. And yet this woman scientist who had discovered more secrets of the orangutan over her lifetime than any other human being had sent her three-year-old son away so that she could do that work. And she is a very compassionate woman. How do you understand that? What is there in an orangutan, in her, that would draw a person so far into that world? I remembered the baby girl orangutan who had clutched me in the clinic. She looked up at me with such large brown eyes that I felt that sense of intimacy that makes you feel full and satisfied.

I kept asking questions about Kusasi even when I went home. From time to time I'd get an e-mail from Garriga in Kalimantan about the big orangutan. "The last two months have been mad work," she wrote. "The most interesting is that Kusasi is due to lose his throne." She typed "trone," the way she would pronounce it in Catalan as *trono*. "Better you respect him," Garriga continued, "because it's just amazing. He is just so big. He is quite calm. He sits there."

But Kusasi was also growing older. The speculation upriver at camp was that he was losing the contest with the other male orangutan and didn't want to admit it. Garriga had been upriver to tend Kusasi.

20

She cleaned the maggots in the festering, Frankenstein-like gashes on his forehead. To do that, Kusasi needed to be tranquilized, and then the small, slender woman could tend the three-hundred-pound brute in peace. But if Kusasi wasn't tranquilized, nobody wanted to tangle with him. The camp flowed in a safe zone around his movements like the current of a river around a huge boulder.

"I had to go to camp, knock him out, and stitch him—loads of wounds—and amputate one of his toes. It was a stressful time, as you never know with such a beast, and the anaesthesia can go all wrong. But he did well and woke up. After such long work I kissed him on his cheek to wish him a good recovery. Such an honor is not granted to everybody.

"I checked him a week after the first surgery. I followed him for several hours in the deep forest and it was good to see he was not doing too bad. He has lost a lot of weight and looks old. I wish he let the new king take the position and retire, but I fear he won't. I bet he thinks he's better dead than without a throne."

What does it feel like to amputate the toe of a jungle king? And why had she kissed Kusasi? It must feel like kissing the rubber of a gritty, old tire. "I don't think I kissed him because he is charming," she wrote back when I asked, "but because he was under anaesthesia and there are very few occasions to be so close to him. I always wanted to squeeze his cheek pads. We always want what we don't have. Also, because he exhausted me after so much stitching him everywhere that I felt sorry, sad, and relieved. Who knows, maybe my kiss is the last one he is going to get from a female."

It was also a small reward for a woman who has dedicated herself to orangutans in an obscure place for so long. "I don't feel like writing now about Kusasi or work," she wrote to me. "Just to let you know that I have the rest of his crushed toe in a pot with alcohol. I was going to throw it away, but somebody told me to keep it. So I did. Not sure for what, or why."

Why indeed. Why do we human beings do the things we do?

*   *   *

I met another person who knew Kusasi more intimately than most, the British wildlife filmmaker Gil Domb. He had returned to Kusasi's patch of jungle to film a biography of the orangutan and was delayed in the jungle waiting, like me, for the chronically late Biruté Galdikas, which gave us time to trade stories about her, as those who Galdikas keeps dangling do. The filmmaker had spent so much time with Kusasi that the orangutan recognized him. Domb had photographed Garriga stitching Kusasi. Kusasi had even hugged the filmmaker. Actually, two long hugs "and a cuddle," Domb told me. Both were, however, affectionate, if "fairly intense."

"He has the reputation of being a brute," I said to Domb as we sat in the jungle where Kusasi couldn't hear us.

"He's a nice guy—once you get to know him," Domb said. "I wouldn't have said that about him before. You have to bear in mind that the way he is in the forest is different from the way he is in camp."

Kusasi is trying to be the dominant male, I said. Is there brutality in that?

"I don't think there is," Domb said. "I think he's very calm and mellow, considering he could easily injure and kill people. He could just snap human limbs and break heads. If he went on a rampage, he'd kill everyone here."

Domb continued, "I think he enjoys not just my company, but the company of my assistant and the Dayak guides in the forest. We don't get too close. Sometimes, when we're going through a particular tangle of vines, he'll look back and check that we're coming. You even get the sense that he's waiting for you. It doesn't bother him, our presence in the forest, and sometimes you get the sense that if he's in a slightly more relaxed mood he even enjoys our presence a bit. That's nice."

What did it feel like to be hugged by a monster in the jungle?

"I got a sense he was playing with me more than anything else. He's known human beings since he was a child. He can't get near them these days because he's so intimidating, so I got a sense when he had me that he was pulling my legs a little bit here and there, and then started using his teeth a little bit on my body, just biting, but very gently, just as if he was feeling, just like I saw him do in play and just like the babies do in play all the time.

"Then, very unnervingly, for a moment, he put my entire head in his mouth and squeezed with his canines on my skull. He was literally just feeling. You know he could crush a skull just like that. You should see the way he bites through things in the forest like nuts we'd use a hammer to get through. He was doing that for a brief moment. It was very gentle. And there was no aggression whatsoever in his whole manner. For my part, obviously, I didn't like that, and I don't seek those encounters whatsoever. I'm not a thrill seeker.

"Kusasi had an interaction with the smallest baby in camp called Penny, who is a few months old, and it was very intimate," Domb said. "It was really like seeing right through him, because you could see that his interest and fascination in the baby was so intense. Kusasi was trying to get close to touch, but the mother was nervous. He finally managed to slowly push his hand close enough where the baby could just reach out and touch it.

"My sense is he's mellowed. You can see it in the way he walks and in his eyes. I like Kusasi now, whereas, when I filmed him six years ago, I respected him hugely. He was at his peak then. I never felt threatened by him. He has a more relaxed demeanor on occasion these days, which is interesting, because he's probably beginning to go on his way out. Nevertheless, he still has the supreme relaxed confidence of someone who's been on top for a long time."

Yes, and that never lasts, does it? Things change. Time flows onward.

Eventually Garriga left the clinic because of the way it was run, because of the way others were trying to dominate her, make the decisions she should be making. Later, she sent me an e-mail from Sierra Leone in Africa saying *aw di bohdi*, which means "how are you" in the Krio language she was trying to master. Somehow she seemed much farther away in Africa than Southeast Asia, although she really wasn't.

In Sierra Leone, Garriga was working with chimpanzees in another rehabilitation project. The largest male chimpanzee of the group, Bruno, introduced himself to her by hitting her in the forehead with a big stone. Chimpanzees can throw. She said that they'd reached a truce since then.

Several years later, she traveled back from Africa to Kalimantan to visit her old clinic again. She told me, "It was special to see the orangutans again and realize how quiet and how different they are compared to the chimps." The number of orangutans at the clinic had swelled to three hundred and fifty. As for Kusasi, after Garriga originally left Kalimantan, he didn't do well. Six months after she left, a message came from Kalimantan. "They haven't seen him for a while." And yet Kusasi will keep returning until he is either killed or crippled badly. Nobody said it was easy to be an orangutan.

Here's another thing that's not easy. It's not easy to think about orangutans the way that we should as human beings. I know that my sense of humanity has taken a bit of a beating since my first foray into the jungle. Sure, there may be personal reasons for that. Maybe it's just my age. Maybe I'm just too sensitive to these sorts of things. Maybe I have some deep need to be upset. You could think of all sorts of reasons why a person would think too much about all this. But ask yourself, is there much real meaning to life if you don't think this way? What kind of deeper experiences do you feel that you're getting in your life? You can never walk on the moon or see with your own eyes what this planet looks like from space, but that doesn't mean that the idea of these things can't affect us. You can listen to what other people say and hear what they have seen. We live in our minds as much as we live in the world. It would be less of a world if we didn't. Just as it would be less of a world without orangutans.

The reality is inescapable. The facts are plain. The twelve-million-year-old species with the slow, leisurely pace and the long, quiet gaze is dying as a species. It is dying because of the way we dominate our planet. The way that our human population continues to grow and the way that we human beings devastate the rain forests, it will ultimately be the end of orangutans in the wild. The species is estimated to have declined from a population of hundreds of thousands at the beginning of the twentieth century in their last refuge in Borneo and northern Sumatra to sixty thousand by the early years of the twenty-first century.

Sixty thousand may sound large, but consider that orangutans are fractured into smaller groups in shrinking fragments of forest. In those fractured groups, orangutans are approaching the critical point where the individual smaller populations can't reproduce fast enough to sustain their numbers. The orangutan is listed as endangered by the World Conservation Union, the United Nations, and other agencies. The Sumatran orangutan, a separate species with smaller numbers, is considered critically endangered. And the speed of the change of the number of orangutans is alarming. The primatologist Herman Rijksen says that during the twentieth century ninety-three percent of the orangutans remaining in Borneo were lost.

And yet, in spite of the way we are destroying orangutans, there are people of dedication and compassion trying to save them. I talked to these people. I wondered at their total abandon, the absolute sacrifices they made when they gave themselves totally to orangutans and the way that it filled their lives. I saw scientists and conservationists working in Borneo and northern Sumatra, where orangutans live, and in places nearby in Southeast Asia. I talked to keepers in zoos, in places like Australia, the United States, the United Kingdom, the Netherlands, and

Spain, who work for years unseen by others behind the walls with orangutans. One was an eighty-three-year-old German woman who lived in a
bungalow she'd built inside the zoo in Jakarta to be near the orangutans.
She served me breakfast with a young orangutan walking by to shake
our hands. Another was a Dutchman whose depth of passion for orangutans almost has the force of a hurricane. Nothing else matters for him.
He would let his passion destroy him like a curse. He reminded me of
the legend of the Flying Dutchman, the lost soul doomed to wander the
earth alone.

I visited them and listened to their tales. Sometimes they raged about
the circumstances of orangutans. Sometimes they wept. But not one of
them didn't have experiences that I wouldn't have traded for my own life
in a weak and vulnerable moment. The choice always felt so close—that
moment when you say, maybe I would sacrifice it all for that. You would
feel that moment when the glint in an eye of a small orangutan shone
with understanding and feeling. I heard them in their sleep as they re-
lived with little raspy breaths the great orangutan passions of the day. I
saw their fear, their joy, their curiosity, their cunning. Those were sweet
moments that made all the difficulties worth it. The world felt like a different place then.

The force of life in an orangutan like Kusasi or Kiki flows strong, like
a small river; it flows, too, in Princess, and Percy, and Bento, and Joshua,
and Siswi, and Aazk, and all the rest—all individual orangutans with
their own thoughts and feelings and ways of being an orangutan that you
have to know personally to appreciate. I remember them. I remember the
way that each of them affects you differently, even if it is only for a moment. These orangutans are not just part of a species. You feel them as
individuals. Some days I wish I had the power and the determination of
the Catalan veterinarian or the Flying Dutchman to abandon my current
existence like them. And yet I also remember the moments of despair, of
pain, of loneliness that I saw in the people who have chosen that life. And
they still have the courage to do what they do. And that's the difference

in them. I'm grateful for the time I spent with orangutans in Borneo and Sumatra and with people I admire deeply who are making a difference.

It will take a huge effort to change human consciousness about what is happening to orangutans and to the rain forest where they live. Both are being devastated. We need to understand what it means that a species of great ape who is genetically akin to us, who thinks and feels like we do, is about to be extinguished. The orangutan in the wild will come to an end because of us. We will lose a creature who is thoughtful, ingenious, curious, gentle with children, wild in ways we don't understand. An orangutan lives in another world. It has a mind that sees dimensions and layers of existence that we don't. It feels time and space in a way that we never will. Catching a glimpse of that existence on the other side of those dark brown eyes is exhilarating, like discovering an ancient civilization. But this consciousness, this way of experiencing the world, this primate culture, will likely be gone before we understand what we have lost. In the end it will likely be our destiny to dominate a world reduced to our own limitations. We will no longer be able to know what an orangutan was. But, before that happens, there is more to learn about orangutans, more about us, in the time we have.

CHAPTER 2

In Deepest, Darkest Borneo

THE WILD ELEPHANTS stared, blinked. Tails swished. Ears flapped. Feet stamped. There was some snorting. The elephants rumbled in low tones like machinery not yet in gear. It didn't feel good. Something was stirring deep in the recesses of elephant brains. Something volatile. The night before the lightning of a storm had flickered in the dark above the darker shades of the tropical forest along the Kinabatangan River, in Sabah, a Malaysian province at the northern tip of Borneo. In the distance, we could hear the thunderous boom of a homemade cannon. It was constructed of aluminum tubes and acetylene, fired to frighten the elephants away from the village of Sukau on the river. The dogs from the village barked in the distance, howling after the elephants. It would irritate the great beasts. Their pace in the night would quicken. Their fitful sleep would be disturbed. They would be grumpy.

The next day, the elephants were standing by the river in the tall grass that elephants like to munch, looking at us, one thin Malaysian and two Canadians, big and little, a father and son. We looked at them. They looked at us. The eyes of the elephants were like tiny round shadows in a flat gray slab of rock. Staring. It was a diplomatic standoff. Then the bellowing started, grew louder. A single elephant charged out of the group, like a great gray boulder rolling through the long grass quick as the wind. The other elephants watched to see what would happen. They were the support group. A few feet from the three of us the elephant stopped abruptly, as though it hit the end of a tether and was yanked back. The beast swiveled around, showed a perky little tail, and then rushed back to its group. Then another elephant took its turn. And another. Swiveling. Perky tails. Menacing and yet flirty, if there can be such a thing.

Yes, we were too close. Elephants have boundary issues just like people. What seemed distant to small human beings like us was too close for a big creature like an elephant. Anthropologists have the term "proxemics" for this, the space around living beings that feels like an extension of them. And the dear pachyderms were feeling some fraying of the boundaries. We were invading their space. The charges went on for a while, until we grew nervous that it might escalate. The wild elephants might be in the mood for mayhem after a night of dogs and booming noises and fitful sleep. Anybody would. We retreated through the tall grass to our small boat. And yet not quite retreated, because in an odd way, we felt stronger, like you do after watching a monsoon or a waterfall. We'd felt the natural power of the big beasts. We were bigger, too.

A herd of elephants like this one is already a rare sight in Borneo and is becoming rarer. The Borneo elephant is a pygmy species, half the size of the mainland Asian elephant, which is smaller than the African elephant. It is listed among other species threatened with extinction like the orangutan, another casualty of the mass destructiveness of the human species. Once the world was big enough to ignore our differences. Now it no longer is. The size of the range of the elephants across the land is being reduced, their forests are being devastated, and that kills them.

In a few years the elephants of Borneo may be nothing but the gray dust raised by the tires of the plantation trucks rumbling along the forest roads. Less than a thousand elephants remain in all of Sabah where three decades ago they ranged across the country. Most of the elephants in Borneo are in eastern Sabah and only a few in north Kalimantan. The group of elephants that we encountered was a small fragment of seven elephants from the larger group of ninety-eight feeding along the river.

In the past, elephants in Asia, like the ones in Africa, were killed as trophies. The museum specimen collector William Temple Hornaday wrote an account of what it is like to shoot an eight-foot-tall Asian elephant from twelve paces. At the time, in 1878, the twenty-three-year-old Hornaday was traveling in Malaysia to collect specimens of crocodiles, elephants, and orangutans for American museums. Hornaday described what happens when you shoot an elephant:

> The great beast gave a tremendous start as the bullets crashed into his skull, threw his trunk aloft with a thrilling scream and wheeled toward us. Before he had time to make a single step forward we aimed for the fatal spot over the eye and fired again. Down sank the ponderous head, the legs gave way, and the huge beast settled down where he stood and rested in the mud, back uppermost, with his feet doubled under him. We instantly reloaded and came to a "ready," just as the tough old pachyderm began to slightly recover and struggle to regain his feet. Choosing our positions this time, a couple of shots behind the ear penetrated his brain and settled matters. With a convulsive shudder and a deep groan the great creature slowly sank back upon the ground, moved his trunk feebly a few moments, fetched a deep sigh and expired . . . In a pouring rain, we cut off his head and took his skull.

The next day, the men found the herd again. The hunters fired and missed. The herd, hearing the guns like savages in the wild would have heard the guns of Cortez erupt, "thought our firing was thunder," wrote

Hornaday. He and his companion were rushed by a young pachyderm that swerved away at the last moment and showed his rump, like the elephants did with us. Hornaday's companion fired at the fleeing elephant and hit him in the ass. At least a bullet would do little damage there. Hornaday recorded it all and it's as much fun to read now as seeing a cat lying smashed on the road. It doesn't matter that it happened years ago. It doesn't matter that he may not have known better. What happened is that he did it and did much the same to orangutans. Sometimes you get tired waiting for the moral evolution of savages.

I wonder whether human beings have the right to be in the wilderness anymore. We're not doing it much good. Nevertheless, I had come to the Kinabatangan wilderness to see the area where the French researchers Marc and Isabelle Ancrenaz are studying orangutans. They are an interesting pair. He, very much the man. Tall, handsome, rugged. She, very much the woman. Smart, beautiful, rugged. Together, very much the couple. Something you can only hope exists somewhere in the world just to prove that romance is possible. Marc and Isabelle met at the zoo in Paris, fell in love, married, and started to finish their science degrees together. Romance, the science way.

Then, after working in Africa, the two had flown to Sabah for a holiday, where they became curious about orangutans. Officials with the Sabah Wildlife Department told them about the Kinabatangan nature reserve, where there was a conflict between villagers and the wild elephants and orangutans. There was a large population of orangutans in the Kinabatangan that wasn't being studied and there was also an unusual opportunity to examine the relationship between orangutans and a rain forest that was degenerating. Isabelle Ancrenaz wanted to determine if wild orangutans could cope with change and what could be done to manage them. A scientist couldn't ask for better challenges. It was perfect for the couple.

By the time I talked to them in Sabah they had established an orangutan study site on the Kinabatangan River near the village of Sukau, not far from the Sulu Sea, and had been conducting research significant enough to affect the survival of orangutans as a species. About thirteen thousand orangutans are believed to exist in Sabah, sixty percent of that outside protected areas and within commercial forest reserves used for timber. About four thousand orangutans are estimated to be in the Kinabatangan, a thousand of them in the Kinabatangan river plain near the sea where the Ancrenazes are doing their research.

The Ancrenazes are working with the villagers in Sukau to ease the village tensions with elephants and orangutans. Their project hires local people and trains them on conservation projects, to encourage tourism projects in order to convert the economy and support conservation. The Ancrenazes have created night patrols to reduce the strife between the villagers and the elephants, who are following their traditional circular route after dark through the village. The patrol from the village tries to make peace between the species to protect the crops with the combination of electrical fences, smoke, and the noise from a tube called "an elephant cannon" that's fired to frighten the big beasts away. The same patrols deal with the orangutans, also hunting for food in the fields and fruit trees and plantations. Marc started by hiring six villagers from Sukau, and by the time I visited Sukau the first time in 2003, that number had grown to thirty-five villagers. Isabelle's project provides intensive training for the villagers as research assistants, including instruction in the English language and in fund-raising.

The wild elephants are followed in the Kinabatangan by a man named Zainal, a thin, bespectacled Malaysian originally from the more urbanized peninsula of his country. It was Zainal who helped us navigate the area in a small boat, wearing, in the tropic heat, a black toque pulled over his head to protect him from any rogue chills. Zainal has adapted to living in the remote tropical forests of Sabah. A naturally curious individual, he is learning about elephants and river sharks and fireflies, which he is able to do without killing any of them. He has a gentle soul and respects nature. It seems as though Zainal has plunged his whole being into the natural world.

Zainal was intrigued by the elephants after his association with Marc Ancrenaz. He sent me an e-mail one time from the jungle that he was making progress with the great beasts: "In the last three weeks Dr. Marc and I got very close to a herd of elephants upriver near my hut. After a few minutes, he managed to touch an adult female for more than ten minutes and rubbed her back. I dared myself and got as close as three metres behind Dr. Marc, just to observe and learn the technique. Ten days later, on another trip along the Kinabatangan, I managed to do the same. Wowwwwww. The best new experience in my life."

Zainal told me that he had seen forty elephants swim across the Kinabatangan River. When the elephants reached the deeper part of the river, he said, "the only thing visible was the trunk and the forehead. Last year, when I saw eighteen in the water from a distance, I thought it is a school of dolphins. I took out my binoculars and saw it was an elephant."

Isabelle Ancrenaz told me that she had seen elephants swim the Kinabatangan River, too. She saw the herd swimming, their feet pumping, their bodies below the water, their trunks held in the air like snorkels to breathe. The mothers push the baby elephants in front of them in the water. "They're really good swimmers," she said.

Marc Ancrenaz told me that one of the reasons he initially wanted to come to the Kinabatangan was the elephants. He is "keen on elephants," he said. He had seen wild elephants before in Africa and had been charged. He said that he was fascinated by the combination of danger, cleverness, and social life in them. "I'm curious about the way these beasts are conducting their life on Earth."

"Elephants are matriarchal animals," he told me. "The herd is comprised of an older female and related offspring. Males, by the time they become adults, leave the native herd and settle on their own in the forest. Sometimes they create small groups of two to five bachelor males. Bulls do not stay with the main herd, unless they are in musth, active for reproduction. Then they join the herd for a few weeks and mate with females, if any of them are in heat. Most of the raids on the crops are done by single bulls in musth who enter the crops to feed on palms to increase their fitness and body condition for mating."

That explained the male Zainal usually saw lingering with the group. "There is only one male bull," Zainal said afterward, and added that we didn't see him that day. "Usually he hides." That didn't sound very male, I thought.

"He never come out into the open," Zainal said. "Either he is feeding or he is behind. It looked fairly dangerous today."

The elephants behaved with us the same way they had with Hornaday when his companion shot one in the ass, but the rush-and-turn tactic was intended by the elephant, according to Zainal, now our personal elephant interpreter, not as an attack but as a warning. The charge-and-reverse maneuver is typical of the Kinabatangan elephant. Zainal recognized two of the female elephants who stood before us by a damaged ear on one and a scar on the neck of the other.

"The female with the scar on the neck, I used to touch the trunk with my hand," he said. "She would reach out to touch me."

"What do you think she was doing?" I asked.

"I think she wants to play," he said. Zainal had perfected the technique for playing with elephants. He said that if the herd stays grazing in a spot for fifteen or twenty minutes while you are there and they turn their backs to you, their tails twitching, that's a good sign. "All you have to do is hold the tail and give a good smack on the back very hard with a branch. Then, after a few times, the elephants will move forwards and they will turn face to face with you. Then they want to play with you."

"How do you play with an elephant?" I asked.

"They will come closer to you, lifting their trunks to try to sniff you and identify you. You just put up your hand. Let the elephant touch you. They come to you, close, about three meters. Then, they will reverse, getting closer to you. Then you have to touch the tail. And give a spank. And start rubbing. After a few times, they will face you. They will run farther out and they will turn back and start pointing their trunk all over your body, just pointing, just close to you. All you have to do is have your hand out and let them touch with their trunk your hand."

He said that during one encounter with elephants a female had held her head out to him, so he held on to the ear and rubbed behind it. When he does this sort of thing, "Four or five females will approach you with a baby. So that is a sign they welcome you."

Zainal said he had done this three times before, but the day we were with him wasn't a good time for play because of the stress the elephants were feeling from the night before and because of the boats of tourists. "I look at the eyes," he said. "If the eyes are open very wide, then that means you can come."

What about the young elephant that rushed toward him and then turned her back?

"The juveniles are notorious. They want to play very rough. It was playing behavior."

"How did you know it was playing?" I asked. The speed and size of the animal was startling and I would never have thought of spanking an elephant myself. Later, I watched Zainal walking along a road dragging his foot from an old injury and realized that he wouldn't have been able to run from the elephants.

"I think the adult female was quite calm," he said.

"And she was calming things down?"

"Yes."

I didn't feel so sure.

I have to remind myself that William Temple Hornaday is dead and has been dead many years and that I am responding to him as though he is living in my time, right now, as though he can still be accountable. Sure, I admit that's being anachronistic. It's reading what we know at this point in time back into the past and finding fault with it for that reason. So you feel it was wrong to have slaves when that was legal or it was wrong to treat women as inferior when it was legal. That's anachronistic. But I feel that we have a right to be anachronistic. I think we should make an effort to unravel time and imagine how it should be different. It jostles time loose for us in the present. So I was absorbed in this way reading what Hornaday had written and was even having conversations with him in my mind. I'm sure I'm not the only person who does that when I read. At other times I was so intrigued by what he had written that I should have been more appalled than I was.

How did this all happen? I made the acquaintance of the old pachyderm hunter through the book he had written, which I found in the back of a small bookstore in Sabah in a reprint with an antique cover that looked good for swatting flies. The story unfolded this way. In 1878, Hornaday was a young American traveling through the jungles of Borneo and made contact with orangutans. It was almost a century before scientists would begin detailed field studies of the red ape. Borneo was then, as it is today, almost a small continent at 740,000 square kilometers, or the third largest island in the world. When Hornaday arrived on the island, it had its own exotic plants and creatures, like orangutans. It was a land with amazing biological complexity and it was difficult to penetrate its terrain of swamps and jungles and remote mountain regions. The real jungle is still that way. Yet Hornaday overcame this and traveled into the interior to find orangutans.

This fascinating opportunity could have been a moment of change in human consciousness. Hornaday glimpsed the intelligence and emotion of orangutans years in advance of science. If he had persisted in understanding what he was experiencing, he could have challenged their status at the time as brute beasts. He published his observations in his book in 1885, seven years after he was in Borneo, the same year that the British were fighting in the Sudan and the Statue of Liberty arrived in New York harbor.

At the time, Hornaday was in his early twenties and a taxidermist by training and he had come to Borneo as a specimen hunter for museums. In that period, naturalists like Hornaday collected living creatures, killed them, stuffed them, and put them on display so that the natural world could be studied and appreciated. It seemed to make sense at the time. But then death and mayhem always seem to make sense to some at the time. People are living it right now in different parts of the world. When Hornaday came to Borneo, places like Africa and Southeast Asia were largely unexplored by Westerners and so adventurers became popular as writers who shared their travels with others.

Hornaday's account of Borneo and of orangutans was likely influenced by the account of Alfred Russel Wallace, the discoverer of the theory of evolution along with Charles Darwin. Wallace had observed orangutans in Borneo during a trip to Sarawak, a small country in Borneo, in 1854, twenty-four years before Hornaday. Wallace published his observations in his book *The Malay Archipelago* in 1869, dedicated to Darwin, just nine years before Hornaday went to Sarawak himself. The experiences that Wallace had and his account would set the mark for a competitive man like Hornaday to match or exceed. It's just the way men are. Always have been.

In all this, Hornaday would likely have known that Wallace had kept a baby orangutan. One day in 1856, Wallace wrote in *The Malay Archipelago*, he shot a large female orangutan. When the body of the orangutan—or *mias* in the local language—was retrieved from the bog, an infant was discovered too young to even have teeth. "After we had cleaned the mud out of its mouth," Wallace wrote, "it began to cry out, and seemed quite strong and active." Wallace was compassionate enough to try to save the creature. He had no milk to feed the toothless infant, so he improvised by putting rice water into a bottle and poking a hollow quill through the cork to allow the liquid to be sucked. "I fitted up a little box for a cradle," he wrote, "with a soft mat for it to lie upon." After Wallace had the infant for three months, it died. "I much regretted the loss of my little pet," he said. "For several months it had afforded me daily amusement by its curious ways and the inimitably ludicrous expression of its little countenance . . . I preserved its skin and skeleton."

Hornaday had his chance to play father to orangutans, too, and it awoke some compassion in him. That's the part that's really fascinating about the man and that created the opportunity for insight into orangutans. One day the Dayak natives of Borneo gave Hornaday a six-month-old orangutan. Because the orangutan is such an elusive creature in the forest, even the Dayaks had few experiences with orangutans, and so Hornaday's association with the creature was an oddity even for the natives who came miles to see the creature. "He was quite peaceable, not even attempting to bite," wrote Hornaday, "but whined softly when I approached him, and rolled up his big brown eyes appealingly." Hornaday cut him loose and made a bed of straw for him, where he curled up. "Thus began a great friendship between ape and man," said Hornaday.

While the other "captives were vicious to the last degree, and died promptly, without repentance, my third pet turned out to be all that the heart of man could desire in an orang." The orangutan seemed to Hornaday ugly by human standards, but nevertheless, "His eyes were large, bright and full of intelligence, and he had a forehead like a philosopher. Because of his bald and shiny head, his solemn, wrinkled, and melancholy visage, his air of profound gravity and senatorial wisdom, we got to calling him the Old Man . . . A thin growth of brick-red hair grew straight up the back of his head and over the crown, making, in certain lights, a perfect halo around his bald, brown pate, reminding one rather forcibly of certain pictures by the old masters."

Hornaday saw that the creature was attached to him and he encouraged it. "The Old Man evinces a decided liking for me . . . but is shy of strangers. Whenever a dog makes his appearance in our room, or it thunders hard, the little fellow makes straight for me, as fast as he can come, climbs quickly up my legs and nestles in my arms for protection."

Hornaday let the orangutan sleep with him. "His favorite position was to lie sprawling upon my chest, affectionately clasping my body with his outstretched arms and legs, with his head on my shoulder and his face close to my neck." But when the orangutan started to snore loudly, Hornaday made him sleep elsewhere. Snoring seems to be a limit to a relationship for human beings. We'll put up with just about anything else.

Hornaday was growing fond of the little orangutan and took him with him, ironically to hunt other orangutans. He didn't see any contradiction. Maybe it was because the older orangutans seemed wilder and more independent. Hornaday watched how the creature behaved like a thinking being. "He leans lazily over the edge of the boat and dabbles in the water with his hairy brown hands as it sweeps past the side." Hornaday called this playful action "true childish instinct" and argued that anyone who still doesn't believe Darwin's theory of evolution should look at the orangutan for proof. "Let him witness their human-like emotions of affection, satisfaction, pain and rage."

In the process of defending the honor of Darwin and science, Hornaday saw human nature reflected in the orangutan. In orangutans, Hornaday found intelligence, affection, expressiveness, playfulness, and other humanlike qualities. If he found this much, he could have gone further. What was stopping him? Why didn't he let his natural sympathy for orangutans blossom? He could have changed our thinking. His name could have stood alongside the other revolutionary thinkers like Darwin and Marx and Freud as a kind of early Jane Goodall. But it didn't happen. Something held him back. Something always holds us back. And the savages lost another opportunity to evolve morally.

What actually happened illustrates a darker side of human nature and it doesn't have to have been that way. In the 1800s when men like Wallace and Hornaday went to Borneo, there were plenty of orangutans to shoot, and orangutans trusted human beings more. Since the orangutan was a creature mainly of the swamp, it was isolated and protected from human beings, from even the Dayak natives of Borneo. By 1900, two decades after Hornaday's venture, there were estimated to be over three hundred thousand orangutans. That number dropped rapidly in the twentieth century to the current estimate of sixty thousand and the warning of extinction. Hornaday killed forty-three orangutans in Borneo as museum specimens. That may not be excessive compared to the thousands of orangutans who have died since his time and the hundreds of orangutans shot every year to separate mother from child for the illegal pet trade. The hunting of orangutans became illegal in 1924 and the commercial trade in live orangutans was banned by twenty-one countries in 1973, but that hasn't stopped the illegal activity. It seems that there are fewer excuses since Hornaday's time.

The tally of the death of orangutans mounts in Hornaday's book, detail by detail, like a ledger. Hornaday wrote how he acted with mercy to end the life of a wounded orangutan. "So I quickly thrust the point of my knife into the occiput of the half-dead animal, pierced his medulla oblongata, and, with a hoarse growl, he instantly expired." Orangutan number fifteen was the biggest and grandest specimen of all, named "the Rajah," or lord, for his magnificence, the Kusasi of his patch of jungle. "Half a mile higher up," said Hornaday, "we heard a deep guttural growl or roar, coming from the jungle back from the river." They paddled closer and caught a glimpse of him. "His body was entirely hidden by the green foliage, so I stood up in the boat and fired at his leg to rouse him. 'The Turk awoke.' He started up instantly, growling hoarsely with pain and anger, and started to swing away. His reach was surprising in its length." Hornaday moved his boat under the tree where the orangutan sought refuge. "I fired twice in quick succession at the orang's breast. He stopped short, hung for a moment by his hands, then his hold gave way and he fell, and landed broadside in the water, which went flying all over us." The men reached to pull him into the boat and Hornaday described the scene, which affected him more deeply than he expected, although he also boasted that he'd killed an orangutan bigger than other "naturalists":

The monster gave a great gasp, and looked reproachfully at us out of his half-closed eyes. I can never forget the strange and even awful sensation with which I regarded the face of the dying animal. There was nothing in it in the least suggestive of anything human, but I felt as if I had shot some grim and terrible gnome or river-god, a satyr indeed! *"Ahdo! Ahdo!"* exclaimed Lamudin in Malay, "the Rajah of all the *mias!*" We were filled with wonder at the huge beast before us. He was a perfect giant in size, larger than any the natives had ever seen before, and the largest ever shot by a naturalist. His head, body, and limbs were simply immense, and his weight could not have been much, if any, less than one hundred and ninety pounds. . . . He has since found a place, with several of his nearest relatives, in a huge glass case in the National Museum at Washington, where he is engaged in a sanguinary "Fight in the tree tops."

As he shot orangutans, Hornaday continued along the Simujan River like Wallace before him and plunged into the forest marshes. He shot one orangutan, number six in the ledger of deaths, a mother with a child. Although he wounded the mother badly, she was so stubborn that she wouldn't let go of her infant. That mattered to her more than her own life. Hornaday missed that implication. "Seeing that she was not likely to die for some minutes," Hornaday said, "I gave her another shot to promptly end her suffering, and then she came crashing down through the top of the small trees, and fell into the water which was waist deep." The baby was submerged for a full minute and nearly drowned, but the human beings were able to resuscitate him. The small orangutan seemed ungrateful, however. Its mother had been killed, its world ripped apart by this strange man, and yet Hornaday saw the seven-month-old as "a little devil" with "the temper of a tiger." He said, "It was restless as an eel and gave me endless trouble."

Hornaday bound the menace, but instead of being placated, "This, of course, increased its rage." The infant still managed to bite him "very severely on the calf," so that Hornaday had to give him "a sounding slap on the side of his head." Exasperated, Hornaday said, "Once it tumbled overboard, and I let it get a good ducking before rescuing it." Otherwise, he tried to be compassionate and understanding of both apes and natives in Borneo, although occasionally even his patience reached the breaking point. One time he found a Dayak longhouse that was so dirty and badly organized that he joked that "the women must read novels to excess." I wonder if the women of Hornaday's time laughed very loudly when they read this.

Maybe Hornaday made some changes to his thinking afterward. After the voyage to Borneo, he would became a prominent conservationist in the United States and a defender of wildlife, as well as an apparently progressive, if also controversial, zoo director. He rose in prominence and was influential in the conservation of wildlife and in the treatment of animals in zoos, although some of his actions also angered people at the time, which means that not everyone thought the same way. Hornaday became the head of a department at the Smithsonian's National Zoo in Washington, D.C., and the director for thirty years of the New York Zoological Park or the Bronx Zoo, retiring from that position when he was seventy-two.

Hornaday saw himself as the modern naturalist-hunter, in an age of science, adventure, and exploration. A turning point came for Hornaday in 1886, eight years after his trip to Borneo, when he went on a hunt for the Smithsonian in Montana to collect specimens of the bison before it became extinct. "He was shocked that the millions of buffalo had dwindled to only a handful," according to the historian Greg Dehler. Hornaday would lobby for laws to protect wildlife and helped preserve the bison from extinction. He was outspoken as a conservationist with "an almost religious zeal," the historian Bill Sharp said. "He threw himself into every cause with the same fervour." Hornaday stopped hunting for specimens and opposed hunting, although only on a scope that endangered wild animals.

In 1906, Hornaday was embroiled in a controversy when he locked a twenty-three-year-old pygmy from the Congo named Ota Benga in a cage at the Bronx Zoo with an orangutan named Dohung. The orangutan was a little shorter than the four-foot-eleven man. It must have been frustrating for the pygmy. He had been captured in the Belgian Congo in Africa in 1904 after he had been hunting an elephant, two years after Conrad's book *Heart of Darkness* was published that criticized the savagery of Westerners in the Congo. Ota Benga had been ripped out of his world and thrown into the prison-like conditions of a zoo. Hornaday didn't see anything wrong or harsh about caging a pygmy, and it certainly helped to make the zoo a popular attraction. After being incarcerated at the zoo and harassed by crowds, Benga told the *New York World* that civilization is "all witchcraft" and the people of New York "all madmen"—which, under the pygmy's circumstances, made some sense. Hornaday released Benga only when he was threatened with legal action. Benga eventually left the zoo, worked in a tobacco factory, and committed suicide a decade later with a gun. When Hornaday died in 1937 in the United States at eighty-two years of age, his obituary called him a "fearless" man with "an uncommon facility of making enemies" who "waged a militant battle in defence of the nation's wildlife."

More than a century after Hornaday was in Sarawak, I came to the Kinabatangan searching for wild elephants and wild orangutans. I made my way to the village of Sukau, which meant a long drive on a road that was dusty and in bad shape because of the beating it takes from the big trucks from the palm oil plantations. Later, I would see the plantations from a boat in the river, spewing the chemicals into the water that some believe are killing fish in the water and destroying the fishing at Sukau. My Malaysian friend Zainal would tell me, "There's pollution from a close by oil palm mill which disposed toxic effluents into the smaller stream. Massive three inches thick of yellowish substances are floating and cover a wide area of four kilometers distance." The dust was so bad on the dirt road to Sukau that it was like driving through a thick fog. Everything from trees to houses disappeared under a layer of gray. The trees looked as though they had been made out of cement. We saw that somehow a foot-long monitor lizard had crossed the road through the cloud of dust without getting squashed. Sometimes you just get lucky. The next time I went to the Kinabatangan, I decided to avoid the dust of the road and Zainal took me from Sandakan to the Kinabatangan River in a small boat, which meant seeing lots but getting drenched in a rainstorm. But at least we felt cleaner after the rain and could see.

At Sukau, it wasn't far by boat to the orangutan study site of the Ancrenazes. We walked through the orangutan site with Jaimal, one of the native participants from the village of Sukau working with the French scientists. It was hot, and leeches got under our clothing without us noticing until hours later. Then it was as though spots of blood had bloomed under our clothing. The leeches were gone, though. Long gone. From our boat on the river, it seemed the wild orangutans were hiding that day, but later, one was visible high in a tree. He watched the human beings cautiously behind a screen of leaves. Only later, when I looked at my photos, did I see that there were actually two orangutans close together.

In the study area we saw the footprints of elephants and croquette-size balls of dung from the creatures. A professor I was with from a Welsh university, Mike Bruford, who was studying the DNA of orangutans, tasted the food of the orangutans as we followed the path. He bit into one large seed and called it "bitter." I was thankful he left the balls of elephant dung alone. Sometimes you can learn too much about nature.

The villagers at Sukau involved with the project were infused with pride and enthusiasm about the work. They'd taken a brief course from Bruford, and when he arrived in Sukau they wanted to pump the Welsh professor for more information about genetics to understand the information they were gathering. The villagers sounded like they were unraveling the genealogical lines of the orangutans like the soap operas they watch on television. Who is the father of Jenny? they asked, and huddled close to hear the answer. They had brought a keg of beer to talk with Bruford and conversed with him late into the night.

In the end the research of Marc and Isabelle Ancrenaz in the Kinabatangan has found that orangutans can adapt to second-growth tropical forests and survive there. That was a contradiction to the prevailing wisdom about orangutans and has radical consequences for the environmental battle to save orangutans and the rain forest. Not everyone wants to hear it. "It's a strange idea for many scientists that orangutans can live in secondary forest," Isabelle Ancrenaz told me. "It's a very controversial issue. At the beginning people would not believe us, or ignored what we were doing. Some people deny my truth." The campaigns to save the orangutan are often based on the notion that orangutans won't survive the destruction of the original rain forest.

But if orangutans can adapt to second-growth forest, then saving the original rain forest isn't as crucial for them. Palm oil plantations and rice paddies could be rotated with second-growth forest. That, in turn, could be used to justify logging, an uncomfortable position for some environmentalists. It undermines the ideology of preserving nature in a pristine state. And yet, "The vast majority of orangutans live outside the protected areas," said Isabelle. She feels it might not be possible to protect enough forest to save the species and so other measures are needed. Secondary forest is "very dynamic," she said. It changes more quickly, which could be a stimulus to orangutans. If second-growth forest can support more males, and if more female orangutans can give birth, and if the orangutans can adapt to that, the prospects for orangutans could change.

Will the effort do any good for a creature threatened with extinction? That's the question, isn't it? I asked this question a lot and got various answers. Marc Ancrenaz seemed more optimistic than most. He told me that he thought the fate of the apes is grim, but the orangutan, he said, "is adaptable, so it could survive." He believed that the people in the Kinabatangan were not hunting orangutans. "This is why we are working in the Kinabatangan, because we show that orangutans and people can survive together, as long as they are not shot. So these people realize that it is in their interest not to shoot the animals but keep them around. They will survive." Zainal, the Malaysian, thought differently and spoke in hushed tones about the fate of orangutans. And yet, with the work of the Ancrenazes and the patrols, ninety percent of the crop damage in the area has been reduced. The economy is also changing to depend on protecting the environment. Sukau has lodges and cabins with air-conditioned units, and some villagers rent rooms to tourists. There is a plan to develop forms of tourism that don't affect the local culture. Nevertheless, Isabelle Ancrenaz told me that she is skeptical of the value of tourism and sees "danger" in it, although even with its problems, tourism is better than palm oil plantations, she said. And so it goes. The arguments weave back and forth.

I was back in Canada and not thinking about elephants at the time when Marc Ancrenaz sent me a clipping from the *Borneo Post*. It was not good news. The head of a dead female elephant was found floating in a tributary of the Kinabatangan River near the village of Sukau. The elephant had been shot in the head. She was a member of the larger herd of those flirty-tailed beasts, although probably not one that we had seen the day we were there, even though I imagined she was. An official said that the mutilation of the elephant was a sign of the anger and vengeance of the villagers. They were afraid of the big creatures and wanted to stop the destruction the elephants caused. You can understand how they feel, but I was glad that I hadn't seen the head floating in the river. It would be like seeing that cat smashed in the road. How do you respond to things like this? It happened, but it doesn't have to have happened, does it?

CHAPTER 3

Forest Murmurs

When I saw Sese in the zoo in Manila I wouldn't say that this was an orangutan who was happy to be there. For years Sese had lived in a cage in the zoo. It was a bare cage even as most cages go, just iron and cement. There wasn't much to occupy her, no other orangutan, nothing but the dull and senseless throng of anthropoids like us who come to stare, like a tide of flesh that ebbs and flows in a bland and meaningless rhythm through the day. No, I wouldn't describe her as a contented ape. I saw Sese on my way through Manila. At the time I was searching in the Philippines for a man who had survived the jungles of Borneo and Sumatra and then had been forgotten. The only way to understand an orangutan fully is to immerse yourself in the jungle like a child of the forest, and this man had done that years ago before others realized it was possible.

I found Sese that day by chance because I always seek out a zoo in the midst of the chaos of a city. It helps me to think and relax. It helps me to ground myself. It's peaceful in a zoo and nobody pesters you. When I saw her, Sese had her face glumly squeezed between the bars of the cage, a little like I felt after almost a day without sleep on the plane to Manila, except that Sese had been in the cage for years and would be there until she died. She just stared out through the bars. I was staring, too, but that was because I was dumbfounded.

Then another dumbfounding thing happened. A stranger standing there asked me how old the orangutan was. Trust a human being to miss the obvious. How evolved are we really? Why is it important to know your age when you are locked in a bare cage in a zoo for the rest of your miserable existence? Now everything seemed to annoy me. The heat. The jet lag. The pixie-size tubs of jam for breakfast in the hotel. I went to the offices of the zoo on a pointless mission to try to track down someone who could make sense of Sese's existence. No luck. I really wasn't in a mood to listen, anyway. Let me take a big leap and say that Sese needed stimulation, the stimulation of the jungle, because in the jungle, there is always something to watch and taste and smell and it keeps you alive, that stimulation. The jungle is part of the orangutan and the orangutan is part of the jungle. Taking an orangutan out of that environment is like taking a bird out of the sky. It really can't exist that way and you can't understand it without that. But the jungle had been taken from Sese.

The man I had come to find in the Philippines had found years ago what Sese had lost. He became part of the rain forests of Borneo and Sumatra in a way that few Westerners had done at the time. He persevered where others failed. He slept in the jungle and wrote about the hum of frogs and crickets down by "the old fig-tree by the river." Over there, a male orangutan is sleeping quietly after gorging on wild mangosteens. He has shattered the jungle nights with the "long series of deep and terrifying roars." "The tree frogs bleeped their songs amid the chorus of the jungle night. From down the slope came grunts from my nesting orangutans and, far away, a strange groaning like an old man in great pain. Sleep came in broken patches amid curious dreams and spells of wakefulness. I woke cold and stiff. A faint grey light filtered through the mist between the ghostly trunks of giant trees. Somewhere

in the distance a single gibbon was singing to the whole forest to announce another day."

This is what it feels like to be alive, to be touched by the blessing of
"leeches, flies, mud, rotan and falling branches." This is what it means
to savor every morsel of the jungle. "Porcupine was delicious and so was
the black tree monitor lizard that lived in the forest. The huge river
monitors, however, were very tough and had to be stewed for several
hours. Often we feasted on terrapins, tortoises or frogs. There was nothing wrong with the meat of a leaf monkey caught by the dogs but I was
rather put off by its yellow fat and was once horrified to find that the
entire head had been left in the pot." That's a life.

And that's what I found buried in a long out-of-print book from 1974
with a plain green cover. And that's why I wanted to meet this man,
John MacKinnon. Nothing I can ever do in my life will match an experience like his. I wanted to know what he possessed to be able to do that.
I also had an odd thought. I wanted some reassurance, that wherever he
is, whatever he is doing, the young MacKinnon is still alive in the old
MacKinnon. I was curious to know whether the flame of his life is still
burning undiminished, still green and vital inside to the core, and that
he hadn't committed himself to a life that is like Sese living in her cage.
If I can't do it myself, somebody else has to do it for me, for us, and we
have to know that he did it and that he is still capable of doing it. So I
searched for the author of *In Search of the Red Ape,* the book that signaled
a change in the understanding of orangutans and what it was possible
to know about them.

From the book I learned that years ago MacKinnon had visited the
Dutch primatologist Herman Rijksen in Sumatra who would later become influential in the science of orangutans. I wanted to find Rijksen,
too. One thing links to another in life. I eventually found them both
at opposite ends of the world. And I slept in the jungle, too, not with
the depth of MacKinnon, but enough. I slept by the river under the
jungle stars and woke to the bone-deep buzz of the morning and saw

the orangutans pee on high from the trees making for us below what the natives call "jungle rain." We all need a little of the jungle in our lives. It makes us more human.

MacKinnon was at Los Banos, outside Manila, the year that I tracked him down. I spent time talking to him while he turned my young son Pearce over to a team of assistants. These assistants were hunting down a huge black cloud rat the size of a muskrat that was living inside the walls of a building at the University of the Philippines and chewing the wiring. When the assistants caught the rat, MacKinnon didn't want the beast killed. He wanted it released into the jungle again as though the life of one big rodent made a difference in the universe. So we took the rat under the trees where MacKinnon opened the cage door. Out of the cage the rat exploded like someone had lit its tail on fire. Everyone jumped back as though they'd been bitten by a snake. The big rat bounded away into the shadow of the trees like it had never been there. That was MacKinnon. He was still deep into that way of life, and I felt comforted and reassured. This was the same MacKinnon who had appeared at just the right moment to survive in the forests of orangutans and to persevere through the hardship of the conditions in which they thrive. It was a moment of change, too, the beginning of the succession of those who would seek to understand orangutans in the wild.

MacKinnon has written so many books that he estimates their number at seventeen and has been a major influence on conservation planning in Indonesia and other countries. He discovered a new species of mammal in Vietnam, a saola, which looks "like a goat," as he explains, but is actually a "primitive cow." Yet all this is largely unknown, aside from the interest that scientists take professionally in MacKinnon's work.

MacKinnon was in the field with orangutans so early that others, like the young primatologist Biruté Galdikas, were being discouraged at that same time from even attempting what he and David Horr were in the jungle already doing. Horr was in Sabah at the same time as MacKinnon and is credited by MacKinnon as the first scientist to clock a thousand hours of watching orangutans in the wild. And yet Galdikas was told at the same time while she was in university in California that it was impossible to study orangutans in their natural terrain. The idea that orangutans were impossible to study had gained credibility in science with George Schaller's report of his explorations in Sarawak and the paltry six hours of observations he was able to log after months in the forest in 1950. The ability of a man named William Temple Hornaday to find orangutans in Sarawak in the 1800s had been long forgotten.

So John MacKinnon immersed himself in the experience of the rain forest of orangutans at a time when others were being discouraged, and published his remarkable observations in both scientific journals and a popular book. It was MacKinnon who gave the name "long call" to the "long series of deep and terrifying roars" that he heard from the male orangutan in the jungle. MacKinnon saw more orangutans at different locations in Borneo and Sumatra than others. To do that, to observe orangutans acting naturally in their natural setting and not in artificial conditions like in a lab experiment, MacKinnon had to adapt himself to the environment of orangutans. He had to be independent, alone. How was he able to achieve that? What character in a man or a woman allows them to accomplish that? If we could all do that, think what a different world it would be.

To do what he did, MacKinnon slept in the jungle in Borneo and Sumatra at night and watched wild orangutans during the day. Once, while he was asleep, an elephant almost stepped on him in the dark. He earned the name *tuan berhani* or "fearless master" from the natives because he swam in the dark across a river with crocodiles. He suffered from a parasite found in dogs and was cured in hospital only to return to the hospital two weeks later with a bout of malaria. His descriptions of thunderstorms and the luminosity of the dark jungle and encounters with orangutans have the power that fiction can only fabricate—and yet this happened.

And MacKinnon paid his dues. One time, a wild boar attacked his young son on a beach in the jungle on the island of Sulawesi, just east of Borneo. MacKinnon was there to study "the black ape," which is really a macaque, and to set up a nature reserve. Both MacKinnon and his son were left gouged and ripped and bleeding from the attack. "We were living," MacKinnon said, "in one of my usual horrid little huts in the forest at the edge of the sea. I heard the screams and came rushing around to help him. He was four. I was in a lot of pain," MacKinnon told me with a laugh. "It was really horrible, because he was pouring blood and we had wounds and flaps. The pig had torn great flaps out. And I had to stitch him up and my hand was squirting blood out whilst I was trying to stitch him up. I used a needle and cotton." Then MacKinnon and his son sat for hours on a pile of fish in a fishing boat to reach the nearest village then hours more to reach the nearest hospital, then more delay to reach a better hospital, which in the end botched the medical treatment of MacKinnon and his son. The boy's broken bone wasn't set properly and had to be set again later in Singapore, and MacKinnon eventually lost his finger to gangrene. The jungle had taken his finger as payment, but the man persevered.

To find MacKinnon took me some time. I eventually located him, then in his late fifties, living a few hours down the road from Manila at Los Banos, near a sleeping volcano and a large, gray, hazy lake that looks like it is evaporating in the heat before your eyes. He was immersed in a project with the university at Los Banos, still absorbed in his work, still with the energy and enthusiasm you had to admire. He was still the nomad he had been in his book, a man in continuous flux, unshackled, unconfined, sleeping not in bed with his wife but on the floor like he slept on the ground in the jungle. And to find him that way felt good.

How is a man like this made? How does he come into being? I asked MacKinnon about his childhood and he told me that he had wanted to be immersed in the wilderness since the time he was a boy in a dull, dirty English town. From an early age he had a strong need to prove that he was independent, self-reliant, and he found it pleasurable to be separate from others. It seemed that the way to do that was by being a woodsman, so, as a boy of fifteen, he would spend a week at a time in a tent by himself in the Scottish mountains, comfortable with solitude in a way that would be useful to him later in the jungles of Africa and Southeast Asia. "The forest is never lonely," he told me when I asked him in the Philippines about this part of himself. "I could feel what it's like to be part of the forest and to be an orangutan." He was calm then, as a boy and later a young man in the jungle, without the responsibility for a family that would later extend to a succession of two wives and three children. "I had nothing to worry about. It was just me and the forest."

He felt different and the jungle allowed him to do what others couldn't do, almost as though he was chosen by the forest for something unusual. "I felt I had some special magic that I could do it better than anyone else," he explained. The difference was that he was part of the experience, that he could be "alien and lost in the green and soaring gloom of the markless wilderness," as the writer William Faulkner once described the mood. MacKinnon enjoyed fading into it, sinking into the pure, dark, smoldering, unrancorous depths of it, vanishing deeper into its deepness "like a fish without any movement of its fins." He knew instinctively that to enter the wilderness he had to divest himself of the trappings of a civilization that isolated and insulated him from it. "I decided to travel alone with only a minimum of equipment, since the added mobility and quietness should enable me to encounter more animals and they would be less shy of a solitary observer."

MacKinnon started early. When he was eighteen he spent a year working at Jane Goodall's chimpanzee station in Gombe, Africa. His uncle, the governor of Kenya, helped arrange it. The life he saw in the jungle at Gombe was what he decided he wanted for himself. It was also in Kenya that, by chance, the young MacKinnon was introduced to orangutans through meeting Barbara Harrisson, the first person to attempt to rehabilitate orangutans and return them to the jungle in Borneo. I would eventually meet Harrisson in the Netherlands through MacKinnon's old contact Herman Rijksen. Later, when the young MacKinnon would have to choose a subject for a PhD in zoology at Oxford University, he would remember Harrisson and her orangutans and make the radical choice to study orangutans in the Far East, partly because he wanted to do what others weren't doing.

At Gombe, MacKinnon built a hut for himself in the forest away from the camp so he could be by himself and learn to track chimpanzees. Aside from Goodall, he said, he was the only one at the camp able to do that. By the time MacKinnon went into the jungle in Borneo, he would already be comfortable with a solitary life in an alien landscape. "Now I was alone," he wrote, as the solitude of the wilderness began to awaken within him. "I felt as though I was being watched, that an animated jungle was studying the pale stranger with unfriendly eyes."

To start his study of orangutans, MacKinnon chose in 1968 the location of Sabah, a province of Malaysia in northern Borneo. There are now an estimated 11,500 orangutans in Sabah, but there were probably more in the late sixties when MacKinnon was there. MacKinnon picked the smaller Sabah over the much larger Kalimantan, in Indonesian Borneo, because Indonesia was still in turmoil from the 1967 revolution. The British colony of Malaysia never had a revolution and war of independence like the Dutch colony of Indonesia. Malaysia made a smooth and orderly transition and even today it feels more sedate and orderly than Indonesia.

MacKinnon headed for the Segama River, which enters into the Sulu Sea, initiating himself by a visit to the Sepilok orangutan project. The Sepilok reserve opened in 1964 as the first official orangutan rehabilitation project for rescued orangutans who had been kept illegally as pets. At the Sepilok camp, MacKinnon was received warmly. "Six eager red apes came to greet me. I was gripped by strong hands and feet while they examined every part of my clothing and anatomy. The bald clown, Jippo, somersaulted in rings around me, hugging himself with jealousy when I paid too much attention to the more introverted and supercilious Cynthia.

Cynthia, an eight-year-old adolescent, was one of the two original animals released by Barbara Harrisson on Bako Island in 1962 in the first attempt to rehabilitate captive orangs."

At Sepilok, MacKinnon, perhaps from his initiation at Goodall's Gombe station, immediately recognized the orangutans as individuals rather than just abstract specimens to study, and felt comfortable anthropomorphizing them as he tried to understand what he was seeing. He explains that it is necessary to anthropomorphize orangutans in order to understand them as a scientist. That sounds like a radical break from the strict empirical method of science, but zookeepers and scientists conducting field studies told me the same thing. MacKinnon said, "These animals are just like people. If I saw you angry, it's the same thing as empathizing how I think that animal is feeling." That makes sense. We need to anthropomorphize other people in order to see below the surface and understand them. If we didn't do that, we'd be living by ourselves in an insular world of purely material objects.

From Sepilok, MacKinnon entered the jungle by river and traveled up the Segama with native Ibans. *"Banyak Buaya, Tuan,"* they told him. "Many crocodiles, sir." "An Iban," explained MacKinnon, "does not feel fulfilled as a man until he has taken a human head. For each man he kills he may tattoo one knuckle of his hand." MacKinnon noticed that his guides had well-tattooed knuckles. When it became harder for the Ibans to justify hunting people, they turned to making themselves men by killing orangutans instead. As MacKinnon went up the river, the jungle opened to him as if it had been waiting all its life just for him. "Eight-foot-long monitor lizards basked on sun-baked rocks and electric blue kingfishers flew by, shrieking. Snakebirds played hide and seek, disappearing for a few minutes under water then surfacing as we drew near and flying ahead to play again." He saw a tree loaded with bats. "Thousands and thousands of these unholy beasts hung in treetops like some rich crop of fruit." By this time MacKinnon was comfortable in the jungle and the jungle was comfortable in him.

*   *   *

But it was his receptivity to the experience of orangutans where Mac-Kinnon really excelled. MacKinnon decided to travel alone in the jungle, moving by day, sleeping by night, to disturb the orangutans less and increase his chances of contact. He was able to locate a big male orangutan he called Harold. Like Jane Goodall and Dian Fossey before him and Biruté Galdikas after him, MacKinnon gave the apes the names of human beings, the type of behavior that would offend the empirical purists as sentimentality. Harold was able to elude MacKinnon, probably because he heard the noise of a human being following him from the bottom of the forest.

"It was four days before I finally tracked him down to a large fruit tree. Harold saw me at once but showed no fear. He was busily feeding on a type of wild lychee called *mata kuching* (cat's eyes)." The orangutan swung over MacKinnon squatting on the trail but "disdained" to notice him. And MacKinnon, for his part, was the same, never yearning for closer contact with orangutans. He was not looking for companionship with apes. MacKinnon heard Harold call at night after a tree crashed in the distance, probably because Harold interpreted the sound of the crash as a challenge from another male. "He reached a bellowing climax, then gradually the sounds subsided to low mumblings again." This is like hearing a cry deep out of the soul of the earth. MacKinnon noticed that Harold had stiff fingers, like Fossey's gorilla Digit. MacKinnon didn't know at this point that he would be missing a finger himself in a few years. Broken and missing fingers make it easy to identify both apes and human beings.

The encounter with Harold happened the same night that MacKinnon was almost squashed by an elephant while sleeping on the ground. To save himself from the elephant, MacKinnon rushed away, wounding himself when he ran past the tiny sharp blades of the *rotan* tendrils. But neither leeches, elephants, nor fever could deter MacKinnon from seeking orangutans. With a severe attack of fever that not even his chloroquin tablets could quench, he forced himself to return to the forest, dizzy and with vision blurred, and encountered the orangutan he named Ivan the Terrible, another Kusasi in another patch of jungle.

"A huge, black orangutan was walking along the path towards me. I had never seen such a large animal even in a zoo. He must have weighed every bit of three hundred pounds." MacKinnon ducked behind a tree and then followed the Russian orangutan. "He was enormous, as black as a gorilla but with his back almost bare of hair."

MacKinnon was too weak from fever to keep pace. "I blundered on, nauseated, dizzy, and failing to see that he had stopped almost crashed into the beast as he sat munching shoots." Ivan was too heavy as an orangutan to swing through the trees, so he was an exile ambling along the ground that orangutans usually scorn.

After the encounter with the huge orangutan, MacKinnon struggled back to his camp. "That night the deliriums of my drugs and fever combined to haunt me with terrible dreams of fiendish creatures taunting my sanity." He was sick with fever for three days with nobody to nurse him but himself. Later he was told by an Iban to eat monkey meat when he had a fever and wanted to keep his sanity.

On his return trip to the Segama, MacKinnon made contact with a large male leader he named King Louis. "I followed Louis for four days and we both spent most of our time sheltering from the terrible rain." MacKinnon continued, "Louis did not like me and made no attempt to hide the fact. . . . By the second [day] he came crashing towards me, descending through the branches as he drew close. I backed away nervously but this gave his courage such a boost that he was soon down on the ground in fast pursuit. Subsequent encounters became rather a trial for, now that he knew I was afraid, he charged whenever he saw me, and, unwilling to call his bluff, I inevitably made a hasty retreat."

MacKinnon decided to challenge the orangutan. MacKinnon crashed through the plants toward the tree where Louis was and started to climb a tree after him. Startled, the orangutan retreated. "For the next hour

Louis remained sulking at the top of the tree like a naughty schoolboy who has been severely scolded." What happened next was remarkable. MacKinnon and the orangutan negotiated the terms of their relationship. It may be the first time in history that such communication and negotiation has taken place between a wild orangutan and a human being. Biruté Galdikas would do a similar thing later in Tanjung Puting with a large male named Throatpouch.

"Somehow," said MacKinnon, "we came to a mutual agreement that he would stop coming to the ground to frighten me if I would stop climbing into trees to harass him." MacKinnon's admiration for the mind of the orangutan grew during this period. "Orangutans have amazing intelligence for solving spatial and temporal problems," he said. "They know the behaviour of other animals. Orangutans have the intelligence to work on new problems that chimps don't. An orangutan sits and studies."

In 1971, MacKinnon returned to orangutans, this time in Sumatra, at the huge Gunung Leuser Reserve in Aceh province in northern Sumatra, where the battle of the Aceh for independence would later flare up again. Here another of the new jungle scholars, the Dutch scientist Herman Rijksen, established the Ketambe station the same year where other scientists would spend years working. This was also the same year that Biruté Galdikas landed in Tanjung Puting at the southern tip of Borneo unaware of MacKinnon.

The strands of what would happen to these people were being woven together, although they didn't know it at the time. MacKinnon wouldn't publish his book for three years, although Rijksen had talked to him in England before Rijksen went to Sumatra, as Rijksen had also met Goodall and Harrisson in Switzerland before he went to Sumatra. At this time the study of orangutans in the wild was still a fledgling science and would continue to be personal and individualistic as it developed through the years. It was never a community of scientists working together in constant close contact. The result of that would be some lost opportunities and some misunderstandings, but also a free and unrestrained process of discovery.

In Sumatra, MacKinnon climbed the slopes of Gunung Umang like a giant in the land of the little people. "The mountain derives its name from the mythical little folk who supposedly haunt its summit, but the only sign of men we found were the *parang*"—or machete—"slashes along the paths made by the collectors of wild cinnamon." Here MacKinnon realized that what he thought was standard orangutan behavior from his observations in Borneo was not. The Sumatran male orangutans were more social than those in Borneo and even tolerated other males. Unlike the male in Borneo, the Sumatran males stay with the female until after the birth of the child to protect mother and child from predators like the tigers not found in Borneo. This may also be a reason for their spending more time in the trees than orangutans in Borneo. The Sumatra orangutans live in densities that would be thought impossible from Borneo studies. In the 1970s, MacKinnon made an important early distinction that some would ignore. He said it was wrong to generalize in a simple way about the behavior of orangutans when they showed such strong differences.

Although MacKinnon started his field studies before the Dutch scientist Herman Rijksen, by 1971 Rijksen was in Sumatra and MacKinnon visited him there. More of the strands of association between people were coming together. MacKinnon found Rijksen and his wife Ans working at Ketambe with orangutans in what seemed like an ideal existence. The Rijksens were living "in their new bungalow adjoining the orangutan orphanage," whereas the MacKinnons had just "a grass hut," MacKinnon wrote. MacKinnon liked the valleys and mountains where Rijksen had settled. "Rising up to the misty mountains," MacKinnon wrote, "the forest was a beautiful blend of every shade and hue of green with here and there a brighter splash of orange or flame."

A rare black wild mountain goat called a serow was grazing on the lawn of the Rijksen home, after Rijksen had saved it from being eaten.

Rijksen was going to release the goat into a wild area in a few days. The goat was so tame that when it was released it came up to different people in the forest, which was the friendly thing to do—until it approached a practical man who simply killed it with his *parang* and then ate it.

A week before MacKinnon visited, Rijksen had found the tracks of a rhinoceros in the sand by a waterhole. At that time, Rijksen was planning to rehabilitate orangutans kept captive as pets and return them to the wild with a degree of human contact he would renounce eight years later. Biruté Galdikas was following a similar style at the same time in Tanjung Puting and would continue that way.

What MacKinnon saw in those days at Ketambe in the lives of the former captive orangutans was encouraging. MacKinnon introduced his young son, Jamie, to sixteen orangutans at Ketambe who had been rescued and were being rehabilitated. They were fed rice and pawpaws and were free to wander back into the forest where wild orangutans lived. "The orangutans were fascinated by this tiny, white ape and came to inspect, smell and kiss the delighted child." At Ketambe, MacKinnon wrote, one female had been rescued after spending "a year locked in the cramped space of a disused car" and another orangutan "had been badly burned by an electric cable." After all the years since then I wondered if Rijksen remembered the orangutan who had been locked in the car. "Yes, of course I do," he told me. "She was raving mad and attacked every human who stood in her way, but was very timid with respect to other orangutans. She had a mad look in her eyes, and when she started to break into our house, I sedated her and put her in a bag and brought her across the river to a place rather deep into the forest. We never saw her again and I suppose she died of starvation, or in the jaws of the tiger."

As for the orangutan burned by an electric cable, named Barbara, Rijksen remembers her, too. "While climbing an electricity pole with live wiring at her captor's house she was nearly electrocuted and lost her underarm as a consequence of gangrene. She could cope very well until she was eaten by a clouded leopard, which cost seven other young orangutans their lives as well." Rijksen said it caused "a riot" among the local people when the leopard was caught so that it could be released alive into another area of the jungle. "They shouted and banged on the car. They were angry." The people would have preferred the leopard dead.

Another orangutan that was confiscated and given to Rijksen, a six-year-old female named Tjali, "could drink like anybody. Just booze. She was kept by an American from an oil rig and he enjoyed himself with Tjali, sitting in a bar in Medan, boozing through the night." The orangutan and the oil worker got drunk together? "Yes," said Rijksen. "Well, the orangutan can have more booze than a person. In the wild there are fruits that ferment on the forest floor and orangutans are crazy about them." Tjali had also picked up the habit of smoking, Rijksen said. She was friendly with people, but didn't like to socialize with other orangutans. After a year and a half she was released into the forest near Bohorok, although she preferred to drink booze and Coca-Cola with the tourists and to smoke cigarettes.

From the time that MacKinnon first visited Rijksen in Sumatra, Rijksen would grow to be well respected among scientists and his station at Ketambe would be a base for other primatologists, like Carel van Schaik, to conduct research. Because Indonesia, where most orangutans are found, was a Dutch colony for years, Dutch scientists like Rijksen naturally gravitated to the place. Rijksen is still greatly influential in this area of science, although he lives in the Netherlands now, in a home that suits his nature—a quiet, genteel, book-lined space with a lily pond outside, set in a forest. I felt intimidated to meet Rijksen, by the sheer stature and respect he had among scientists. In person, Rijksen has the handshake of an ironworker, firm and crisp, like his mind, with round-rim glasses accentuating the intense light blue eyes of a sage. He seemed tempered and chastened by too many years spent watching humanity destroy its environment. His manner can be harsh when he talks about the lapses of science and humanity.

Rijksen was born in 1942 at Zeist, in the center of the Netherlands, "the relative highland, river dunes outcrop of the central Veluwe." The time of his birth was during the Nazi occupation of Holland. After he grew up, Rijksen wanted to study biology in university, but that was initially blocked by his father, who "decided that it was not a profession" for his son. Instead, Rijksen graduated with a degree in veterinary medicine. "I never practiced," he says, "since I wanted to study apes from my first year at the university, in 1962." Rijksen and his wife, Ans Graatsma, were sponsored to work with orangutans by the director of a Dutch research organization, Jan H. Westerman, a career diplomat who had been posted to Indonesia and Australia. Rijksen wanted to study gorillas in Africa, but Westerman convinced him to study orangutans instead. "He wanted to re-establish the wider nature conservation ties after the post-colonial turmoil of the Sukarno era. He knew that the situation of the orangutan was bad, and he feared that it would go extinct unnoticed, if there was no new scientific attention focused on the ape. I was part of his survival campaign."

Rijksen studied orangutans in Sumatra from 1971 to 1974, collecting enough information to write a doctoral thesis, and then he returned to Sumatra and Indonesia on an annual basis to pursue his interest in conservation. "Pure chance" brought him to the Ketambe site in Sumatra. "A poacher who knew the area intimately recommended the location. He became a dear friend, and teacher, and my employment and frequent company kept him from poaching."

"We lived across the wide Alas River, two kilometers from a resthouse along the forest track between Kutacane and Blangkejeren. When the river was swollen or flooded we were stuck for days, and lived off rice, bananas, papayas, and tinned fish. Quite often we had to ford rivers on our way to Medan, since the primitive timber bridges were washed away. It was very primitive, but incredibly special."

Rijksen started field studies of the orangutans at Ketambe and continued to return there for twenty-six years. In later years, Carel van

Schaik would follow the same group of orangutans at Ketambe and establish another station at Suaq Balimbing in south Aceh where van Schaik could study an even more densely packed group with the help of Beth Fox and Ian Singleton.

It was hard work for Rijksen to find wild orangutans. "It cost me almost a year of daily searching and a handful of chance encounters, to learn to find, anticipate, and smell out orangutans." Fortunately, he had the orphan orangutans he was rehabilitating to give him encouragement until he could find wild ones.

I asked Rijksen if one orangutan impressed him above all the others. He talked about Yoko, not yet ten years old. "She was extraordinarily intelligent, using tools for all kinds of activities, thoughtful in all her actions, and kind. Smart and friendly without a trace of subservience or fear."

Trouble for Yoko came from an orangutan named Binjai. According to Rijksen, "One robust six-year-old rehabilitant female, Binjai, showed enormous self-esteem and resourcefulness. She was so wild and self-assured and that's something orangutans need to survive. She quickly established a high social position among the wild group—became a resident, and lived for at least thirty years in the study area, during which time she had three offspring and became a grandmother. Her character was quite brutal, when feral.

"Around her ninth year, Binjai adopted a young, two- to three-year-old rehabilitant and cared for him as a mother. She also sometimes helped the one-armed small female rehab, Barbara. She quickly rose to top female rank in the group and established her dominance with every female newcomer by manually raping her on first contact. She could direct even the males of the same size as she was. And she raped other females. That's the way that orangutans show other orangutans they are dominant. John MacKinnon was the first to mention that orangutans rape other orangutans, which caused a riot among primatologists. Orangutans are preoccupied with sex.

"Binjai hated Yoko, who had entered the rehab group before her—and wasn't raped as far as we know—and always looked for opportunities to attack her. I believe Binjai went for the kill, but Yoko was invariably too clever to get involved in a serious confrontation, and also could count on protection of the oldest sub-adult male rehabilitant in the group. Binjai was quick to attract wild boyfriends who consorted with her from her tenth year. Binjai had four children and her first two children also have children.

"Yoko came from south of Lake Toba and she was totally different in character. She was more thoughtful. She was extremely friendly. She understood things that I would never have dared to believe. She was attacked in the forest by a clouded leopard and very badly mauled and she dragged herself to my house. We weren't there, but she was waiting for me on the doorstep. She had never been to my house before. I was amazed to see her there. I said, 'What's up?' She started whimpering and only then did I see that she was very badly hurt. She had wounds all over her body. She came to get help. So I treated her and, like a patient, I spoke to her when I treated her. She had to keep still with her wounds that I had to treat every day. We put her in a big box, an open box, near my house, so that she would be safe. She stayed in the box for weeks even though she could go anyplace. She understood what was happening with her. And when she was healed entirely we took her across a river that no orangutans had ever crossed and she was back at my house before we were ourselves. I have no idea how she got across the river. We had to wade through the river. She was a character. It was her friendliness, her way of very quickly sensing or understanding what the best way was of dealing socially with other orangutans and with me. She liked to come to you and sit and groom, which is unusual for orangutans. Eventually she disappeared."

Disappeared? "Does it feel like something is missing in your life not knowing what happened to Yoko?" I asked Rijksen.

"Yes and no. Yes, because one is curious to know what happened to her." But he felt it was best that the orangutan leave and not become dependent on human beings like himself.

Time passed. Rijksen went his way. MacKinnon his. With his early start with orangutans, MacKinnon could have become the world's foremost expert on orangutans, like Jane Goodall with chimpanzees and Dian Fossey with gorillas. He would have been offered a fat post at an important university in a Western country and with his talent as a speaker and a writer he could have written popular books and filled lecture halls. But, after his 1971 expedition to the jungle, MacKinnon pursued other interests with the same nomadic and solitary nature that he appreciated in an orangutan in the jungle. "I had found," he wrote in his book in 1974, "the orangutan to be a solitary nomad. His large bulk and relative immobility forced him into a hermitlike existence for few trees could bear the ravages of more than one red ape at a time." MacKinnon concluded his book with the observation, "The most outstanding feature of orangutan life was its solitary nature."

Over time, MacKinnon established, like a male orangutan, a companionship with the jungle that he found fulfilling. "My whole attitude towards the jungle had mellowed," he wrote. "It was no longer an enemy but a friend. Even the leeches had their uses. Tied to a creeper tendril and lowered into a stream pool, they proved irresistible to the small fish. I had become used to my own company and was no longer bored or lonesome in my solitary life." An orangutan moves through the forest as though he is inside the outward manifestation of his life, history, and memory. In the same way, "Every part of the forest was filled with memories of previous experiences, good or bad," wrote MacKinnon. "Gradually I became a part of the jungle and felt at home there."

Years later in the Philippines, when I asked MacKinnon again about solitude he said, "You have to be able to deal with solitude. I certainly like my own company." Unlike other scientists and cerebral types, he never established a nest for himself in academia. His independence gave him the intellectual freedom that university professors can only debate. He remains reflective in solitude and seems to favor the more solitary side that some people share with the *mawas* or orangutan, as distinct from the more social gorillas and chimpanzees. "I was following rather solitary nomadic animals," he wrote in his book, "so had become a solitary nomad myself. I travelled when my orangs travelled, ate when they ate and slept when they slept. I was reminded of the story of the man who stayed too long in the jungle and turned into an orangutan; I wondered if I wasn't becoming half a *Mawas* myself."

Thinking about it again after all this time, he said, "I don't know why I wanted to be independent. I was probably overconfident" when young, he said, and the years have also brought dimmer eyes and arthritis. He cited the influence of his mother, a strict Presbyterian, for his independence. As a girl she'd save thrupence by walking home for an hour from school rather than take the bus. "It wasn't as though she had to," he said. "Why does anyone do anything? I still most often sleep on the floor. I have no idea why. I'm very comfortable on the floor. There's nothing I want to go back home for. Britain is now so parochial." His current wife is Chinese. They have two children, after MacKinnon had a son, Jamie, with his first wife Kathy.

But maybe it's not exactly a solitary existence. Maybe it depends on how a person looks at it. Consider the difference between orangutans and chimpanzees, said MacKinnon. "Chimpanzees," he said, "can meet and a few hours later meet again as though there were a long interval of time. But an orangutan can greet another that he hasn't seen for three months and not bat an eyelid. To him, the interval isn't long. They don't feel that they've been separated. The orangutan doesn't feel he has been alone. He doesn't feel solitude. He's thinking a lot." So maybe there's a way to see the world more like an orangutan than a chimpanzee. We don't have to be like chimpanzees all the time.

CHAPTER 4

Touched by an Ape

THE WORLD LOOKS different through the eyes of an orangutan. The world also looks different through the eyes of a man or a woman. It's a difference we'll never quite understand. It's like trying to see a firefly in the dark. All you can catch is a glimpse of a quick flash in the night and nothing more and yet you keep trying, as though if you can stare long enough you'll see it and understand it. I'd think about the meaning of the differences while discussing orangutans with someone like Ulrike Freifrau von Mengden or Barbara Harrisson or Biruté Galdikas. All strong and independent women. All different from each other. All different from men. How did that affect things? How is a woman looking at an orangutan different from a man looking at an orangutan? How does a woman like the Catalan veterinarian Rosa Garriga see a male orangutan like Kusasi? Remember that she amputated the toe of the big brute and then kissed him. How did she feel? Or how does a man see a female orangutan? My friend Gary Shapiro knew Princess intimately because he acted as her surrogate father to teach her sign language. He would bring out a side of her that a woman might never know. Actually, he says that lady chimpanzees and lady orang-utans find him attractive. That's understandable. He has a nice voice and a pretty gleam in his eye.

One woman told me how delighted she was to forge a bond with a difficult male orangutan that others couldn't reach. That experience may have had another dimension for her because she also told me that she never had a good relationship with her father. Was the success with the difficult male orangutan partly compensation for what she never had with her father? I don't know. Maybe she doesn't know, either. Of course, as a father with a daughter of my own I would think about these things as I talked to women. I'd wonder what kind of relationship the women had with their fathers and how that had affected their lives. I felt a bit guilty, too, because I took my son with me to Southeast Asia and not my daughter. I didn't think that a huge Muslim nation in the Far East was ready just yet for a spirited seventeen-year-old female from the West who didn't know the meaning of the phrase "You can't do that." Later, I took my daughter with me to the Netherlands when I talked to Barbara Harrisson, who was rehabilitating orangutans in Borneo before anybody else. Harrisson had many adventures with orangutans, and you should imagine the words of hers in this chapter as the tale of an eighty-three-year-old woman told to a seventeen-year-old girl.

Harrisson told us that years ago she had the courage to stay in a small camp in the jungles of Borneo. "I spent a lot of nighttime in the forest," she said. By yourself? I asked, glancing to see if my daughter Caitlin was listening. She was. My daughter is intelligent and listens and makes up her mind more quickly than her dad. "Yeah, sure," Harrisson said. "That's the only way to do it. Sometimes for two, three days and nights. Sometimes for a week."

I asked if she wasn't afraid to spend a week by herself in the jungle, all the while watching to see if my daughter was still absorbing this. "Why should I?" she said. "This is a stupid question. I wasn't seventeen any longer."

I said that my daughter was seventeen and then asked, "Should I say to my daughter, 'Go into the jungle in Sarawak by yourself for a week'?"

"Why not?" she said. "It must be that you find someone locally that could give her good advice, but do not say don't go. That would be stupid. That would be entirely old fashioned." Good answer.

At the end of the tale of her adventures, Harrisson turned to my daughter to advise her that men only last for so long, so be wise in your choice, and have a backup career to your "dream," which makes sense if you know what happened to Harrisson. Her husband was killed in a car accident after betraying her with a Belgian woman. "I found this very, very frustrating, I must say," she told my daughter and me. "I had an absolutely miserable time, but there was nothing I could do."

She returned to school in her middle age and reinvented herself as a successful professor teaching in a university in the Netherlands far from the land of the exploits of her younger days. "Keep your independence," she said to my daughter. "By this I mean don't get involved with a man who has no hope. It's a terrible danger. I never regretted being married to my husband because he was a very amusing guy. He certainly wasn't a man with no hope. He was only hopeless after getting too old." Good advice. I would have said the same to my teenage daughter, but it wouldn't have had the same effect, and you can guess why.

So my foray into the jungle of gender went in this way, like chasing fireflies through the dark, as I tried to reach an honest understanding and record it here. The final words in this chapter from Terri Hunnicutt, a keeper at the St. Louis Zoo, of how she reached a deeper understanding of orangutans, should be read partly as the accomplishment of a female mind. I would guess that more men than women may have conquered the terrain of the orangutan, but more women may have conquered the terrain of its mind. I would also guess that when a man interprets another man he interprets him as an individual, but when he interprets a woman he is reacting on some level to the whole gender. The same with women reacting to men. That's why, when someone is hurt by the opposite sex, we say, "I don't trust men" or "I don't trust women." And science may not be much different in the way it has come to understand gorillas, chimpanzees, and orangutans. But you will have to be your own ape on this. I've done my gender best.

Saying that Ulrike Freifrau von Mengden is a strong and independent woman is like saying a hurricane is a kind of wind storm. Ulrike Freifrau von Mengden, or Ulla to her friends, is the curator of orangutans at the Schmutzer Primate Centre inside the Ragunan Zoo in Jakarta. I talked to her when she was in her eighties and still living in a bungalow she had built inside the zoo in 1966 to be close to the orangutans she loved. Before scientists began studying orangutans in their tropical forests, before the crucial breakthroughs in understanding apes by Jane Goodall and Dian Fossey, there was Freifrau von Mengden. And she was quite blustery.

Before Jakarta, I'd heard that von Mengden was a fearless, self-reliant woman. Born in east Prussia after the First World War, she came to Jakarta in 1954 with her husband, who was a high official at the German embassy. She traveled widely across Indonesia in small boats at a time when it was unusual for a Western woman to do that. Now, years later, I heard that she lived "apart" from society and "doesn't fit in. She's very complex," said someone who knows her. "There's a lot of frustration in her, unhappiness."

But, according to the orangutan conservationist Willie Smits, "There's the orangutan babies. She needs them." She is "a fanatic" for animals and has an unusual ability to help premature orangutan babies survive, Smits said. "These orangutans are the children she never had," he told me. Smits described her as intelligent, ambitious, stubborn, adventurous, impulsive, someone who sometimes put trust in the wrong people—the same qualities that I'd seen in Smits, another person intensely devoted to orangutans.

I spent a night in a room inside the zoo—a quieter, safer sleep than I had enjoyed in some hotels in cities from Los Angeles to Kuala Lumpur—and woke to the sounds of the jungle. I had breakfast with von Mengden at her home on the grounds of the facility. The noise from the monkeys made the jungle feel close, although trying to understand von Mengden above the crazy hoots and screams of the gang of gibbons was making me deaf. I'd heard that von Mengden had been curator of orangutans for forty years.

"For forty years? I am working for forty-six years," she yelled at me, and repeated the words even more forcefully for emphasis as though talking to an idiot. "The longest one on Earth. We were so poor in the zoo and I worked like hell, building it up with my money and I never asked for a penny." The gibbons were hooting so loudly that she had to stop talking for a moment. "THIS IS A BIG SHOW," she shouted. "TODAY IT IS A BIG SHOW."

She laughed. Fragments of phrases like "German embassy" and "when I was young" struggled to survive between the hoots and cries. "At the university at Bonn I was working with animals as a nurse. The Indonesian governor, Ali Sadikin, asked me to stay here and take over the very small primates endangered when the city was burning"—burning in a figurative sense, she meant, as I learned later after I wondered how she had survived the flames and smoke. "Save them and make them strong and send them back. He gave me the ability to stay here for my life until I die here. I build the house, my house—This is marmalade. Do you like marmalade?" And she lapsed into a flood of German. "It is a good place. Everything is perfect, perfect."

She smiled as an eight-month-old oriental pied hornbill, large and black with red eyes, hopped to the table on her small patio. "He gets breakfast," she said. "He sleeps at the end of my bed. This bird was brought in a shoe box, by a smuggler. He could have been smothered. The tail was too long and the smuggler cut it off. But the smuggler was caught." She tossed a piece of bread to the bird.

"Why do you want to live in a zoo?" I asked.

"Warum wollen Sie in einem des Tiergarten leben?" she mused. An Austrian journalist who was traveling with me discussed the question with her in German and she answered in German. *"Ja, weil der Gouverneur mich beauftragt hat, hier innerhalb des Tiergartens zu bleiben, und er hat mir die Erlaubnis gegeben, mein eigenes Haus zu bauen.* Yah, because the governor ordered me to stay here inside and he gave me the permission to stay here and build my own house," she said, taking advantage of a lull in the ruckus.

"Why do you want to live on the grounds of the zoo rather than in the city?"

"Warum mögen Sie hier inmitten des Tiergartens anstatt in der Stadt leben?" More discussion in German. "That is the most funny question you can say," she said. *"Idiotische Frage.* Idiot question. I like to stay near to animals," she said, pronouncing each word with firm, precise Prussian emphasis. "I'm touched by animals. I'm born like an animal. Maybe in former life I have been an animal. I'm crazy with animals. To be outside, impossible."

"How has the zoo changed over the years?"

"When we started it was very primitive, because when we went outside they were killed, all the officers. It was a political, dangerous time, a communist time." That was the 1965 Communist uprising crushed by Suharto when she helped to move the animals from Cikini to Ragunan using only beer as a sedative. "I was sometimes alone here in the house and, for the food, there was nothing for the big animals. We fed them only with the help of one chicken. It was a hard, hard time in the beginning."

Grasping for questions, I blurted out, "What makes the orangutan special for you?"

"He is equal with me," said von Mengden. "We are the same. We give honor together. I respect him. He respect me. We are the same." More German. More hoots.

"How many orangutans have been born here while you have been here?"

"*Ich glaube sieben.* I think seven." There was a consultation in German and the pronouncement she made next was lost forever among the chorus of gibbons. "In ten minutes," she said, "the orangutans will come to play." The exercise area for the young orangutans was beside her house with lots of monkey bars. It looked like the typical play yard in a school for children. My thirteen-year-old son Pearce was with me and I'm so glad I didn't say, "Why don't you go play with the others?"

"I am very straight," she said. "Never, never hit an animal." Then, to an orangutan strolling past to the play area, she said, "Ratner, come here." Ratner came to the table to shake hands with my son. Ratner impressed us as being polite and dignified and diplomatic. He must be accustomed to strangers. "The rule is never punish," said Freifrau von Mengden.

"The rule of my life from the beginning, to me the small ones should be able to live the normal life, the normal animal's life, with luck and family and without the bloody human beings. The most lowly, I hope, they find the freedom. And I tell all these animals here, 'You have already got the ticket from me for the freedom in your little pocket. And I hope I can keep your freedom.' I hope I can keep my promise. I do the best for them so they are strong and healthy. In forty-six years not one has escaped. They tell each other, 'Don't go outside. Stay with the old woman.' It is a friendly atmosphere. We are a family here. We respect each other."

Orangutans have been a mystery to human beings for centuries because they were difficult to find. Initially orangutans were the subject of a few wild myths by natives who caught glimpses of them in the forest swamps. These sightings were so rare that the indigenous people did not leave much of a record of orangutans in the traditional forms of painting, carving, or folklore, as I discovered talking to a curator at the national museum in Jakarta. "Most tribal communities never saw an orangutan," explained the Dutch scientist Herman Rijksen.

The orangutans remained remote for good reason. "The few interior Dayak tribes that hunted them," said Rijksen, "used their skin, meat and skulls for the soul-substance it conferred upon the hunter and his clan." When I asked about the myth of an orangutan taking a human wife and losing its human voice, Rijksen said, "I believe that the few fairy tales around orangutans have been repeated and exaggerated time and again since they were recorded by the first colonial explorers, as though they were common among many peoples in Borneo. They are not. Orangutans have tried hard to avoid people, and most natives never ventured deep into the forests where the ape survived away from the few paths and stretches of navigable river." Then, in the late nineteenth century when tribal existence was disturbed, he said, more orangutans were seen as the natives went deeper into parts of the forest they'd never traveled before and Westerners were intrigued by the idea of exploring "the jungle."

The red apes were occasionally glimpsed by Westerners in Borneo and Sumatra from the time of the Dutch traders and the British male scientist Alfred Russel Wallace. The early twentieth century saw some work with orangutans in captivity, such as the studies that the Yale University scientist Robert Yerkes conducted with an individual orangutan at a private estate in California during the 1920s. Yerkes described the temperament of the orangutans he saw in captivity as "solemn," "non-committal," "distrustful," and possessing a "tragic" sense of life, which could be a reflection of their captivity.

The more revealing experiences with orangutans had to wait until 1956, when the German Barbara Harrisson, another independent woman, came by chance to care for infant orphan orangutans in the yard of her home in Sawarak, in Borneo. It was a remarkable moment when people like Harrisson started to see an orangutan or a gorilla or a chimpanzee as an individual like us and to treat them that way. The breakthroughs in understanding orangutans and the other great apes depended on the willingness to see them as individuals rather than just abstractions and members of a species. But that idea was controversial at the time and would lead to tension and disputes between scientists.

By luck I found Harrisson in her eighties in Jelsum, an old village in the Netherlands with an old church tower where owls have roosted for over a century. At the time I was visiting Rijksen and two exceptional orangutan zookeepers, Leo Hulsker at the Apenheul Zoo in Apeldoorn and Ton van Groningen in Amsterdam. Van Groningen liked to take walkabouts in the jungle of Borneo. I had my daughter with me and Harrisson told us that her orangutan venture started because her husband Tom became the director of the Sarawak Museum. Tom Harrisson was an eccentric British adventurer who was parachuted into Sarawak, on the island of Borneo, during the Second World War to organize a local guerrilla army unit against the Japanese occupation. It was Tom Harrisson who found in a cave in Sarawak the teeth of the species of orangutan that once ranged across Malaysia, India, and southeast China. When I talked to Harrisson, then eighty-three, she spoke about her life in Sarawak, before her husband had betrayed her, when her husband used his power as a government official to confiscate orangutans. Tom Harrisson brought home an orphan orangutan and Barbara took the responsibility for raising it. Raising it meant learning about it.

There was little that Harrisson could learn about orangutans from Western male scientists at that time. Aside from the scant information in books and in Dayak lore, Harrisson had nothing to help her but her own common sense and an ability to observe. As a woman, she wouldn't feel limited by that. Why should she? The credentials that were created in the universities made it possible for men to practice science. But orangutans were being misunderstood at the time because they were being seen through a veil of human desire and abstraction and gender, as they still are. It's just human nature. Harrisson thought, in simple and practical terms, that a mother has to educate herself to raise a child and that it would be similar caring for orangutans. "How do you get to know a child that's growing up?" she asked me. "It's just the same kind of story. It grows on you."

To understand orangutans, Harrisson made trips into the jungle with Dayaks to learn about orangutans in their own world and to prepare to release them into the wild again. "The forest is so beautiful and so full of life that there is no end to it," she said. "But, if you start being afraid, you've had it. I remember I was one time in Sabah. Suddenly there was a great crashing noise quite close. I froze against a tree. I was too terrified to move. This crashing noise came from an elephant. Elephants are quite huge creatures when you are alone."

In the jungle, Harrisson learned about the long call of the male before John MacKinnon gave it that name. She called the "singing" of the male "a low vibrating growl which gradually increases in intensity, like the sound of a motorcycle approaching from a distance."

One belief that Harrisson developed about rehabilitating orangutans was that it was "essential to provide a substitute" for the loss of a mother in the life of the orangutan. Practically that meant a human substitute after the natural mother had been killed. The idea of using human beings as substitute mothers would become controversial later and one of the dilemmas of trying to help orangutans. Some scientists argue that the contact with human beings trying to repair the damage in the development of orangutans caused by other human beings only interfered with the wild nature of the creature even more. Others, like Biruté Galdikas, believe that the relationship of mother and child is so essential for the development of an orangutan that it needs to be duplicated, even if that means using human surrogates.

At the time when Harrisson was given orphan orangutans there were no orangutan rehabilitation projects, and she saw only a choice of either helping them or letting them die. "For me it was just a natural thing to do," she said. Harrisson wrote in her influential book *Orang-Utan* in 1962 that it was only by seeing orangutans in the jungle that we can understand the importance of the jungle to their mental health. "Their minds," she wrote, "had taken to the trees—for there you can best develop a mood of slow, relaxed contemplation and curiosity." Harrisson understood that the vitality of the mental and emotional life of the orangutan needed the kind of stimulation they get in the jungle. Their strong, natural curiosity, which is part of their intelligence, needed exercise. But she also wanted to return them to the jungle as quickly as possible. If they died, that was life.

Then there was Arthur. Harrisson's project to return orangutans to the jungle might have gone well in Sarawak, which had almost no wild orangutans, if not for the independence of the large, four-year-old orangutan. Arthur was a bold and lively fellow. He frightened Harrisson by his strength, although she was able to keep his respect. He had been captured and confiscated on a border area between Sarawak and Kalimantan where there are few orangutans. The large scar on his forehead could have come either from human beings or another orangutan.

"At first I thought I might send him to a zoo," Harrisson said. "But then he was enterprising. I thought he might be the right person to get around in the forest." Arthur had the personality of "a very naughty teenager and a strong one, not frightened by anything. He would sit up high in the trees to observe every boat that came in and then he would come down and see who it was. They are tremendously curious animals and you see this also in the wild populations. They sit for hours on a branch somewhere and they love observing."

The government of Sabah gave Harrisson a patch of protected forest that seemed safe and secluded enough. It was separated from a seaside area used by the Malaysians by a mangrove swamp, but Arthur found a plank walk through the swamp. "Now Arthur, one morning, took it on himself to escape over the plank walk and get down to the beach. No one was bitten, but hell was raised, and because this was something the government could not tolerate, I was told I should move the project away as soon as possible."

Harrisson found an ally in a game warden who arranged for Harrisson's orangutans to be moved to a new camp in neighboring Sabah, a development that eventually became the famous Sepilok orangutan rehabilitation center, the first of its kind. So, in a sense, thanks to the orangutan Arthur, Sepilok was created. The trip took two or three days then by boat with the orangutans in cages. "Arthur had a fairly substantial cage and I thought this was safe. But he spent his time taking the cage to pieces from the inside and I spent time from the outside trying to repair the damage. It was impossible. But we managed." In Sabah, the cage was heavy and it took six men to carry it into the jungle, far enough so that Arthur would not even be close to the camp. "Arthur got out and went up into the trees and all seemed fine. The animals, including Arthur, did not know this forest, so I spent a week with them trying to encourage them to go further and further into the forest.

"Then I had to go back to Kuching, to Sarawak, to resume my normal life." After Harrisson went into town to get her ticket to return home, "I got back to the camp and was told that Arthur had been shot dead. I was so devastated that I thought I will never again have anything to do with this because this is just terrible. A ranger shot Arthur claiming that he had killed Arthur in self-defense. Arthur had suddenly come out of the forest near the camp, wanted to explore it, and get to know everybody and everything, and had fearlessly invaded some kind of store, where he had gorged himself with bananas, and then he went on to the camp and this man had felt threatened and had shot him." Sepilok was officially established a few years after that, in 1964, as a sanctuary that allows tourists along fenced walkways. It has a separate compound for scientists to conduct research. Aside from the Camp Leakey facility of Biruité Galdikas in a national park in Kalimantan and the small rehabilitation project at Bukit Lawang in Sumatra, it is one of the few places in the world where people can get close to orangutans who are free to wander. At Sepilok, I noticed that there is no monument to Arthur, who paid for his independence with his life, and few outside those devoted to orangutans know of Harrisson.

Harrisson marked a beginning of a change with orangutans that awakened intriguing possibilities. From what she learned, Harrisson was able to devise ways to help the orphan orangutans grow and develop. Others took encouragement from her experiences published in her book in 1962, during the same period that Jane Goodall was studying chimpanzees in Africa. The early orangutan researchers who wanted to work with orangutans in the field and to rehabilitate captives started by contacting Harrisson. At this time in the 1960s, because the science of orangutans had a slow start, it was able to benefit from the new work Jane Goodall was doing with chimpanzees and Dian Fossey with gorillas. Goodall and Fossey perceived different aspects of apes because they saw them as individuals with an emotional life, despite the resistance in the science community to considering the importance and role of emotions. The idea of individualizing of apes gained support and credibility through the popularization of the work of Goodall and Fossey in *National Geographic* magazine.

Goodall and Fossey had started to work with chimpanzees and gorillas because of the influence and assistance of the paleoanthropologist Louis Leakey. Leakey had chosen women to study apes for reasons of gender. He thought women were naturally good observers, could endure years of field work, and were not limited by the conventions of male-dominated science. Leakey now asked Harrisson to consider starting field studies of orangutans, neglected to this point, and told her that he could find funding for her. In a remarkable decision, when Harrisson was being offered the unique chance to have a life like Goodall and Fossey, she said no. "I must say I was very tempted by it," she told me, "but I was married and, if you do that, you have to completely abandon everything else." And that was it. Leakey continued to look for someone to study orangutans in the field and eventually found a willing person in the young Canadian anthropology student Biruté Galdikas.

Meanwhile, the young Brit John MacKinnon, who had spent time with Goodall in Africa, immersed himself in the tropical forest in Sabah, starting in 1968, to learn about orangutans. He was followed by two researchers who established permanent stations in the jungle, the Dutch scientist Herman Rijksen in Sumatra in 1971 and Galdikas in southern Borneo later the same year, in some ways the male and female branches of orangutan science. Since orangutan studies were in their infancy then and unorganized, contact between researchers was sporadic. Galdikas worked in isolation until her 1975 cover story in *National Geographic* magazine catapulted her into the public realm in a trajectory made familiar by Jane Goodall and Dian Fossey. By the time that Galdikas arrived, the public had been taught how to read the life of a female scientist in the jungle through the stories and photographs about Goodall and Fossey.

Harrisson remembers the "young and idealistic" Rijksen coming to discuss orangutans with her and the equally young and idealistic Galdikas. "I admire Herman to no end now because he persisted, instead of becoming angry and frustrated." Rijksen listened to her advice, she said. But Galdikas was different even then. She had her own strong ideas and emotions that determined her direction. Galdikas and Rijksen would take different directions; this explains the differences in thinking that still exist in the work being done with orangutans.

The two articles written by Galdikas in *National Geographic* in 1975 and 1980, read in the glow already cast by Goodall, helped Galdikas to prosper and find support for her work. But it was also the beginning of a rift in this area of science. The popular type of publicity from publications like *National Geographic* disturbed people like Harrisson and Rijksen, who saw it as part of the cult of the ego and the use of a wild creature for the glory it created. Yet Galdikas knew from watching the success of Goodall and Fossey that publicity was a powerful way to focus public support, put pressure on politicians and governments, and raise funds. The long and close contact that Galdikas had with individual orphan orangutans being rehabilitated in a tropical forest would also become controversial because of the way some said it interfered with the health and development of the creature. What revealed the most about orangutans and could build support to save them from extinction might also contaminate the integrity of their wildness. The way people were saving orangutans might destroy them. The issue remains controversial.

But the study of orangutans was changing even more. There was a radical departure coming from the empirical tradition of science and the way human beings saw the world. This departure was largely because of the growing influence of a female consciousness and the power it was attaining through the chance emergence of three women from three different countries following a similar path and making a joint contribution to science. Jane Goodall, Dian Fossey, and Biruté Galdikas, from England, the United States, and Canada, each had a flash of insight into the personal nature of an individual ape they were studying. That revelation encountered resistance from the male scientific establishment of the time, and there is still a residue of that resistance today.

Goodall said that when she began studying chimpanzees at her station at Gombe in Africa in 1960, the scientific community had forbidden the discussion of emotion and personality in the great apes. It wasn't considered science. But Goodall hadn't been indoctrinated into the science culture that policed and perpetuated these ideas. She didn't know the conventions that allow science to operate as a society unto itself. Her mind worked independently, and that allowed her to make breakthroughs. For this reason, Louis Leakey had chosen her and encouraged her to study chimpanzees. Goodall was also working during a historical period in the sixties when there was a social ferment in Western society in the struggle for liberation and independence.

"I didn't realize that animals were not supposed to have personalities, or to think, or to feel emotions or pain," she wrote. "I had no idea that it would have been more appropriate to assign each of the chimpanzees a number rather than a name when I got to know him or her. I didn't realize that it was not scientific to discuss behaviour in terms of motivation or purpose." She used empathy and intuition to understand chimpanzees and wrote unabashedly about the "forbidden" terms of their lives.

When Goodall tried to interest other scientists in what she had observed about the intelligence of chimpanzees, "There was a chill silence," she said. In her first paper for publication she ran into opposition for her use of the gender pronouns "he" and "she" for apes. To treat a living being like a living being with gender and not an inanimate object was considered sentimental and anthropomorphic. But Goodall persisted in her belief that chimpanzees were beings, not things, and prevailed. She made breakthrough observations in the use of tools and in the character and behavior of chimpanzees—observations that Goodall noted were similar to those made decades earlier by the researchers Robert Yerkes and Wolfgang Kohler, but had been easily forgotten by a science community that didn't want to acknowledge them. Because of her quiet, tranquil, saintly manner, and the popular support she received through the pages of *National Geographic,* Goodall became unassailable. But the debt she incurred by breaking the conventions of science would be paid later by more flagrant and assailable targets like Fossey and Galdikas.

The recognition of the individuality of apes began with Goodall making contact with an ape named David Greybeard. Goodall described this threshold experience and it sounds rather uneventful on the surface. She gave a nut to a chimpanzee and he dropped it. Similar things happened to Fossey and Galdikas. A gorilla momentarily touched the hand of Fossey. Galdikas touched the hair of a young orangutan being held by its mother. Not much happening there, at least outwardly. And yet these were momentous events as the women understood them. It was about what was taking place inside the ape that mattered. It all depended on the ability of a person like Goodall to understand the depth of meaning in the experience of a chimpanzee as the chimpanzee understood it.

Goodall described what happened. Sensing the rightness of the moment, she saw a ripe palm nut and held it out with an open palm to the chimpanzee David Greybeard. "He took the fruit and, at the same time, he held my hand firmly and gently in his own." Then he dropped it. It wasn't the nut that mattered. It was the touch of skin and the gaze of the eyes and the mood in that instant between the two of them. It was how the chimpanzee and the human being understood the gesture between them. Goodall realized what David Greybeard was trying to communicate "through a primitive emotional channel" and, because of that, "The barrier of untold centuries which has grown up during the separate evolution of man and chimpanzee was, for those seconds, broken down." Either the world changed in that instant or it was all in the imagination of Goodall. But some scientists don't like the risk of that kind of mental leap.

A few years later Dian Fossey had a similar breakthrough experience with a gorilla. She had been studying gorillas in Africa, in the mountains of Virunga, where she was later murdered in 1985, and discovered that the brutish gorilla was actually "a gentle but maligned" creature. Fossey wrote about her threshold experience in her 1983 autobiography *Gorillas in the Mist*. Peanuts, the youngest male gorilla in the group, was a few feet away "when he suddenly stopped and turned to stare directly at me. The expression in his eyes was unfathomable. Spellbound, I returned his gaze—a gaze that seemed to combine elements of inquiry and of acceptance. Peanuts ended this unforgettable moment by sighing deeply, and slowly resumed feeding." Fossey was "jubilant" and cabled Leakey that she had been "accepted" by a gorilla.

Two years later, Fossey wrote, "Peanuts became the first gorilla ever to touch me." Fossey and the photographer Bob Campbell found the group feeding in a ravine, and the two human beings settled down to watch in a "moss-cushioned *Hagenia* tree trunk." Then Peanuts wandered toward them. "Slowly I left the tree and pretended to munch on vegetation to reassure Peanuts that I meant him no harm." The curiosity of Peanuts was aroused and he watched her. When she thought he was bored watching her feeding, she scratched her head, and he scratched his. "Since he appeared totally relaxed, I lay back in the foliage, slowly extended my hand, palm upward, then rested it on the leaves. After looking intently at my hand, Peanuts stood up and extended his hand to touch his fingers against my own for a brief moment. Thrilled at his own daring, he gave vent to his excitement by a quick chestbeat before going off to rejoin his group." Fossey added, "The contact was among the most memorable of my life among the gorillas."

Fossey saw nothing wrong with a scientist like herself having human emotions, and she didn't pretend that they don't exist. For that reason, like Goodall with chimpanzees, Fossey saw the emotional life of gorillas and the role it played in the existence of the creature. Fossey used the emotional reactions of gorillas as a way to analyze what they were thinking and to understand the structures of their relationships and behavior. In one unusual moment—the only time in her life that she experienced this—Fossey saw a gorilla sob and shed tears. It was a young gorilla named Coco whose family had been slaughtered by order of the park superintendent to acquire a gorilla for a zoo in Europe. Fossey confiscated the gorilla and wanted to return her to the wild. But the creature was sick, worn down, and dispirited. Coco went to a window to look at a mountain where there were gorillas like her and wept.

After the breakthroughs of Goodall and Fossey with individual apes, the Canadian anthropologist Biruté Galdikas, after spending an incredible fifteen years with orangutans, had a threshold experience with a female orangutan named Akmad in the mid-1980s. The description of Galdikas making contact with the orangutan has the same terms as Fossey with Peanuts and Goodall with David Greybeard.

Akmad was an orphan Galdikas came to see as an equal. Galdikas had known Akmad for years and saw a sweetness of character in her, despite the brutality she had probably suffered of seeing her own mother killed in front of her and being "kidnapped" by human beings. The orangutan had "a gentle way about her," said Galdikas. "Even her squeal had a daintiness that the vocalizations of the other orangutans lacked" and so even among "her own tranquil species, Akmad stood out as being exceptionally calm." Galdikas saw her as a distinct personality. "Akmad always dropped food remains and fruit skins very gently and slowly. She would put her hand behind her back as if to hide what she was doing, as though she didn't want to be caught littering." And the scientist was so familiar with the orangutan that she even recognized her odor, just as another orangutan would, as a "deep, slightly sweet, musky odor, the odor I called *Rawa* (or swamp) No. 5."

After years of this sort of observation, the moment came when both Galdikas and the orangutan felt the connection between themselves. Galdikas described the scene after the orangutan had unexpectedly attacked a strong native named Achyar at Camp Leakey, the facility in the jungles of Kalimantan that Galdikas named after Louis Leakey. Akmad lunged at the man with her long fangs, and he only escaped being "mangled" by leaping out of the way. Galdikas responded by going to Akmad who was with her infant. Like a mother would a child, Galdikas pulled a fern out of the hair of the orangutan's child. "Akmad did not even blink to acknowledge me. Her eyes were focused elsewhere." Galdikas then touched the infant to position a photo. The man watched with amazement.

Galdikas realized the obscure meaning of the incident as one species making contact with another. She wrote, "Up until that moment I had never imagined the degree to which Akmad accepted me . . . what I had taken as indifference and rejection was the orangutan expression of acceptance." Some would say this was a fantasy in the mind of Galdikas. Others would say it is a rare human accomplishment. Which choice you make, in essence, helps to define you.

It may be that an orangutan can only begin to be understood by a person with specific personality traits. Some of the most successful keepers of orangutans in zoos in Australia, the Netherlands, Spain, and the United States like Leif Cocks told me that an angry, egotistical, or self-centered person will have trouble coming to know orangutans well enough to deal with them. It requires maturity and mental and emotional balance merely to start a relationship with an orangutan and then there is the difficulty of learning how to develop the relationship. Some of the keepers of orangutans in zoos have had unusually close relationships with orangutans over a long period of time and have seen things that scientists haven't.

Terri Hunnicutt, a keeper at the St. Louis Zoo, is typical of a perceptive keeper, male or female. Hunnicutt told me that she understands orangutans on a "gut level" and thinks that women "try harder to form a bond with them because women are more relationship oriented. I have seen orangutans feel overjoyed, depressed, malicious, grief-stricken, mischievous. I have looked into the eyes of an orangutan and seen love, heartbreak, joy, despair and mirth, among other things."

Understanding orangutans and their individual ways took Hunnicutt time. "I did not understand then what I know now, which is that an orangutan needs no one. But sometimes, as with everything, even an orangutan can use some help. One of the males at the zoo, Minyak, was literally dying, and no one seemed to be able to reach him. Minyak was dying of a broken heart. His woman, Tupa, had been euthanized the year before due to recurrent pneumonia. Minyak did not want to live without her. My heart went out to him and I began to spend a lot of free time around him.

"I learned so much from this time with Minyak and I felt a terrific kinship with these strange, detached creatures. It seemed to me that he was often too proud to admit that my company mattered, but somehow I felt it did. With Minyak, oh, my god, I had never felt such sadness. So I continued to come and sit with him, bringing treats, singing songs, feeling a little foolish at times. But in the end it worked. Minyak stayed alive long enough to go to the Los Angeles Zoo, where he is now living with a beautiful young Bornean female who is expecting his first child.

"This experience primed me for Merah, a Sumatran girl. She was born May 3, 1969, at Wassanaar in the Netherlands. Her mother, Nonja, lived in Miami and was the oldest orangutan in the United States. When I met Merah, she was suspicious and really downright mean sometimes. I had learned that to make friends with an orangutan, especially one who has suffered, you need to be prepared to give much more than you ever can take or expect to take. So I took that approach with her. She fascinated me, feeling the kinship that I do with them. And to this day, I don't know why I identify with orangutans so much, except to say that perhaps I have a similar personality."

Hunnicutt continued. "I began to understand the things Merah was trying to tell me. I had to look at her as an equal. I learned that Merah had a pretty decent life before she came to St. Louis, but there weren't a lot of keepers who were that interested in orangutans during those years. Orangutans sense such things keenly and respond accordingly. They are the most sensitive to it and also the best at hiding it. I believe this wholeheartedly because I have seen two very different orangutans, Minyak and Merah, respond positively to love that they did not appear to care about or want. I believe that one failing we have as humans is to believe that we should only give love where we feel it is desired. And that is what happened to both of these orangutans. They failed to demand attention and they didn't get it, which resulted in their becoming a shadow of themselves. In Minyak's case, it almost killed him.

"So once I realized these things about Merah, it was possible to make progress. Getting to know Merah was tough. There were many times when I wondered if I was getting through. Over time, Merah came to at least tolerate and respect me. Maybe she even likes me, I dared to hope. I made sure, and still do, that a fuss is made over her for every cooperative gesture she offers. And she is quite cooperative. But oddly, she reserves most of her best for me. I have taught my fellow keepers how to deal with her, I hope, but she does not always do so well with them. In fact, she bit a woman's fingertip off.

"To see what is probably her last child, Rubih, growing up is such a gift. She's climbing and taking food early and curious. The baby is both skittish and brave at the same time. She struggles to be free of Merah's grasp to climb and venture out a little, but if I look at her too long or she hears a loud noise, she squeals and Merah is right there. Not once has Merah blamed me for her baby's cries, a fact that I am proud of. I have noticed that she will leave Rubih with me and, even if the baby squeals, Merah harbors no grudge.

"There was one day. Her baby girl was about five months old at the time. On this day, Rubih was moving around a lot. She had just learned to maneuver the caging and the ropes and was usually anxious to try her new skills out. Merah, an experienced mother, would watch the baby closely, but generally let Rubih clamber around as she liked. Merah was sitting in a nest at the back of the holding area and Rubih was climbing like crazy around the mesh, looking for all the world like a little stuffed toy, all orange hair, big eyes, hands and feet. I often watch the baby and I think I was smiling. It's impossible not to smile when watching a happy baby orangutan. It's also impossible for me not to watch Rubih without feeling a sense of awe for her mother, Merah.

"So I looked at Merah with love and respect and she smiled at me, then crossed her arms over her chest and slapped her chest with her open hands. She did this several times and I felt I should do it back, feeling that she was telling me something and I didn't want to miss the moment and not respond. When I copied her actions, she threw her head back in a playful open-mouth laugh and then reached her arms toward me, palms up. She repeated this several times. I was incredibly moved and felt that something profound had passed between us, something that felt like love. It felt like we told each other we loved each other. I will never forget that moment."

CHAPTER 5

Sumatra: The Other Side of Paradise

I DON'T THINK reality should stop you from dreaming, but it can be somewhat of an obstacle. It's probably fair to say that there's a dreamer deep in me like there is in all of us. I long for the last idyllic places on Earth—the spots you don't quite believe exist but that keep your hopes alive, like Fuji or Bali or Iceland. Okay, maybe not Iceland. But the island of Sumatra definitely. Sumatra ought to be paradise. Sumatra is huge, the sixth largest island in the world at almost half a million square kilometers. To the east of Sumatra are the Malacca straits, with the Malaysian peninsula alongside Sumatra's northeastern portion. Borneo is more distant to the southeast. On the western side, the island has the open water of the Indian Ocean stretching all the way to Africa. That explains the strong waves on the western coast. Sumatra is what you always wanted in your life. It is a land of sun and sea and mountains and rain and tropical forests that make you feel that the Earth was made just this moment for you. The earth and the trees smell warm and clean here. Even the dust has a richness to it, light and spirited in a little wind.

And it is here that orangutans are born, to be nourished, to be ripened, to be made fully Sumatran in the sun and the rain, like they could in no other place. Orangutans are the calmest, most patient, most content of all the primates, with none of the nervous energy and constant bickering of other apes. By "other apes" I mean us, too. Why are orangutans like this? Is it possible that living in some of the sweetest tropical forests on the planet may have affected their mood and temperament? I wondered about that. I wondered if it would affect my mood, too. Maybe I'm really Sumatran at heart.

But I have to say that Sumatra would be a little better if its main airport wasn't located at the city of Medan. I thought *The Rough Guide* was being a little severe with Medan, the fourth-largest city in Indonesia, when it said that the city "has acquired a reputation for being filthy and chaotic." But I saw what the guide book meant. There is a dirty smudginess to the city, as though it is rubbing soot deep into your skin. Aside from that, Medan is a typical Indonesian city with heat and gasoline fumes and fast traffic. The people of the city drive motorcycles while wrapped in scarves or encased in motorcycle helmets. The city sprawls as though it doesn't quite know what to do with itself.

My son and I sought relief from the city in the Rahmat International Wildlife Museum. We thought we'd learn about the wildlife before we saw it. But this wildlife was killed and stuffed by a businessman who built the museum to commemorate himself. The day we were there a troop of schoolchildren was going through the building to see what had been killed and stuffed. I wondered if some day these children would be stuffers of birds and animals, too. That would be a way for them to work off their frustrations from living in Medan.

But the nice thing about Medan is that it makes you appreciate the mountains and the sea more, and that's positive. You don't want to complain about the city when you have the whole of the island to enjoy. That would be the wrong attitude. I'm sure that's how the Sumatrans feel. You're not in paradise unless your mind finds a reason for gratitude.

*   *   *

I was feeling quite grateful when I flew to the island. I'd never been there before. I'd come to meet the orangutan conservationist Ian Singleton, a durable Brit who has an ability to cope with a big and unmanageable country like Indonesia where the individual can be crushed. Singleton was busy for a few days when we arrived, so he suggested my son and I see Bukit Lawang and the orangutans on the mountain slopes before he showed us his orangutan sanctuary. I wanted to get to the countryside because I didn't feel that Medan was really the best example of what is good about Sumatra. It's the mountains and forests and rivers that make Sumatra what it is. The city is just a distraction.

But the car broke down on the edge of the city, which felt predictable in a way, as if it should be happening just because it was Medan. Maybe in Sumatra there is a rule that something bad happens before something good happens. Maybe we were earning the good times to come. Isn't there some kind of balance like that to the universe? We had to push the wounded vehicle to a small garage where the mechanic was eating lunch. We sat waiting on a sofa that hadn't been treated well. Some children came to stare at us like we were specimens in the Rahmat International Wildlife Museum. Then the mechanic started to take the vehicle apart piece by piece to get inside it as though he were going to rebuild it. Now that's dedication, I thought. By the time he has finished rebuilding the vehicle it probably won't need a mechanic for at least a year. Delays like this would have bothered me at home. Here, it made sense. I had to get outside my fussy self. In paradise, you have to think on the bright side. You can't let paradise do all the work. I decided not to leave anything to chance. I hired a second vehicle before the mechanic could take a break for dinner and we made it to Bukit Lawang before night.

The village of Bukit Lawang sits by the Bohorok River at the edge of the slopes of the Barisan Mountains and has the kind of beauty where it seems that nothing bad could happen. The word *bukit* in the name of the village means mountain. People stay here who want to explore on foot Gunung Leuser National Park where orangutans are protected. The orangutan reintroduction center was established here in 1973 by Regina Frey and Monica Borner from Switzerland before it was a tourism destination. The funding for the orangutan center where Singleton works comes from the Sumatran Orangutan Conservation Program operated by Frey and Borner.

Bukit Lawang was still recovering from a flash flood from the river six months earlier when we arrived. The government lodge where we stayed was high on the rocky south side of the river, which is why it had been spared from the destruction of the flood. To get to the government lodge, we had to cross the river on a walking bridge that creaked and danced in rhythm to our bodies. Bukit Lawang is the most scenic orangutan site that I visited. Its vistas lifted the soul above the ground and created a liberating view of everything around. It made you feel like a proud bukitineer.

To see the orangutans at Bukit Lawang, we hiked along the shoreline of the river, through natural tunnels carved into the rock, past people bathing in the current of the river, and on past tourist houses demolished in the flood. We saw the power of the flood in a large house that had a huge log through it as though it had been speared by a giant. In another of the demolished houses, a squatter was cooking dinner over a fire. We saw a few mattresses laid down in rooms that were empty and had no doors or shutters on the windows. Our guide was Tomin, a thirty-six-year-old man born in the village. He found a large poisonous centipede in the leaves beside the empty buildings and showed us how he played with centipedes on a stick as a boy. I wasn't too happy with him planting the joy of poisonous centipedes in the mind of my son. Past the buildings, we crossed the strong current of the river again, this time by a canoe connected by ropes to both sides of the shore. Then there was a climb up the slopes that seemed as long as the steps up a pyramid.

Bukit Lawang is an airy and invigorating place to live, unlike the swamps other orangutans inhabit. If I were an orangutan, I'd want to live here. Tomin told me, "This area is protected because the orangutans are here. The orangutans save the jungle." Tomin said that when he was a boy fishing or bathing in the river in the 1970s he saw orangutans on the south side of the river, where they fed on the sweet fruit of the durian trees. The river preserved the peace with the orangutans on one side and the village on the other. The boys thought the orangutans were "red monkeys, but is not monkeys," Tomin said. "Of course, for us, an orangutan is not exciting." I asked if there were any tigers still in the area. "When I was around ten years, cow in plantation, one time it is attacked by tiger. The cow was killed." I asked if parents in the village worried about a tiger in the area. "Yeah. All that time after that accident we not allowed to go out at night. Was tiger somewhere. We just stay in the house."

Tomin took my son and me on the back of his motorcycle to see an eighty-two-year-old man born in the village named H-Monel. He lived in a small, plain house, squeezed together with others like packing crates. A single plank served as a walkway over a drainage ditch, and bright flowers grew all around. The old man had ten children and sixty grandchildren; his wife had died the year before. Around him, in a room without furniture, five boys were watching television. He still swam in the river at five in the morning, after his Muslim prayers. The river kept him healthy, he said, between swimming in it every day and drinking its fresh mineral-rich water from the mountains. When he was born in Bukit Lawang in 1922, the village had twenty-two people. As Tomin translated, I heard that H-Monel saw plenty of orangutans in those days, as well as eleven rhinoceroses and the occasional tiger. When he was eight years old, a man fishing in the river was caught by a tiger and killed. The rhinoceroses were not dangerous, he said, because they ran from human beings. Sometimes the orangutans came into the village and sometimes they were killed and eaten.

It was painful to walk the blasted shoreline of Bukit Lawang and see what the flash flood had done. I wondered how nature could be this beautiful and this brutal at the same time. Paradise has a nasty side. In the dark of the night a churning wall of water, boulders, and logs hit the village. Two hundred and sixty people died in a few minutes. Four tourists were also killed. The people either drowned or were battered to death. The river rose slowly at first for several hours, so the villagers weren't worried. After dark it burst through a series of irrigation dams, releasing a torrent of water at the part of the village that was vulnerable because of a sharp bend in the river. The houses on the shoreline were pulverized. I saw rubble, bits of broken crockery, a few pieces of clothing, a bone or two. The destruction was so total that it was even difficult to walk through the rubble, except by following paths created by the villagers. The only building left undemolished on the shoreline was a small office for changing money. It had muddy windows.

I talked to survivors who heard the roar of the water as it broke through the dams. "It was like the end of the world," one told me. Another told me of running while he held the hand of his seven-year-old daughter. Pieces of cement from the irrigation dam for the village's rice paddies were strewn around. I heard how a huge red boulder thrown by the water crushed those in its path. I saw where the channel of the river had changed in one night. It was as though the power of hundreds of years had been focused in a few minutes. Some of the resorts were completely demolished, ruining employment for the people of the village as well. "One guest house washed away. One resort called Bohor River, it is gone." One advantage of the flood, though, Tomin said, was that "thirty years ago Bukit Lawang look like this. Is clean and quiet."

We climbed the steep shady slopes to see orangutans being fed, past a demolished orangutan station lower down and closer to the river where there were empty iron cages for the orangutans. Five orangutans were inside the cages the night of the flood. They fought to survive by keeping their heads above the water. I wondered what kind of fear the orangutans would have felt fighting for their lives in a cage as the darkness of the water rose. It made me shudder inwardly. That's no way to dic. Do orangutans feel the same type of fear in a situation like that as a human being would? None of the orangutans in the cages died, although the corpse of a wild orangutan was found in the river. It was probably sleeping safely in its nest when a landslide washed the tree into the flood. I saw a large male orangutan near the river and wondered if he had any memories of what happened. He was carrying food and didn't pay attention to us. Why should he? We were as fleeting to his existence as the flow of the river.

Tomin's parents were living in the village near the river the night of the flood. They'd come from Java years ago to find a small, peaceful spot in Sumatra to raise their family of six children—four boys and two girls. The village was less than a century old and had grown, with a rubber factory and a palm oil plantation for employment, to a thousand people by the night of the flood. I asked Tomin what happened that night. "Nine thirty, the lights went out. Many people running and screaming, 'Help, help. *Bangir, bangir'*"—the word for flood. It was raining hard. "Everybody run to try and get help, to survive, because it was dark, suddenly dark."

Tomin lived in another village two kilometers away and borrowed a car to see what was happening. "We drive with a car. When we were in the middle between here and the village, the road is almost full of people running. In my mind, I think only how do I find my parents." He found his sister on the road. "My sister said, 'Our house is gone. Our house is gone.' I don't know about our father and mother and our sisters. I just running, with the water to my waist. I just go to find my parents. I do not believe it, because I cannot see my parents' house. It's gone. So, I thought, 'My parents is finished.' So I try to find someone." Tomin kept looking that night and eventually found his parents. "My parents lucky they're still alive."

At that point, he tried to help the others. "We can try to search for the people, rescue who is still alive. People calling, 'Help, help.' Some of them under the big trees. Some of them under the broken house. Some people on top of the roof. Some people in the trees. Because at that time there is no light, only little torchlight. We find many people that get injured." Tomin used his car as an ambulance to take people to the hospital. "My job, go to village, put them to clinic and back again here. Many die." There was a special burial, he said. The victims who had no relatives to claim them or who were unrecognizable were buried in one mass grave.

For six months the villagers couldn't drink the water because it was so dirty. Like others in the village, Tomin's parents had no insurance for the house and possessions they lost, but they were alive. A year later people still hadn't recovered. A group of thirty-five were living in a shelter in the bare rooms of the bus terminal. Their children couldn't go to school because they had no money for tuition. Then the giant tsunami hit Sumatra and Thailand at the end of 2004 and smaller tragedies like this one were forgotten.

From Bukit Lawang I rented a van to take us back to Medan. The driver decided to avoid the main road this time, which was in terrible shape, and take the back country roads. That meant stopping here and there for cows sleeping on the road. It also meant crawling across a system of logs and planks temporarily erected across the rivers and ravines. We crossed at least half a dozen of these plank bridges. And I liked it. It made my heart pump faster. Lots of adrenaline every time we crossed another rickety bridge. A good cardiovascular workout. This is a more interesting way to travel than by main road and I would recommend traveling Sumatra by rickety bridge to anyone.

This kind of travel is what Singleton probably meant, when he told me later that everything is interesting in this country. "It's much more of an adventure," Singleton said, "when you get in a car in Medan or outside of Medan. You don't know if the bridges are down. You don't know if there's a flood. I've had to raise my legs on the motorcycle driving past snakes. You just raise your legs and hope they don't strike at you. It's the same in the forest. I always have the urge in the forest to leave the trails, to get lost, to push myself, challenge myself."

Have you succeeded in getting lost? I asked him. "I never get lost. I knew I was in the forest," he said. "Seven months ago I got stuck in the forest and nearly killed myself of exposure," although he emphasized that he wasn't lost, "just stuck." The ordeal started because it's risky getting directions through the jungle from local people who give an optimistic version of the difficulties.

But then Singleton likes the difficult. "I went to a place where somebody told me there were orangutans, but nobody had ever confirmed it and it's high, above the clouds most of it, at Punchak Sidiakan near Sidikalong, five hundred kilometers square of forest. I went down and followed the river, found some orangutan nests, and then found an orangutan. It was cold. Dark already. It started to pour rain. I hadn't eaten all day. Eventually I got out of the forest along the road about three in the morning, wet, hungry, exhausted. Once you get to a certain stage, you don't think logically anymore. I've been dehydrated before, after three or four days, and hungry, and you can't walk straight. You get a headache and you start to wobble till you drop dead, or fall and break a leg. It was horrible at the time. I was already thinking about my wife and child and when am I going to see them again. I started to get out of the forest at three in the afternoon, so, by three in the morning, I'd spent twelve hours going up and down this mountainside in the pouring rain, freezing cold. But once I got out, I was happy. That was an adventure. I hadn't had one for a while."

I was eager to see Singleton's orangutan sanctuary and later to meet Mike Griffiths, the man behind the huge and unusual Leuser conservation project. Through the twentieth century the number of orangutans in Borneo and Sumatra began to dwindle to dangerously low levels. Now the Sumatra orangutan, a separate species of orangutan, is closer to extinction than the orangutans in Borneo. The main hope for the survival of orangutans in Sumatra is the huge and unusual Leuser conservation project created by the former oilman Griffiths. The mountainous 800,000-hectare Leuser National Park has one of the largest populations of orangutans in Sumatra, 3,500 out of an estimated nine thousand on the island. This group of orangutans is expected to decline quickly and drastically, along with the others, in the next few years because of illegal logging.

Meanwhile, outside the park, Singleton, a former British zookeeper, leads a rehabilitation project to return orangutans to the forest after they have been kept illegally as pets. Singleton took me to the orangutan quarantine station forty-five kilometers outside Medan. The orangutans are taken from here to a release site south of Medan, on the edge of Bukit Tigapuluh National Park, about twenty-four hours from Medan by vehicle. The last few kilometers of rutted dirt road to the quarantine station were bad, even by the medieval standards of Sumatra. But the scenery was great—glimpses of rivers and ravines and forest slopes.

At the end of the road, the station is surrounded by a waist-high cement wall topped with wire fence topped with barbed wire, with a sign that reads in Indonesian "Anyone who touches this wall will be shot to death and chopped into little pieces by machete." Actually, I can't read Indonesian, so I don't know what the sign said, but it would be forbidding whatever it was. The front gate was overseen by the private security guards who are everywhere in this part of the world. One of the security features of the orangutan station is that a small village full of eyes is situated at the last juncture in the road. Singleton always chats to these people in Indonesian either from the car or by stopping. He stopped when we were with him to talk to what he said was "the local mafia," although all I saw was a man in a white undershirt.

Sitting with Singleton at his orangutan quarantine station I heard more birds calling from the trees than I'd heard anywhere else in Borneo and Sumatra—magpie robins, bulbuls, jungle babblers, barbets, flowerpeckers, plus long-tailed macaques and leaf monkeys. He found beauty in the forests of Sumatra and its orangutans and showed me what hc meant. We walked through the forest and I could feel how his delight in being there fed him. He had such energy among the trees. He is more at home on Sumatra than on the other island where he was born, Great Britain. Singleton married a woman born in Medan of Javanese descent and has a son with her who is "filling a little gap in my life that I was missing." He likes the hot and spicy food and he drives as badly as any Indonesian, maybe even worse. He is part of Sumatra now.

Singleton has come as close to perfection as anyone in finding the life that he would have dreamed for himself. But not without a cost. It's like you feel as a parent when you watch your children grow up and you can't protect them from time and circumstance. The same with orangutans. The same with the rain forest. Singleton saw all these beautiful things that come out of the earth full of promise. He wanted to live with them.

As a boy in Great Britain, Singleton was fascinated by the things of the earth. He worked for a reptile supplier as a teenager and then he fished commercially around the oil rigs in the North Sea. Then he decided he wanted a degree in environmental science and a position in Lawrence Durrell's revolutionary Jersey Zoo, in the English Channel. Initially he was hired at the Edinborough Zoo, but in 1989, in his early twenties, the Jersey Zoo offered him a position. He stayed for the next seven years while his desire to work in the jungle grew. "Like everybody else, I'd taken a strong interest in gorillas," he told me, "but never thought about orangutans. I was to be ape relief." He would fill in for whatever ape keeper was away. By luck, after a couple of weeks, the orangutan keeper departed and Singleton took his job, also on the weekend looking after the gorillas, a creature that, in the zoo world, he said, has the prestige that orangutans don't. The primate zookeepers ranked themselves according to their species of primate and orangutans were at the bottom, said Singleton. "Gorilla keepers are revered," he said. "Everybody was focused on gorillas and chimps." Why the ranking? "People," he said, "assumed that gorillas were socially complex and therefore difficult." Orangutans seemed less sophisticated, less interesting socially. They didn't need much care and were dull and boring and moved slowly. "But," he said, "the reality is that both gorillas and orangutans are complicated."

At that time, Singleton was influenced by the gorilla keeper at Jersey, Richard Johnstone-Scott, who had worked at a radical zoo in Kent that took a new approach by allowing the keepers to bond with the animals. It was a "maverick" operation, but it had its successes. The bonding concept was what Durrell called "green-fingered animal keepers," said Singleton. "You just do it instinctively. My boss, Richard Johnstone-Scott, spent ten years establishing the biggest gorilla colony in the world. Animals are happier," said Singleton, "when they trust and know the keepers. None of this standing outside the gate waving keys and shouting. Richard went in with the gorillas in Jersey. But, if you go in with an orangutan male, however, you'll die. I've only heard of two keepers who go inside with an adult male orangutan and one of them is Leif Cocks." A few weeks later in a conversation I had with Cocks at the zoo where he works in Perth, Australia, Cocks explained that certain traits in individuals make orangutans accept them better, such as independence and a quiet self-assurance, which people like Cocks and Singleton have.

At the Jersey Zoo, Singleton used his status to advance to the next stage of his ambition, to immerse himself in the jungle. In 1990, he traveled to Camp Leakey, the jungle facility of Biruté Galdikas in Kalimantan, in Indonesian Borneo, and mingled with the orangutans that wander freely there. A big independent male orangutan called Zoro chased him down a jungle path, like he does everybody else, the Dayaks included. It is part of the initiation rites at the camp.

Singleton remembers Galdikas talking to him about issues that were broader and more spiritual than the practical and empirical subjects that preoccupied other scientists. "Biruté was always talking about the forest and orangutans," he said, "the bigger spiritual things and relationships. She was talking more about orangutans as orangutans, and the forest as a spiritual place, and the Dayak in Indonesian culture and tradition." After that, Singleton attended a workshop in Medan and met two of the leading orangutan scientists, Carel van Schaik and Herman Rijksen, who invited him to come with them to the orangutan station Rijksen established years before at Ketambe, in Sumatra, not far from Medan. Rijksen would tell me later about Singleton, "Ian is the toughest I've ever seen. He can do without food for weeks in the forest. I once saw him come back looking like a skeleton. Ian is totally in love with orangutans, absolutely. He's besotted with them."

Singleton went to Ketambe, he told me, because he wanted to wander by himself to test whether he could adjust to a tropical forest. "The thing I like most is being in the forest on my own," he said. "If there are other people, I don't enjoy it as much." He said it stimulated him to put himself in situations "where I'm stretched to maintain control. In the forest, if you get lost, you have to maintain a level head and stay in control. You're vulnerable, but you have to see if you can stay in control." At Ketambe, he said, compared to what he'd seen in Borneo, "I suddenly realized how much better looking Sumatra orangutans were. I realized then quickly how much richer the forest was. Orangutans were easier to find, because they were in higher densities. I saw how much more luxuriant and green and hilly and more beautiful the terrain was." He knew that he could handle the terrain and thought that a PhD was the excuse he needed to acquire funding to spend the two years he wanted in the tropics. "I loved Jersey," he said, "but I knew at some point I had to get out, otherwise, I'd never leave and I'd end up regretting not having gone off and done other things."

The location Singleton chose for his PhD study was the hellish swamp forest site established by Carel van Schaik at Suaq Balimbing on the west coast of Sumatra in south Aceh. Suaq, as swamp all year round, is more difficult terrain, said Singleton, than the hills of Ketambe in Sumatra or the flat and relatively dry stretches of Galdikas's research camp in Tanjung Puting in southern Borneo. In this location, Singleton would document for the first time the extended ranges of orangutans outside the trail systems normally used in a research zone. "My task was to patrol the edge and when they leave, go with them, with just a poncho to sleep under and a bag of noodles for a few days. John Mac-Kinnon did the same thing, but he did it years ago when there were no trail systems."

By chance, when it came time for Singleton to write his PhD thesis, MacKinnon was lecturing at the same university in England and became his supervisor for a few months. Singleton had read MacKinnon's adventurous book *In Search of the Red Ape* before he conducted his field-work in Sumatra. Singleton found in MacKinnon a kindred soul who was unpretentious and unpreoccupied with the fierce, apelike ranking of the academic world. "John always carried a pig's leg around with him in the forest," Singleton said, "and he would eat that every night when he made a fire. He'd just hold the leg over the fire and cook it again. As opposed to starving, it's really a sensible thing. You can just recook it. You don't have to use pans. This is what he told me, anyway."

At Suaq, Singleton slept by the edge of a river in a wooden hut raised on stilts where the air was cooler and the floor was above the termites. He slept under a mosquito net with the window wide open to listen to the insects. The days were spent in the swamp, where sometimes he slept on a patch of dry ground. To follow orangutans, he rose at three in the morning to go into the swamp. He got wet from the waist down and became covered in a biblical plague of boils—"I got five massive boils and about a hundred small ones"—risking fever, being sliced with grass and rattan, itching "to bits" till sometimes as late as ten at night. Or not coming back at all.

Sometimes he'd sleep in the swamp under a Malaka tree, which has "a leafy dome underneath it." He made an impromptu tent for himself with the poncho he carried. He'd make a fire that never lasted, which was lucky because it might attract tigers. Yet he slept because he was "too exhausted" to care about anything else. "Never sleep on a trail," he warned me, "because tigers use the trail." "It was a fantastic adventure," he said. If he was isolated, he didn't notice. He was living a solitary life pursuing a solitary creature. "I'd been working on my own for a long time," he said. "One of the things I liked in Jersey is that I looked after the orangutans and nobody came there. I find I'm more productive when I'm on my own. They say people are like the animals they work with and there's a lot of truth in that, maybe."

At the Jersey Zoo, Singleton came to know orangutans more intimately than he could in the wild. It is an irony that we come to know the apes better when we keep them in captivity than when they are free to be themselves in their own world. The field studies of orangutans had started in the late 1960s, at a time when science was also affected by the liberalization of thinking in culture and society. And yet there were differences between the way that scientists and zookeepers came to understand a creature like the orangutan. The scientists focused on specific intellectual problems and tended to work within the boundaries of their discipline. Scientists naturally associated with other scientists, often within specific niches in their different fields. The zookeepers, separate from that, had a more social attitude and less restricted thinking, which affected the way they saw orangutans. Zookeepers also had the practical task of managing orangutans and their well-being, and that required other forms of insight into the nature and behavior of the creature. Like Wallace and Hornaday years before, Singleton would raise an infant orangutan and learn more about orangutans in the process.

At the Jersey Zoo there were three Borneo orangutans and six Sumatrans, and Singleton still remembers them. He can list them by name with their dates of birth. "Giles, Bali and Kupo-kupo, Gambar, Gina, her oldest son Mokko-mokko, her youngest daughter Mawar, Maias and her daughter Selaatam. I learned a lot from those animals." Singleton spent two years raising an infant female orangutan named Manis, after her mother, Bali, the consort of Giles, her father, died and left the two-month-old infant alone. The father couldn't raise the child. He'd be more likely to kill her. Later, after Singleton had raised the orangutan long enough for her to survive, she was accepted and protected by Kupo, the other consort of Giles.

"She became my kid for a while," he said. "Twenty-four hours a day, clinging on. I was working with her clinging on my neck."

"How would you get her to go to sleep?"

He did what parents typically do. "You put her on her mattress and sit with her until she falls asleep. You ungrip the hands from your shirt and sneak away. I used to nip out to the pub when she was asleep. It was always a battle to get her to go to sleep before ten o'clock. As soon as she wakes up, she starts screaming."

"You were, in a sense, the mother of an orangutan."

"Hmmm," he said. It didn't sound as though he liked that reference. "Often," he said, "the keepers used to give them to their wives, back in the sixties and the seventies." Singleton was unmarried at that point and didn't have that option. "I lived," he said, "in the zoo as well, in a room."

It was exhausting for him. Did raising the baby orangutan affect him emotionally?

"I was very tired," he said, dodging the question.

Were there limits to the relationship?

"I was very attached to her and I liked having her around a lot, but she was always an orangutan. She was never my substitute child. She was also an ideal subject for me to learn more about orangutans. I basically got her back into the cage with other orangutans as soon as possible. I did it very quickly compared to other standards."

Singleton said that some human beings prolong the infancy of the orangutans because they like having babies. Maybe for some people compassion is a biological urge they can't control. "Every orangutan is different," he said. "The important thing when you're dealing with orangutans, especially in captivity, is flexibility, the ability to change and adapt according to the individual needs. When they're really vulnerable and need it, they need attention, but, once they're strong enough to be independent, they need to be independent. And, if your aim is to release them in the wild, they need to be more independent."

"Were you conscious of a line in the bonding process?" I asked him. "Two years is a long time to spend with a creature like that." I mentioned that Biruté Galdikas and Gary Shapiro said that they literally regarded the orangutans they raised as their children, although they also made distinctions between a human child and an orangutan. For Galdikas, the bonding process is necessary and natural for the healthy development of an orangutan, a position she took to an extent that is controversial among scientists.

"I never went that far," Singleton said. "She was my responsibility," he continued. "To that extent, she was my kid. But, emotionally, she was an orangutan that I had to get to the stage where she could get back with orangutans as quick as possible."

"Some people have bonded strongly with orangutans," I persisted.

"I certainly did as well, but it was always an orangutan. I got her back into a group with her dad and auntie, Kupo-kupo and Giles, and that was a big achievement for me. A lot of people had been scared in the past of reintroducing youngsters to adult males, and Giles had been suspected of killing infants, so that was not an easy decision to make. We did it anyway and it worked. So, when I got her back to that group, it was a relief for me. Suddenly I had more time to myself. And yet she was still in the zoo, so I saw her every day. I'd just open the door, and she'd come out and play in the kitchen. But she didn't need me anymore."

"Was it sad that she didn't need you?" It's a question on the minds of all parents.

"No. It was a relief. It meant I could go surfing. But, the sad day was when, shortly after that, we decided to build a new enclosure for the Sumatran orangutans and get rid of the Borneans. We found a good zoo in France, with a very good enclosure, and we sent all the Borneans there, Giles and Kupu and Manis. By that time, Manis was already semi-adopted by Kupu. Kupu would protect her from the male. And the day I left them in Paris, I took Manis out one last time and took her for a walk and sat down on the park bench. That was quite emotional, yeah. Well, very emotional. I'd invested so much time and love and care into this orangutan and I might never ever see her again. I just wondered if I'd ever see her again. And I thought, 'I hope she does well.' I didn't want her to come down and knock on my door every two weeks. I wanted her to be an orangutan. The relationship is the same as a daughter, but she's not my daughter."

"What happened to her?"

"She had a baby when she was about ten years old and they told me she didn't rear it. And then, since then, I don't know. She's only fifteen now."

To change the subject I asked, "What are the differences between Sumatran orangutans and Borneo orangutans?"

Singleton laughed. He understood the idea behind the question. It is well known that he makes extravagant claims about the beauty of the Sumatran orangutans. It seemed to be one ideal he still holds dear. Scientists see the Sumatran orangutan as a distinct and smaller species with more delicate features. "Sumatran orangutans are prettier," he said.

"Prettier in what way?" I prodded.

"They're slimmer and their fur is more golden, more petite, delicate. The males have a much bigger, long, flowing beard. Borneans tend to be more rotund in the face and in the body and have much darker hair. Their beard is much shorter, not a big, impressive, long, flowing thing. Sumatrans—I won't say they're more intelligent because—"

"Well, you did the other day."

"Yeah," he said, "but they do use tools. It's not a question of individual intelligence. It's more ecological factors." He became more empirical and explained that the orangutans in Sumatra have a richer and denser supply of food in the forest. That allows them to gather more in groups and, in those groups, they learn to use tools better than the orangutans in Borneo. The result is that they display their intelligence more visibly.

"When you said Sumatran orangutans were more intelligent the other day, were you joking?"

Singleton didn't want to answer. Instead, he talked about how orangutans in zoos show their ingenuity in using tools. Zookeepers observed the ability before scientists in the field were able to see it, he said. "They are always thinking. They have the mental capacity to invent tools. Take them from the wild anywhere, in Borneo, Sabah, anywhere you like, put them in a zoo and they'll probably use tools tomorrow."

Several days later I asked him again. "Are Sumatran orangutans really more beautiful, or is that a jest?"

"No. It's true."

"So, that's not craziness?"

"No. It's real."

CHAPTER 6

Too Smart for Us

THE HUMAN BRAIN rambles far too much and thinks it is much smarter than it is, which is how our brains soothe us and keep us happy. They fool us. We really don't have a good record of understanding intelligence when you think about it. To write this book I had to talk to some human beings whose minds do more than just ramble and keep them happy. They have to use their brains for real thought. One of those people was Biruté Galdikas, who has an exceptional mind, although sometimes it doesn't seem to be quite in the same universe as the rest of us. One time she blurted out to me that another scientist, Anne Russon, is smarter than her. That's interesting, I thought. That's quite a concession among human beings. You have to be secure in your own intelligence to praise the mind of someone else. And that's even truer in science, where intelligence is the Golden Fleece, the Holy Grail, the pot at the end of the rainbow, the Super Bowl cup. It's much sought after. Now I was looking forward even more to talking to Russon, who has devoted herself to the study of the minds of orangutans. That's a supremely ambitious enterprise. Some might wonder if it is even possible.

To find this scientist meant traveling to the orangutan rehabilitation station at Nyaru Menteng, near the dusty town of Palangkaraya in a marshy area on the Kahayan River, in the Dayak heartland of Central Kalimantan to a facility funded by the Borneo Orangutan Survival Foundation created by Willie Smits. Palangkaraya isn't a destination. According to *The Rough Guide*, "Most travellers only pass through it in transit between Pangkalan Bun and Banjarmasin," and you don't want to linger in those two gardens of paradise for long either—unless you are deeply interested in orangutans or Dayaks, which Russon is. Russon likes the small, isolated Dayak villages clustered in central Kalimantan where life is still close to the forest. She could easily have become an anthropologist studying the Dayaks in these villages, but she made a different choice in her life. Orangutans.

The facility at Nyaru Menteng was established and managed by a Danish woman, Lone Dröscher-Nielsen, who is smart in the kind of life she has created for herself and her orangutans. The facility at Nyaru Menteng prepares orangutans to return to the wild after they have been rescued from illegal captivity, which makes it an excellent place to be close enough to orangutans to learn about them. In the wild, it takes years of observations to put together snatches of insight, and those conditions aren't ideal for probing more difficult questions about intelligence. So the orphan orangutans are useful to scientists.

When I was at Nyaru Menteng, there were two hundred and seventy orangutans. The orangutans were being prepared for release in a forest in a Dayak area on the Mantangai River and their spots would be filled with about eighty new orangutans a year. Another infant had arrived just the day before. Dröscher-Nielsen said it was likely that because the forest was being cleared for an oil palm plantation, the mother of the infant had come into a village and was butchered for meat. The infant then became a commodity that could be kept as a pet or sold as part of the illegal wildlife business. It's a kind of baby trade.

One morning we picked Dröscher-Nielsen up at her small home.

She had spent the night there with fifteen small orangutans because the Nyaru Menteng facility was full and she wanted to ease the stress of crowding on the orangutans. "Last night," she said, "I had three orangutans in the bed with me. Sometimes I have four, sometimes I only have two, depending on how tired I am." She had the new infant in bed with her and said that a female orangutan who has become attached to her showed her displeasure at the new arrival by lifting one eyebrow. Yes, that expression works for orangutans, too. "The little one was sleeping up on my chest. She immediately got jealous. She moved down to my feet and just did not want to come up to me again."

I asked Dröscher-Nielsen how she got any sleep with that many orangutans in her house. It wasn't meant as an insult. "I don't look that tired, do I?" she said. "You have extra energy to do these kinds of things because it's your child. These orangutans are my children in some ways. But I have too many of them. You cannot love them all the same. There's always some that you favor over others and I don't think that's fair, but it's very difficult to avoid those emotions of favoring some." Is that mere sentimentality or something else? It was a question I would ask Russon later to understand her relationship with orangutans.

Dröscher-Nielsen is one of those unseen, dedicated, pragmatic souls who make things happen. People like her not only save individual orangutans but make it possible for scientists to do their work. That is not easy in this part of the world, especially with the biases against women and foreigners. Even the orangutans have those biases.

"I've got some grown-up females I don't get along with at all," Dröscher-Nielsen told me. "To them I'm just an adult female." She was bitten so badly by the orangutan Mellie at the Camp Leakey facility of Biruté Galdikas that she was in the hospital for a week. She still has the scars. "I never blamed her. It's humans who made her the way she is. She had been in a logging camp for eight years. She was used to drinking alcohol, smoked, and I would not be surprised if she was raped as well."

By men? I said, not sure if I understood fully what I was hearing. "Yes," she said. But being hospitalized by an orangutan didn't stop Dröscher-Nielsen from working with them.

Dröscher-Nielsen started when she was fourteen years old and volunteered to work with the great apes at a zoo in Denmark. The zoo had two baby orangutans. She wanted to study biology at university, but she liked her freedom and independence more and spent her twenties roaming the world, until she volunteered to work with orangutans at Camp Leakey. There she met and later married a Dayak named Odom, the nephew of the Dayak husband of Galdikas, who was working with orangutans in Pasir Panjang. It was with Odom that Dröscher-Nielsen, after growing disillusioned with the way that Camp Leakey and the orangutans were managed, started Nyaru Menteng.

In the years that followed, Dröscher-Nielsen married and divorced Odom. She said he had changed from the man she had fallen in love with. "What I really admire about him," she said, "is his capabilities in the forest, but he changed too much. He went from being that wonderful forest person that lived with the spirits and lived with the traditions." But orangutans are more permanent and enduring. I asked her if she could see herself looking after orangutans for the rest of her life. After all, earlier in her life she had had a strong need for freedom and independence. "I could never leave them," she said. "I wouldn't trust them to anybody else."

It was to the orangutan station at Nyaru Menteng created by Dröscher-Nielsen and maintained by her energy that Anne Russon came to do science, after growing disillusioned with Galdikas and leaving Camp Leakey like Dröscher-Nielsen. And it was at Nyaru Menteng that I met Russon, a short woman with a thick swath of hair that was graying, dressed in a robust way in field clothes and hiking boots. Like Dröscher-Nielsen, she was decisive. She seemed confident of herself in the way she moved and talked. When we talked about moral issues, she would say that it's "not an area of expertise for me," which I doubt. The Russon I saw was preoccupied by morality in her thought and actions. If she weren't, she would not have talked about orangutans the way she did.

Every year since 1988, Russon, a professor at York University in Toronto, Canada, has been making the trek to Kalimantan in the summer to study the rudiments of intelligence in the minds of orangutans. Over the years, the orangutans—Bento, Bimbim, Manggis, Maya, Mojo, Sumo, Panjul, and the others—have come to know her and she them. The blustery male Bento protects her as though she were a female orangutan, with one of those brute hearts of we males that might be forgiven for its sincerity.

It isn't easy for someone like Russon to study orangutans in the equatorial jungle. A full-grown orangutan stands as high as four feet, is stronger than a human being, has a mouth full of teeth as large as a tiger's, and lacks human restraint. That makes it very different from the comical way the orangutan behaves in the Clint Eastwood movie *Every Which Way but Loose*. Think of what a creature with strength, ingenuity, and few inhibitions can do. Then think of a scientist trying to deal with a creature like this, in the heat of Dante's Inferno, in a jungle that can lash out at any moment, in the culture and political system of Indonesia that even Indonesians don't understand completely. Russon was bitten on the elbow by a female orangutan on an island in the Rungan River and needed seven or eight stitches. It could have been worse. It didn't deter her. She has that kind of mind.

About Russon's friend, the bold one, Bento. My choice of an orangutan as a companion would be the sweet-tempered Princess rather than the troublemaker Bento, who is getting even more irritable with age, like some of us, but Russon is not me. Bento is not smart or graceful or particularly friendly with other orangutans, and over time, he has become even more difficult to handle. But, no matter. Russon liked Bento the moment he sauntered out of the trees. He was still a youngster then, greeting the human female in his smug, self-possessed way, testing her, getting a measure of her by touching the skin of her face with a finger, then sniffing it. The female didn't flinch. She looked him in the eye. She was different. It was quite a match. And that says something interesting about Russon. She likes the ultimate mental challenges in the world around her and yet she enjoys the simple pleasures, too.

I asked Russon about herself as we sat outside in Palangkaraya with geckos chirping a little too insistently overhead. Russon is a professional thinker. In Athens, thousands of years ago they were called philosophers. Now they are psychologists who study "cognition." It takes years of study to be able to do this with no guarantee that you will do it well. I wondered how far I was out of my depth with a member of the cognoscenti like Russon. Maybe we should leave thought to the professionals. But maybe not. I was curious how the mind of Russon had developed. And how did someone like her have the kind of mind that could understand an orangutan, the last remnant of the old consciousness of the deep Asian tropical forest?

Russon is a private woman, solitary, an independent and unconventional thinker, without husband, without children. After twenty years of traveling to Kalimantan, she has "better friends" there than at home. It is a combination of detachment and intense involvement, "like living life from the outside," she said. She quoted the religious sentiment "in the world but not of it" to explain. "I didn't get companionship from orangutans," she said, although she enjoys being with them and it gives her an unusual satisfaction. "I get to be part of a piece of the world that isn't normally a part of human experience."

Russon is the oldest of five children raised in Regina, Saskatchewan. Her father was a psychiatrist who specialized in the mental problems of prisoners and delinquent children, which he interpreted as the result of a dysfunctional society. He received his medical degree when his daughter was a year old, at the end of the Second World War, from which he abstained as a conscientious objector. Instead of fighting, he performed national service and helped to eliminate the diseased trees from the woods in the Rocky Mountains. "When he talked about it," Russon told me, "you got the impression that was a really valuable experience. Nature, living out in the woods, were what he communicated to me as things that were good."

Regina didn't have an abundance of wildlife. "As a city kid, I only knew there were two kinds of butterflies in the world. There were cabbage butterflies and monarchs. And that's all I thought there was to nature." For the young Russon, the natural world was limited to the wildlife films her father watched on television and "camping three weeks a year in the summer from the time I was five until I was sixteen." She picked blueberries and spent so much time in the water that her family called her a fish. The countryside had the smell of pine trees and "sulphur from sawmills in Kenora, Ontario," she said. "They were my dad's values. He valued living outside. He valued communal living. He was a strong influence."

At university, Russon originally decided to be a mathematician. Numbers suited the precise, orderly nature of her mind, a characteristic that orangutans have, too. She earned a master's degree in mathematics and worked for five years as a computer programmer. Then she realized that the mental challenge was missing. "There's only so much of your life that you want to sell your brain for. In my mind, that's probably worse than selling your body. Also, the people that I met that were involved with computers had different ideas about values in the world." She wanted the kind of mental activity that doesn't make interesting things "boring," that doesn't "take all the fun and all of the interest out of things" and trap the mind "in meticulous details of methods," that doesn't "kill" the "joy" in thought. Her father was radical in his notions of treating the problems of prisoners and yet the colleagues she had chosen to work with were different. They had a conventional, materialistic bent. "They were more interested in the inanimate world and not very interested in the human world and that's what I grew up with." Russon switched to the family field, human psychology, and still she found that was also missing something she needed. She switched to the psychology of primates.

"What did your dad think about your choice to study mathematics and psychology?" I asked.

"He never said anything," she said. "Although he was firm, I didn't get, like some kids, parents dictating which way you went."

"Did you have an idea of where you fit in?"

"No. Our family was outside the norm socially. I think it was partly my dad. He was the first person in his family to go to university. His social preferences were for spending time with people working in the trades. If he had friends, they were plumbers or electricians, not dentists or doctors and other professionals."

"We expect psychiatrists to be really social people. Was your dad?"

"No, he wasn't. In fact, I don't think I know why he ended up in psychiatry. I don't remember him ever talking about it."

I told Russon that when Lone Dröscher-Nielsen was driving me around town, she blithely called herself "antisocial." Yet in Dröscher-Nielsen there was strong compassion for the plight of orangutans mixed with strong independence and a pragmatic attitude, which I saw in Russon, too. I said that.

"In some ways I'm more of a loner than other people in the kinds of areas I work in. I fade into my own funny little space more easily than others seem to."

"What space is that?"

"I work on things on my own. I don't like conflict very much. I can be cranky, but, if there's a big academic debate, my tendency is to avoid getting involved. In some ways, digging in and engaging with the dialogue can be much more productive. But my tendency is to want to withdraw and find something else and work on that on my own. The way it plays out in my mind is, 'This debate is silly, I think most of what they are saying is nonsense, but I am not going to waste my mind fixing other peoples' thinking.'"

"Is that typical of your family, your dad?"

"Yes, in a way, he kept out of the mainstream."

"What do you think is the most valuable lesson you learned from your father?"

There was a long pause while she thought. I was wondering what my own daughter would say to the same question. She resumed, "I like his idea of supporting the underdog. That sticks. His message was to treat people fairly and treat them as equals and treat them with respect. And I'm pretty sure living off in the woods is something I got from him." Orangutans are the underdog and they live in the forest.

So what about the intelligence of orangutans? How smart are they? The intelligence of an orangutan in reasoning and solving problems, Russon told me, can reach the level of a three-and-a-half-year-old child, and yet "they don't have a child's mind," she said. In orangutans, years of knowledge and experience have accumulated in their powerful memories and can be put to use. It's like their minds are a library that they can consult whenever they want. "The more items you can hold in memory at one time, the more complex the problem you can solve," Russon said.

Is there much scientific evidence for intelligence in orangutans? Except for a few orangutans like Princess trained to use symbols or sign language, orangutans can't be tested like human beings, using language and questions and problems that make sense to human beings. We can't even be sure that our current notions of intelligence in ourselves are completely valid. Nevertheless, scientists studying the minds of the great apes have grappled with these issues and have drafted a list of the kinds of behavior that they believe can be examined for intelligence. The list includes the ability to learn, to solve problems in creative ways, to learn symbols to communicate, to have a concept of the self, to distinguish the differences in thought and feeling of another creature, and to use the eyes to communicate. All of these are aspects of our ability to think that we use as human beings all the time. We are so accustomed to them that we are often not aware that we use them.

For example, orangutans have the ability like us to communicate and to read the intentions of other creatures through subtle signs in the behavior of the eyes, the behavior of the body, and other small clues. As part of this activity, eye contact is a way that one creature uses to understand the intentions and state of mind of another. Scientists have found that orangutans point by using their eyes rather than a finger like a human being would. But this ability is far more elaborate in both human beings and orangutans. For instance, I can read the state of mind of my students in the university through their eyes as they drift mentally in class. Some minds are quick, resourceful, versatile; some are moving cautiously and inflating their egos to protect themselves; some are happily carried by the mental currents and tides, each of them swimming in their individual seas of thought and feeling. In their eyes you can see that they are attentive, bored, intrigued, confused, distracted, frustrated, relaxed, anxious, angry, jovial, thinking of food, thinking of sex. In the same way, an orangutan can read the thoughts, feelings, and intentions of other orangutans through their eyes, and they send and receive messages through the eyes. And like us, they have an awareness of others. They can distinguish between what they are thinking and what others are thinking and realize the significance of the differences. Knowing the differences creates the opportunity for forging alliances and accomplishing more as a group than an individual. This awareness is believed to develop in a human child about the age of three and can be impaired in some people, producing the insensitivity that destroys social relationships.

There is another interesting implication. Once a creature knows that it has different thoughts and feelings, it can also develop mental abilities such as lying and deception. That begins early in human beings, earlier than we may sometimes want to acknowledge. We like to see a purity and innocence in ourselves when we are young, just as we like to see it in orangutans. It is a form of self-deception to protect us against reality. "The better you are at reading another's mind, the better deceiver you will be," the American psychologist and researcher Julian Paul Keenan told me. "Deception that involves mind reading really is a sign of high intelligence. Kids around the age of two start lying and they soon see how adaptive it is. By the age of five, around ninety to ninety-five percent of children will lie."

Knowing how others lie and the differences in lying between the sexes can be useful in society, the psychologist said. "The average person tells at least one lie per day," he said. It is how people adapt. Since he was an expert on lying I thought I should ask him how often he lies himself. How truthful would he be about lying? "I do not lie too often," he said, explaining that he does it to spare the feelings of his students. "To be a good teacher, you have to do this. If a student hands in a horrible paper, the last thing you want to do is be cruel. Deception in this situation can be encouraging with the idea of raising the enthusiasm of the student."

Okay, good or bad, deception requires mental ability. But don't get the wrong idea. Intelligence can be benevolent, too. There is the brilliance of a Gandhi. It's not all a Machiavellian jungle out there. More about that later.

How do the orangutan cognoscenti put their mental abilities to use? The benevolent Princess was an orangutan with a strong ability to think and calculate and express herself. She had the intelligence to learn sign language better than other orangutans, and Russon believes that Princess even created her own ways to communicate. For example, she made a throaty huffing sound to tell an infant it was time to nurse. "It was as though," said Russon, "she had taken a sound or movement that had just been a normal reaction to the world and she turned that into something to communicate with." Princess was "the sweetest" among apes, Russon told me. That trait may have also helped her adapt too well to the human world, which she wanted to be part of, and then, said Russon, Princess was "not part of orangutan society." Princess did not have "good forest skills. Her six-year-old son is better than she was." It was things like this that made Russon wary of too much contact between human beings and orphan orangutans. Turning an orangutan into a companion could change an orangutan in a way that is disruptive.

"Princess was never irritable, wouldn't steal, would give things to you," said Russon. "You never felt that you had to be wary or careful around her. And some of the other orangutans you wouldn't turn your back on them for a second."

Ten years later, Princess wasn't so mellow anymore. "She was an adult female, but she was pretty subordinate with the other female orangutans, so she probably really needed friends. But she had got very pushy. I remember she was pregnant and she'd want to sit beside you and she'd want your arm around her. It was just entirely captivating. She used to organize things. Orangutans are all so meticulous. I remember one time she was sitting there and picked up sticks from the ground and very systematically broke them all down so that they were about the same length and then laid them all out parallel to each other. They like things to be neat. Human kids will do the same thing too, little kids with blocks. Orangutans do some of the same stuff." Russon talked about the nest of a male orangutan high in the trees where "around the outer edge of the nest were small leaves all very neatly laid one beside the other like in a pattern all the way around. They clean things off a lot. They like things to be very neat. I think it's a standard part of the way their minds work."

Orangutans are schemers, though, some better than others. I remember the devilry in the eye of an orangutan I saw in quarantine in Warariset. He took his penis in hand and aimed a spray of pee out from his cage at the Dayak I was traveling with. There were three of us standing there and the orangutan chose the Dayak. It was calculated. The orangutan had never seen the man before, but he didn't like him and thought he'd have some fun. I told the Dayak it was because his ancestors had eaten orangutans. But whatever the reason, the orangutan knew exactly what to do to embarrass a human being who apparently had all the advantages over an ape locked in a cage. That's using your brains.

One of the most skillful schemers at Camp Leakey was the orangutan

Supinah. Russon remembers Supinah as an intelligent young adult female who worked so hard at being human that the camp "almost voted her a human. She seemed to want to be human and to be part of the human world more than she wanted to be part of the orangutan world." Supinah was tough, aggressive, cranky, and concerned about status in the female hierarchy of the camp where the primatologist Biruté Galdikas was clearly the ranking female among both human beings and orangutans. Supinah attacked women and took "swipes" at Russon. "She had a real bad chip on her shoulder," said the scientist. "I got the impression she just wasn't happy with her life. She'd break trees. With women visitors to the camp she could get very aggressive. She tended to like to bite the cooks. She got really pissed if there were other women around that tried to tell her what to do or acted like they were superior to her. She would, for the most part, keep it under control, but, if she got a chance she'd make a grab at you; she'd bite you. She'd lie in wait for some people and then bite them." Supinah was attached to Galdikas, partly because Galdikas was like a mother to her, partly because Supinah recognized the power of Galdikas and was irritated by women who might come between her and Galdikas. The Galdikas I saw in camp is quite aware of her power and uses it, which sometimes irritates other human beings.

Supinah had been taken from the jungle illegally by human beings as a pet. Then she was confiscated by officials and given to the Orangutan Foundation International to try to rehabilitate her and return her to the wild. "She had been raised with a human family from very early in life," Russon said, "so she was much more in tune with the human world than she was with the orangutan forest world. She didn't seem to like being in the forest much and broke trees when she tried to climb high." Orangutans don't have an instinctual ability to climb, but have to learn it and even overcome a fear of heights, according to Gisela Kaplan and Lesley Rogers. Russon told me that Supinah was "very, very smart, but seemed bored or in a bad mood lots of the time. When she was involved in a project, she was absorbed, focused, interested. When she wasn't, she banged things around, harassed people, and otherwise just was in a bad temper."

But Supinah was very intelligent. She would hammer nails, sandpaper wood, sharpen an axe blade on a stone, sweep the porch with a broom, chop wood with a hatchet, and hold a discarded cigarette butt to a burning stick. One time she even hammered a grave marker into the ground. If she spilled paint, she wiped it up. Then there was the time when Supinah tried to start a fire under the camp mess hall. She carried sticks to build a fire underneath the cabin, but she was caught and stopped. Another time Supinah wanted to give rice as a gift to Galdikas on a plate like she'd seen others do. She didn't have a plate, so she improvised with a flat piece of bark instead. Galdikas told me that Supinah was being shrewd with her generosity with the rice because she didn't like rice. Supinah was thinking that she could score points with a person she recognized was important by giving away what she didn't want. She thought it might improve her status. Always thinking.

"Supinah often used to sleep over night in a small hut near the park office," Russon continued. "She was followed a lot, almost every day, partly because she was such a troublemaker and somebody had to keep on her tail to make sure she wasn't causing havoc, and partly because she was very used to being followed and apparently got depressed if she wasn't. If she really wanted to get into trouble and couldn't because a human being was watching her, at the end of the day she'd head for her little hut near the park office and climb in as if going to sleep. The camp assistant following her would note that she had gone to bed and, when it seemed clear that she was settled in, he'd go home. Supinah knew that. Once the assistant was gone, Supinah would sometimes head out to do damage, such as break into one of the houses. So her going to bed was deceptive. She did it on purpose to get rid of what from her perspective were the camp police."

Orangutans will act out a plausible "script" to conceal their intentions. Princess did that one time, spending five hours fraternizing with human beings to hide her intention to do some pilfering by sneaking into a cabin nearby through a tear she spotted in a screen. In this case, the human beings had to ask Princess to unlock the door of the cabin for them.

But why weren't human beings smarter at learning the behavior of a Supinah or a Princess and anticipating their tricks? Why can a human being be fooled by an orangutan? In the case of Supinah, the human beings "wanted to go home at the end of the day," Russon said, "and left the problem for somebody else to fix." Okay, laziness, indulgence, lack of consideration of others. We can understand that. Otherwise, it seems that human beings are easy to dupe because we always assume we are the smartest primate. Our brains can't imagine being outsmarted. As for the devious Supinah, she wandered into the trees one day and was never seen again. Galdikas believes that the park rangers killed her to put an end to her attacks against women, not to mention the irritation of having her in camp. Or maybe they thought we'd be better off without an orangutan that smart.

Understanding orangutans requires that we not let our brains get in the way. Not everyone can do that. That's what the Greek philosophers were doing in Athens thousands of years ago, learning how to prevent their brains from getting in the way of thinking. It's the ability to think simply with an uncluttered mind and to observe clearly. It is what distinguishes the mind of a Darwin from others. Russon has that kind of intelligence. She can see what others don't.

In one research project, Russon compiled a list of fifty-nine examples of intelligent action by orangutans at Camp Leakey. The list is amazing for what it suggests that an orangutan can accomplish when its interest and curiosity are aroused. Russon said that orangutans go beyond imitating an action and imitate the "technique" of a human being, like we might imitate John Wayne's saunter or the way that Barack Obama speaks by weighing his words with care and consideration before he speaks. The list of imitations that Russon compiled included applying insect repellent to the knee of a human being; brushing teeth and spitting the foam over the porch edge; examining a sick infant as nurses do; hanging a hammock on a hook and riding it; putting a T-shirt on over arms and head; and siphoning fuel from a drum to start a fire.

Orangutans are ingenious and that makes it a constant battle at Camp Leakey to protect the buildings and supplies from them. They steal the canoes, as I saw when I was there, splashing the water out of a canoe that human beings had sunk in a shallow part of the river to protect it from the apes. The orangutans at Camp Leakey also learned how to construct bridges after watching a native assistant one day. The assistant was sent across the river to feed the group and an orangutan sank his boat. The man couldn't swim and so he improvised by dragging a log to the river, walking over the log, and pulling the log up so that the orangutans couldn't follow. The orangutans watched the man carefully. Before long, two orangutans were improvising and dragging everything they could find to the river. One crossed on a thick vine and the others followed. That's the orangutan sense of enterprise.

Orangutans want to try everything and experience everything that they see preoccupies the human beings who are part of their world, including painting and drawing. An example of that is a big female orangutan named Siswi who gleefully draws swirls on paper. She gets pleasure from imitating what she has seen both people and orangutans like her mother do with paper and a pen. Siswi also likes to draw swirls in the sand with a stick or her finger. I was there one day while Siswi was drawing and she turned to me and showed a big mouth of orangutan teeth. It was a kind of Cameron Diaz smile—wide and full and with her whole being thrown into it. Siswi was trying to show me that she was having fun and she wanted me to see that she was having fun. Siswi is also the camp flirt. I only learned later from Russon that "she used to drape herself on the deck like she was Mae West, very voluptuous." So maybe I was being played yet again by the charm of a clever female. Maybe there is a flirty intelligence.

Siswi was never a captive herself, but she was born at the camp from a former captive. As an adolescent, she had her boyfriends. Siswi spent time with the steely-eyed Kusasi, which was a good choice for her because of his emerging power and his physical size. Siswi was the daughter of the ranking female Siswoyo, so although she was younger than Princess, she could still boss Princess around. "She had the status," says Russon. "She'd been born into and grew up around the camp. That was her area, the camp. She was the camp hostess. She would come down and meet people by the dock and she'd take them on a tour of the camp."

The first time that an orangutan like Siswi wanted to draw, Galdikas said she was "shocked." Galdikas was making notes and the orangutan grabbed her notebook and pen and started drawing. Her husband laughed and said the orangutan was making a map of the "day range" of an orangutan. "It wasn't random," Galdikas said. Orangutans have been observed at Camp Leakey matching the precise way that people paint and using the same brush strokes in the same direction or plucking on the strings of a guitar like a human being. The orangutan Princess was interested how the volunteers at camp painted the buildings. One day, when a volunteer was painting and stopped, Princess climbed the ladder to finish the work in her typically methodical way. "She started painting where the person left off," Galdikas said. "There wasn't a drop that fell from her brush. And she didn't put the brush in her mouth." Princess also found a way to cool the coffee she had come to like by pouring it from one container to another.

When Siswoyo, the mother of Siswi, used pen and paper, she was careful not to run off the edge. Galdikas interprets the action not so much as pure imitation as social bonding. The orangutan is saying, according to Galdikas, "If you can do it, I can do it." Simple imitation would be a machine-like duplication of what another is doing without involvement in the process. Galdikas believes that an orangutan is making a social statement through imitation that the two are equals. It is a kind of sharing. In the same way, we share food to be friendly, not to demonstrate that we know how to imitate eating. Galdikas said that Siswi understood that working with a pen and paper was important to Galdikas, and that added significance to the task. Siswi would be "very intent" and curious what Galdikas was doing. "She was trying to figure out the importance of it."

Russon remembers Siswi as full of schemes to get what she wanted. One time Siswi wanted to borrow an infant from another orangutan after she lost her own child. "Siswi was fat and looked depressed and regularly plagued Princess during that time—because Princess had a one-year-old infant, Peta, and Siswi very much wanted to hang around Peta. I got the distinct impression Siswi would have taken Peta from Princess if she could. Princess was uneasy about it, especially when Siswi got too close. Several times, Siswi tried to 'buy' Peta. After trying to get close to Peta or touch her without success, Siswi picked up a stick and, once, a piece of clay, which orangutans eat to calm their stomachs, and offered it to Princess as payment."

Russon spent almost four hundred hours observing twenty-six orangutans at Camp Leakey for a research project. Her subjects were mainly adult female orangutans and their children, since the females stay closer to camp and don't roam in the jungle as much as the males and were less aggressive. Russon concluded that the ability of orangutans to imitate the actions of a human being was complex and required mental acuity. She followed the spontaneous imitation of the orangutans at Camp Leakey, according to what the orangutans wanted to imitate, rather than selecting actions for them to imitate and rewarding them for doing it. In that sense, the orangutans were conducting the experiment and the researcher was watching how they did it.

Russon recognized a basic creative activity in the kind of imitation the orangutans were doing. It involved absorbing an act performed by another and translating it into action for themselves. The imitation could be a new way of getting the seeds out of a neesia fruit, unlocking a door with a key, or starting a fire with fuel and a match. Russon said that orangutans must have some kind of ability to "analyze" the behavior they see and make "instructions" for themselves to "drive their own activity." In human society, imitation has often been seen as the beginning of education, in language and thought and art, until some kind of leap of understanding or inspiration takes place, which teachers like myself don't quite understand. This means that we haven't understood how creative the act of imitation is.

According to Russon, the orangutan Davida was able to break an action into smaller elements to try to put on a T-shirt. "She managed to analyze the complex action into a number of key components. She then tried to put all these components together into an organized routine that solved the problem." Princess showed similar mental ability by adapting a mosquito coil to work like a pen and use its tip of burning ash to make marks like an artist or a writer. What orangutans do with an action is like taking a machine apart and assembling it again. Others have noticed that orangutans also like technical activity, such as figuring out how to use tools, using keys to unlock doors, and even trying to work machines such as outboard motors and generators. There are signs of "technical intelligence" and "engineering" ability in what interests orangutans, say Kaplan and Rogers.

Russon says the signs in orangutans of intelligent action are: a clear function or purpose; an ability to break down the actions observed into smaller elements, each of which can be reproduced separately or put together in different combinations; the ability to substitute an old element for a new element; or the proficiency to take actions learned separately and put them together for a new purpose. Russon says that the goal of an orangutan in imitation is sometimes social or simply to understand and learn what they see. Their curiosity draws them to gather information for its own sake, like a human being. It helps them get in touch with their inner orangutan.

*   *   *

And then there is Bento, who I was told by one person is "a mean little shit." Bento is partly like a child, and yet not a child, either. He is a male orangutan reaching maturity, which makes a relationship with a human being more complex. But should human beings even have relationships with orangutans?

Russon is wary of fraternization between the species, and we talked about her first encounter with Bento the bold. "I had heard about him, that he was a bad guy. He was only about six years old, but he had a reputation even then for being a bully, and most people were afraid of him. When I met him it was my first year in Sungai Wain, and before then I'd been at Camp Leakey and I'd spent a lot of my time around adult orangutans. Having anybody be afraid of a six-year-old just struck me as absolutely silly."

One day Russon and a native assistant were in the forest and the assistant said, "Oh, here's Bento coming." Russon continues, "He was just ambling along the path. Even though he was just a kid, he was the biggest orangutan in his area, so he figured he's the big boss. It's his job to come in and see who's there. So a six-year-old orangutan came over and I just squatted down on the ground and thought, 'Let's get it over. Let's have a meeting.'" At that point Bento walked over to sniff her. "And he just walked off. And I never had an ounce of trouble with him, I think because I wasn't afraid of him and because I did the greeting. If you make it clear that that's okay, that you can come up and check who you are, it seems to make it better.

"He mostly wanted to play. I never played with him. We weren't supposed to interact with the orangutans. Sometimes he'd come tearing past me and grab one of my legs and I'd just give him a shove and roll him down the hill. He was always a jerk. He was a bully with the other orangutans. He couldn't think for himself. And he was lazy. He wouldn't start on his own. He wouldn't make his own decisions where to go.

"I knew him from the time he was six to about eighteen. I always got along with him. He never did anything bad to me. I just got fond of him. He was my old crony. Even though he was a really big guy, he could have done a lot of damage; he never did anything, at least not to me anyway. He'd come and he'd sit with you."

As he got older, though, his temperament changed. He was getting stupid with teenage hormones and had "a hair-trigger temper, like adolescent human boys. You just looked at him sideways and he'd just get furious and start chasing you. He was really a problem that year. But even when he was causing trouble, I always had the impression he never would mean me any harm, but what always worried me about orangutans of his sort, the adolescent males or the subadult males, is they're risk takers and they've got all these hormones and they're stupid, so without meaning to cause any damage he could cause a lot," she said, laughing.

"I watched him grow up," said Russon. Bento came to know Russon and be protective of her after years of association. Russon tells us that even after she has been away for a year, Bento remembers her. When they are walking in the forest together, Bento now stops and waits for her to catch up. He considers her part of his group. One time Bento saw Russon talking to a stranger and chased the man away. Afterward, Bento came over to look her in the eye with an expression that said to her, "I shouldn't have been talking to a strange male because I was part of Bento's group and you don't do these things."

Russon said that the ability of orangutans to remember makes it difficult to rehabilitate them to return them to the wild. For orangutans like Bento, she said, "There's a big catch in having a phenomenal memory. They don't forget." Orangutans remember the human influences of their captivity, Russon said, to the point that there are stories like the one of an orangutan coming out of the woods, waiting on a road for a bus, and when it stopped, climbing aboard. Orangutans remember the human food they have acquired a taste for and feel free to raid gardens and houses and search through the pockets of people.

Their minds also make them more vulnerable to the cruelty of human beings. Russon has seen them confined in cages too small for them to stand up or an infant left alone all day at the bottom of a dark oil drum. Others were in such bad shape they died soon after they were confiscated. There was also the psychological damage, she said, of orangutans deprived of companionship who sank into an "autistic-like" state. She wrote that the "scars from captivity cannot be removed." Russon continued, "Dealing with ex-captive orangutans is like dealing with pollution. We made the mess, so, it may be expensive, but it's our fault. So, it seems to me that the onus is on us to try and do what we can to fix up the mess we made. We should be treating them with as much respect as we do other humans."

That's a simple ethical principle. I was curious whether orangutans have a sense of fairness, too. "Do you think orangutans have a sense of right and wrong?" I asked.

"They show things like shame, guilt. Several of the orangutans will get annoyed if a friend of theirs is attacked and they'll come and intervene. One of the orangutans, Manggis, decided that my student Laura was her friend. Another orangutan came along and tried to bite Laura. Manggis came in right away and stopped the other orangutan from biting Laura."

"That's interesting because it is helping a member of another species."

"Yeah. And there's another little one called Munmun who doesn't like to see people fight. It doesn't seem to matter who's fighting, she doesn't like it. So, if she sees an orangutan biting or attacking, she comes over right away and stops it."

"The peacemaker," I said. We need more like that.

Russon gets her own peace sitting at Nyaru Menteng at the end of the day, as the small orangutans return from the forest. I sat with her there and we didn't talk, just watched, absorbed, listened. Sometimes that's the best thing to let your brain do. Let it cool off. Don't think too much. Just let the ideas drift. Feel the thought. Don't overpower it. You make discoveries that way. That moment with Russon the light was softening as the sun went down and the orangutans were playing and hugging before bedtime. There was a sense of companionship, because orangutans, like people, need companionship. Russon has seen young orangutans in captivity cry in desperation because of the isolation.

"I'm more social here than I am at home," Russon told me later. She fraternizes with the local people and the Westerners, and the orangutans treat her as part of their extended family, their aunt Russon. They don't see her as a scientist. She is like an aunt who wanders in and out of their lives. Russon talked about the orangutan Bento again—the bold, beautiful, teenage male who expects her to respect his authority. He must think her naïve in some ways, in the forest that is his country and his heritage. She looks forward to the time she spends in Kalimantan, remembering the call of the gibbon, with its "long soaring note at the end that reminds me of a loon's call. It's a very clear, haunting sound. I find this a much more interesting world. The environment is more complex. The forests are more complex. Things that happen here seem to be more real. Borneo attracts people who are interested in some vision of the untouched beyond."

Russon said that orangutans can be "an addiction, like you saw Willie getting his orangutan fix." I traveled with Willie Smits for a week and saw him tense and sleepless most of the time, until he sat down with young orangutans at the Nyaru Menteng station at sunset. The tension washed from his face, his muscles relaxed, and he smiled like a different person. Russon said that working with orangutans also gave her a way of being in the world and a way of seeing it from a point of view she can't get in Canada.

Sometimes orangutans make gestures of friendship to her, such as the time an orangutan offered her blades of grass to eat out of gratitude. "I was sitting on the ground with Pegi in my lap. I'd taken her with me

to watch the Camp Leakey assistants play volleyball at the end of the afternoon. I trucked Pegi around with me a lot. She was depressed, probably because her human family had abandoned her to rehabilitation, and it seemed to me the best I could do for her was to be there and to introduce her to the camp and its surroundings. She had been so depressed that she wasn't eating, hardly drank, and had diarrhea. She had been getting better. We found her a water bottle that she liked, especially if it had Gatorade in it, and we managed to find some foods she'd eat.

"So, with careful tending, she was coming along. This day, I'd been feeding Her Highness grass shoots while we were sitting on the ground, then quit because I got tired of it and turned to watch the game of volleyball. I was absolutely stunned when she offered me a blade of grass to eat. I just had a ticklish feeling at my chin to start with, then, when I looked down, she was looking earnestly up at me and offering me the blade of grass. Of course, I had to eat it. How could you possibly turn it down? One thing that was stunning was the level of understanding—certainly some version of imitation, but so much more than that. This was also one of the most touching moments I've ever experienced, not only because of my relationship with her but also because it meant she was starting to come out of her depression and take initiative in the world again."

Is all this sentimentality? Is it using our brains too much to think that orangutans think like us? Are we anthropomorphizing them, making them images of ourselves?

No, said Russon. It is legitimate, she said, for scientists to anthropomorphize creatures like orangutans to understand them better. It is a view that some scientists are coming to accept and is argued particularly well by Frans de Waal. De Waal even goes so far as to say that social behavior, which would include emotion and morality, is a sign of intelligence in apes. I'd asked Russon if most studies of cognition in orangutans examined what they thought or what they felt and she said what they thought. But, at this point what I wanted to know from her was whether, with the similarity of emotions between orangutans and people, how far it was possible for ape and human to have a full relationship.

After some preamble, I said, "When there is similarity between emotions there are grounds for a relationship with orangutans."

"Sure. A different kind of relationship."

That was an interesting qualification, so I asked, "Would you put a limit on the relationships?"

"Yeah," she said. "I set limits because in my view humans don't deal well with what happens if you allow those relationships to develop freely. What happens is that at some point orangutans assert what they want the world to be like and humans assert what they want the world to be like and the two are not always the same. When that happens, the orangutans always lose."

"Do you think a limit should be put on relations between our species?"

"Why? Why put a limit? With dogs and cats, we work things out fairly well."

"But we'd have to give them some rights and that might be uncomfortable for us at times."

"Yeah. What it would mean is backing off on the notion that we always get to make the decisions and accepting their making the decisions on some things. We want the same land. We want the same foods. We like all the same things, so we're in direct competition in so many areas that it's really hard to find a way to live together. We have to accept that the decision should sometimes be in their favor and that means that humans will lose."

"If somebody says that you've got a sentimental attachment to the creature, that you're not thinking rationally, what do you say?"

"I don't see what's wrong with having some sentiment involved." Russon has written in support of the Great Ape Project to give gorillas, chimpanzees, bonobos, and orangutans basic legal rights and "to prohibit research that is not in the best interests of the apes themselves." She said that, rationally, orangutans are enough like us to be entitled to rights. "They're entitled to equal treatment or equal respect. We should be treating them better. A hundred years ago we didn't consider human a lot of people that we now consider human. The classic one was an African pygmy, Ota Benga, who was brought over and put on show in a zoo. He was not considered to be human then. Now he would be. So we can quite clearly extend our notion of who is human and who is not."

The following year an e-mail came from Russon in Palangkaraya. The world was a year older, but not a more humane or a more intelligent place to be. Both Russon and Bento had been busy during that time. Russon had written a couple of research papers and given a paper on the intelligence of great apes at the conference of the International Primatological Society in Italy. Bento had been wounded badly by a machete attack and was in jail—at least he was in the orangutan clinic to recuperate with people who care about him. Then he was paroled back to the jungle at Meratus for his next adventure.

Russon saw him in a quarantine cage before he was released. "I think he looks bigger," she said, "but that could be partly because I saw him in a cage rather than out free in the forest." Bento still didn't have the cheek pads of a dominant male then, although it wasn't for lack of bluster or swagger. If he survives, Bento is the type who will be a leader, but his boldness and his familiarity with human beings also make him vulnerable.

"He had been at the clinic for almost three months," Russon said, "brought in because he had a *parang* wound on his back from an encounter with illegal loggers that was not healing. The forest at Meratus is in bad shape. The illegal logging continues and has made its way even deeper into the protected forest. So I'm worried about Bento's fate and the fate of the other orangutans who have been sent there. Bento is likely to go back to the human camps he knows, even if he got hurt there. There's a good chance that he will get wounded again. We can only hope that he won't be killed. At least Bento looked healthy when I saw him, although he was out of shape after three months in a small quarantine cage." Bento recognized Russon immediately when he saw her and the old gleam came into his eyes. It was the female that he thinks needs his protection. "He held out his hand right away from the cage and got just a little worked up."

CHAPTER 7

The Little Schoolhouse in the Jungle

I MET THE ORANGUTAN Princess several times when we were drifting through the trees in Tanjung Puting in Borneo. We were both enjoying the forest in our own way. At those moments you let your mind wander from the texture of a leaf in the sun to the sound of a bird in the shade to the rasp of the earth under your feet. It is whatever you and circumstances choose together and it feels good. I'd already learned from others that I had nothing to fear from Princess, even if she had been a consort of Kusasi's years ago. I knew the trust and respect that people had for her. She was a good mother, and by the time she was in her midthirties she had raised five children one by one as a single parent, which is never easy. Knowing all this made me relaxed to see her and she may have sensed that. I was a bit in awe of Princess, too. I'd heard what an exceptional student she was years ago when a researcher came to the jungle to see how much an orangutan could learn to communicate. That meant something to me as a teacher. A teacher lives for a good student. It makes you what you are. And orangutans are good students; they are curious and they want to learn. There are days when I wish that my students in the university were all orangutans. But they are only human.

One of the times that I met Princess, I was walking through the trees with my son Pearce and she stopped and sat down with us in the same sandy path I'd seen her three years earlier. This time she had her wee son Percy with her. Percy was then almost two years old and dared to dart out toward my thirteen-year-old son, who must have seemed huge and dangerous to him. Once and only once did he touch the human child with a small, leathery finger. "It took a lot of courage for him to do that," my son said later. I hoped that Princess thought my son was as brave and as strong as hers. I'd heard about Princess from the stories that others told me and I knew the pain and dilemmas of her life. She had been a captive, which is illegal in Indonesia, then brought to Tanjung Puting to be rehabilitated in the forest. It was here that she was taught sign language by the American researcher Gary Shapiro and it was here that her intelligence and potential were able to develop and thrive.

But there were also questions whether the development of her abilities and her friendships with human beings made her an exile among orangutans and maybe even an unnatural sort of human-utan creation. Maybe yes. Maybe no. It's not a question that's easy to resolve. I was aware that Princess knew sign language, and I would have loved to have greeted her with the sign for "hello," one primate to another. But I could only smile and hope she understood, uncultivated brute that I am. You are not always your best with an orangutan.

Princess would not be the orangutan she is without Gary Shapiro and an unusual experiment to see how well orangutans could learn to communicate and use sign language. It was one of those moments that made both of them who they are. We like to think afterward that these things are destined—and maybe they are—but it is more likely that someone like Shapiro seizes the opportunity of a series of chance interactions and relationships that lead to something that seems like destiny. The elements to watch in this story are chance and relationships, particularly relationships, for that was crucial in what happened between Shapiro and Princess.

For Shapiro, his destiny unfolded this way. When he was twenty and a zoology student in a California college, Jane Goodall came to speak at his institution. He was enlisted as the driver for the day for Goodall. That led to a meeting with Allen and Beatrix Gardner, who had recently published their first groundbreaking paper on teaching sign language to the chimpanzee Washoe. The chimpanzee had been taken from the African jungle for American medical research, then declared surplus goods and acquired by the Gardners when she was ten months old. The Gardners would later use a young researcher named Roger Fouts to help them. The relationship of Fouts to Shapiro as a teacher and a mentor would help send Shapiro on his way into the jungle with orangutans. But that's getting a little ahead of the story.

Shapiro continued on to study animal behavior and earned a master's degree, choosing as his thesis topic comparative psychology. "I knew," he told me, "that orangutans were intelligent and that no one had worked with the species in the language arena." For eighteen months he used a young female orangutan named Aazk at the zoo in Fresno in an experiment. I would later visit the zoo in Fresno to talk to the keepers who knew Aazk. Shapiro's experience with this particular orangutan was crucial in helping him make the choice later to try the same experiment of language with orangutans in the jungles of Borneo. It also taught him the importance of having a relationship with an orangutan. But that's getting ahead of the story again. In Fresno, Shapiro learned that he could go inside the cage of the orangutan. He learned with this orangutan that he could see her as a child and as a friend, although she had a reputation at the zoo for being aloof and difficult. Working with Shapiro, the orangutan was able to put symbols together on a board to make sentences. The relationship was important in this.

Shapiro went to the University of Oklahoma for his PhD to work with psychologist Roger Fouts and his program of teaching chimpanzees sign language. Then, like a bolt of lightning, Biruté Galdikas phoned Fouts in 1977 looking for someone to teach orangutans sign language at Camp Leakey in Borneo. The only person Fouts knew who made sense for the job was Shapiro. Shapiro was single again after a divorce and so had more freedom to travel. The relationship with Galdikas and her husband Rod Brindamour would be important. Shapiro met the pair in Los Angeles and Galdikas wanted a two-year commitment from the young graduate student. That was two years in the same jungle that Galdikas's husband Brindamour was coming to see as a "green prison." It was monotonous heat, monotonous diet, monotonous passage of time. No relief. Just monotony. But Shapiro wanted to go.

So in 1978, a year after the Los Angeles meeting, Shapiro, almost twenty-seven, arrived at Camp Leakey, upriver of a fork of the Sekonyer River, in an area of abandoned rice paddies grown green and soft with elephant grass, with some patches of swamp forest. Brindamour wouldn't arrive until two months later, followed by Galdikas, finishing her PhD at UCLA three months after that. Shapiro would be there for two years until 1980.

When Shapiro arrived in the jungle, it was isolated and solitary. There were only natives who spoke Indonesian. But Shapiro was so enthralled with the romance of the intellectual life of the scientist and with the thrill of collecting new information about orangutans, that he could tell himself it didn't matter. Now, looking back, he knows the frustration and emptiness of having no one to share his findings with. He needed relationships. Some of the excitement of what he was learning about orangutans was being lost in the isolation, like a parent who can't share with a spouse what is happening with their child. "I was getting all this great data," he told me. "I couldn't express it to anybody but my diary."

When Brindamour arrived, Shapiro says that he "purged" himself in a single mighty outpouring of what he'd learned: orangutans could communicate. "It was a release of all that built-up knowledge," he says. "We got really close." In that way he needed Brindamour. In the stories that are told about the successes at Camp Leakey the role of Brindamour is an important factor. Shapiro said that Brindamour had earned the respect of the local people and was missed when he left after the break with Galdikas. I heard the same from others—such as Herman Rijksen, who liked Brindamour, too—who echoed the same sentiment and believe that Galdikas's success in the jungle that built her fame and career came from the practical support of Brindamour. From the relationship.

Shapiro recorded in his diary the incidents that happened to him at Camp Leakey and his mood swings in his isolation from human contact. The first orangutan that Shapiro saw at camp was Gundul, who Shapiro knew as the orangutan who had raped the cook there. Gundul looked "like a terror," but was smaller than Shapiro had expected from the stories. The next day the camp boat was discovered downstream after Gundul took it for a ride.

Life in the jungle for a scientist has emotional rhythms that scientists don't often discuss. Every six months Shapiro would be overwhelmed by the isolation and by the frustration of the slow pace of work in a jungle. He labored long hours, then worked late at night tabulating his data with the flame of the kerosene lamp as his companion. "Every six months there seemed to be a psychological barrier I had to break through," he said. "It slowly wears you down. I think being isolated out there, it does cause the mind to be compromised. I remember every six months going through this breakdown period. It was almost like clockwork, where I would go down to the river and have a big cry and it would pass and I'd feel stronger after that. Being confined in this remote area, it does take its toll when you can't share with somebody certain things." At the end of the first six months, he was also dreaming in Indonesian.

"I think both Biruté and I used to experience very similar phenomena where we would stare off into the trees," he told me. "I said one day, 'You know, I think this is the fruit stare. We're like an orangutan looking up into the trees.' It was a common moment between us."

"How long would you stare?" I asked. I wanted to know in case it started to happen to me.

"It could go on for quite some time," he said.

That sounded rather open ended. I thought we should do an experiment and see who could stare into the trees the longest.

Shapiro recorded in his diary the kind of erotic dreams that erupt in people kept in captivity or isolation, like prisoners and university students. And then there are the jungle romances, because human beings drift into relationships whether they want it or not. They can't help themselves. Female scientists came to Camp Leakey during that period and Galdikas told me she was baffled one day when a female scientist came to her complaining that Shapiro was plotting to kill the woman with scissors. The psyches of Westerners are just as vulnerable during long periods in the jungle as orangutans held captive in human society. Galdikas said that she stopped the female scientist from fleeing in the camp boat by grabbing the mooring line and holding on like Hercules. Galdikas told me stories of the occasional escape from the isolation of Camp Leakey by Westerners. There would be a panic, a small psychotic episode, and a camp boat would be commandeered for the breakout. Galdikas said that she suspected it was a side effect of the malaria pills, but then she doesn't seem as susceptible to the effects of solitude as others and always had a partner or friend with her in the jungle. I know I was feeling the same effects of isolation as Shapiro after only a few weeks.

I asked Shapiro about the mental and emotional changes he felt in the jungle. "I think there were some intense, almost paranoid relationships at that time," I said.

"What do you know about that?" he said, his voice rising.

"Galdikas told me about an episode where one woman thought you were going to kill her."

"Yeah, things happen when you're in a situation like that where you're isolated from town and you cannot leave. There were a couple of women out there at the time that were helping me out. They were told they couldn't leave. They probably felt like they were in danger and the reality was it was all in their own minds. People can create all kinds of fiction. For whatever reason, they got a bit paranoid."

"The conditions you're talking about," I said, "the isolation and solitude, it creates intimacies. It creates discord."

"Yeah. That was one of the issues with those two women. I had relationships to both and once they found out, I think that's when the problem started. I learned a lesson."

"What's the lesson?"

"If you're going to do research out there, bring a wife."

But I said, it's also typical of Western culture to find extreme states of mind in the wilderness, one ideal, the other demonic—the noble savage and the heart of darkness. I knew my jungle literature.

"I've seen it oscillate getting close to both sides," he said, "to the point where one could get very paranoid out there."

"Did that happen to you?"

"For me the incident with the two women was the closest thing to it. It was probably only a reflection of one bouncing off the other causing an amplified feedback loop. Yeah, there were times when you're off in the forest by yourself, it's dark and one can feel paranoid."

"That's the whole mythmaking capacity of human beings."

"Oh, sure." He said that writing his diary and then reading it later helped him appreciate the mundane reality of his experience. "It gives you a sense of objectivity that may have been lost as the story is told over and over and over again."

"When you go through your diary now do you recognize yourself as the same person?"

"Same person," he said. "The seduction that took place, it happened much sooner than I originally thought, within a week of arriving. I'm still trying to figure that one out."

*   *   *

It was a different time then. Shapiro started in the jungle with orangutans when the Sekonyer River was still clear and black, not the muddy brown it is now. He would swim across the river, wade through the mud of the swamp, and then sit down on a log to wait. One of his first students was Rinnie, an orangutan in her late teens, who was not as playful as the others and darker in the face. "Rinnie liked being groomed and being attended to," Shapiro said. "I called her Queen Rinnie." When she saw him, she'd come out of the trees, sit down beside him, and for an hour they would have the kind of relationship that is natural for a primate. It is how orangutans learn. One orangutan learns from the other on its own initiative. Their style of education is to cultivate a relationship between two creatures without the domination of one by the other.

Shapiro remembers Rinnie, "the way she'd slouch and sit with her arms down on the side and lean on them a little bit." Shapiro learned the individuality of orangutans, their moods, their gestures, their character. He told me that Rinnie was "very curious" about him and interested in the food he brought. The biologist carried cookies in his pockets to reward his student orangutans, which is why a child at the camp, Binti, the son of Galdikas, called him "Mr. Cookie." Shapiro learned that orangutans treat a relationship seriously, any kind of relationship, even student and teacher. Orangutans can love and hate, be generous and jealous, forgive and be unforgiving, and these emotions are woven into their process of education. It is how the mother orangutan schools her infant in the history and culture of being an individual of their species for the first eight years of its life. The relationship with Rinnie started to develop quickly, on Shapiro's second day in the jungle, quicker than Shapiro expected.

Rinnie had been rescued as an illegal pet and returned to the wild. She could be relaxed with Shapiro because he came to her in her jungle home, according to her will, her schedule. For orangutans, that kind of freedom and respect is important. "Within a week or so," Shapiro said, "she began making signs and, very soon after that, sentences. I couldn't believe how fast she was progressing. Signs were taking shape, sentences were getting longer, and she began inventing signs as well. Then, on the day of my twenty-seventh birthday, Rinnie took me by the hand and led me to a ground nest she made behind a tree. There she sat in the nest, laid back and spread her legs. At the same time she began pulling me toward her. I read this as an attempt to seduce me, and, thinking about it later, I came to understand that perhaps she was responding to my bringing her goodies, holding her hand as part of the process of shaping the hands for sign language, and showering her with affection for good signing behavior. She was, perhaps, interpreting my behavior as a potential suitor. Certainly, my red beard and dominant role with the other youngsters during the training may have impressed her to take a liking to me. But what a birthday present! Her attitude changed noticeably when I rebuffed her proposition, signing "no" and walking away. She was much cooler toward me after that for a while. However, it wasn't that long before she was back as the motivated student."

Shapiro was searching at the time for an orangutan of the stature of the chimpanzee Washoe, the first primate to break the language barrier in a substantial way by communicating with sign language. Washoe could use one hundred and thirty-two signs by the time she was five. Speaking was really not a practical possibility for apes. Apes can make sounds, and do use sounds to communicate, with the males having a different repertoire of sounds from the females. But they don't have the type of physical vocal apparatus needed for proper speech.

Shapiro and others also say that apes, unlike other mammals such as whales and dolphins, don't have the neurobiological wiring in their brains for speech. A researcher reported in 1916 only being able to teach an orangutan to say the words "papa" and "cup," and even those syllables were barely articulate. But the ability to communicate in other ways is another matter. Chimpanzees, orangutans, and monkeys have a series of hoots and gestures they use to talk to each other. And sometimes they use their language to deceive. The vervet monkey, for instance, has a call to warn about leopards, which he uses to deceive other monkeys of the species and frighten them away from food he wants for himself.

But then there is sign language, which the psychologist Roger Fouts used with Washoe and which a researcher named Patterson used with gorillas. An orangutan named Chantek learned more than one hundred and fifty signs with eight years of training and within two months could combine signs into sequences. In fourteen months, Shapiro taught four young orangutans at Camp Leakey about four signs each in that shorter period of time. He saw that orangutans could communicate with sign language, but he was not sure whether they did it creatively or in a mechanical way without insight. "We don't know," Shapiro says, ever the empiricist, insisting on conclusive evidence before he'd make up his mind.

One difference Shapiro saw was that orangutans aren't social creatures like chimpanzees and so don't feel the same need to communicate with their species. They are preoccupied with themselves and not as anxious about their social ranking as other primates. Although Fouts saw chimpanzees using sign language to communicate with each other, Shapiro said that the attempt to encourage the same behavior with orangutans failed. Science will never know if orangutans can use language creatively, Shapiro told me, until someone can read their minds. And that may be a long time coming.

But Shapiro saw the potential of an unusually strong and willing student in Princess. He found her in a cage used to protect the orangutans at Camp Leakey, who were being killed by wild boars and snakes. Like the others, she had been kept captive as a pet and was naïve about the ways of the jungle. "Princess actually selected me," Shapiro said, "as an adopted parent when I was looking to find an orangutan student to compare sign learning to that of Washoe in a long-term study of sign language. After I opened the holding cage with the half dozen or so juveniles inside, Princess leaped out into my arms." Shapiro was troubled, though, by the way that science sometimes separates orangutans from their wild existence. "I felt privileged being able to do the research and most importantly, relieved once the study was over, because Rinnie was able to go back to the forest and continue her life in the wild. Princess, too, was not caged once the study was over. She is free to come and go as she pleases, something that apes in North American scientific studies are not allowed to do. Princess recognizes me when I make my visits. She sits down with me, goes through her lessons, and stays well behaved. That is one indication she remembers me. I don't think she would do this with just anyone."

Shapiro had good success teaching sign language to Princess, who was younger than Rinnie and thus had a greater potential for the relationship that would make her a student. Shapiro said he would have preferred finding an orangutan mother for Princess, but that wasn't possible, and so he became her parent himself. His involvement with Princess was attacked by one individual who tried to stop it by complaining to the organizations that funded Galdikas. The person was outraged by what she believed was tampering with a wild orangutan by changing its behavior, although Princess had already lost some of her essential wildness in captivity. The thinking was that, since orangutans don't communicate this way in the jungle, they shouldn't be taught to do it, even if they have the potential. It raises the question of why an orangutan should be denied the ability to develop. Should orangutans have the same chance to develop beyond a natural state as human beings?

Princess was a lively, sociable orangutan then, smaller than the others at her age, about three or four years old. Shapiro treated her as his daughter, wheeling her around the dirt paths in the jungle in a cart, swimming in the river with her on his back, and she became his best student. Shapiro says Princess "adopted" him immediately. That's typical with young orangutans because they need a long and intense relationship with a parent, normally a mother. It is also the reason that human beings are easily seduced into an emotional relationship with the creature. A young orangutan's need for intimacy is intense and absorbing and overwhelming. It makes you feel like you are the center of the universe.

Princess learned thirty-seven signs in nineteen months and had a limited ability to combine vocabulary. One time Shapiro opened a can of fruit and she put together two hand signs to call it "sweet fruit." Shapiro recalled those moments: "Princess was a darling orangutan with an impish look. She wasn't the best student because she preferred to stay in the trees and play with the other youngsters. She would tolerate the sign lessons, as she was able to play with me between trials. She enjoyed tickle games that were used as the referent for one of her action signs. She also loved to come with me to the river to play with the laundry and soap. Activities like these were used as a context to do the sign training. She was so bonded to me early on that she would cry when I needed to part from her to do something else, such as work with other orangutans. Over time, Princess became a bit more independent and I could leave her with some Indonesian students or camp staff without her making a fuss."

Princess showed her difference in other ways. She had an "elegance" of movement, said Shapiro, unlike the male Pola, who'd "stomp and drive his fists into the ground" when he walked. Shapiro noticed how expressive Princess was with her mouth. That was how she conveyed her mood to him, and when she wanted to know his mood, she watched his mouth, not his eyes. Princess would curl her lips or pull them away from her teeth in different expressions and sometimes laugh. Orangutans and other primates use kissing naturally in the wild the same way human beings do. "Their lips are very sensitive," said Shapiro. He said that a young orangutan learns about the choices of food by watching the mouth of the mother while she is eating. Shapiro did the same with orangutans and let them teach him about the food of the jungle.

He followed Siswoyo, the clever and dominant female at the camp, into the forest to imitate her. In order to imitate her like an orangutan would, he had to have faith and trust in her judgment, which is difficult for human beings to do with apes if they think of them as inferior. "I got my first taste of red weaver ants when I copied her ant-eating behavior one day," he said. "She came across a tree covered with a swarm of the biting insects and, as they crawled on her hairy arm, she would pluck them off with her lips and eat them quickly. I was daintier about it, carefully grabbing a single ant by its head and thorax and sucking on the abdomen. The taste was very sour, perhaps owing to the fact that the species belongs to the family *Formicidae*—a group of ants that produce formic acid."

With Princess, Shapiro found that he had a small orangutan that needed to cling to him for most of the day. It was part of the bonding that would determine the success of his work as a scientist. But it also affected him emotionally as an element of his research, as it did Goodall, Fossey, and Galdikas. The new female primatologists of the 1960s and 1970s made unexpected discoveries about primates through relationships with them. So Shapiro let Princess sleep with him on his narrow cot. It didn't make sleeping easier in the heat of the jungle with the warmth and rough fibrous hair of an orangutan scraping against him. He said that it made him itch like he had sand fleas. "It was my first experience with fatherhood," Shapiro told me. "I enjoyed it. We developed a routine. I'd get us out of bed early in the morning, take her outside. I'd hold her away, and she'd pee on demand and we'd go back to bed."

So now the teacher in me wants to ask a question. It's typical of me to want to take a mental detour down the quiet back roads and sweet country lanes of abstract inquiry. Here is Gary Shapiro in the midst of important research in the jungle with a peeing orangutan and I want to break away. But you must understand that learning is a preoccupation of mine as a teacher. And we should want to know what Shapiro and other orangutan scientists have learned about the natural process of education in apes. It is relevant to our own system of education. We are apes, too, and descended from a common ancestor with them. Scientists like Roger Fouts say that our first experience of learning may have been like theirs. Maybe we can learn from what they do well.

So I asked the scientists about this and from what they told me, being able to learn in the jungle depends partly on curiosity. Don't think that curiosity is just a pleasant attitude. It is essential for the survival of the species. It also affects the kind of life you lead. If you have a real sense of curiosity, you will be happier, get more out of experience, and maybe have a better chance for success. I see that in my students in the university all the time. The curious ones are open and alert and get more stimulation. They have a gleam in their eye. The others eventually go belly-up in the goldfish bowl. Their brains are starved of the incentive they need. The next time you are in a crowd, try to read the eyes this way to see who is alert and alive with curiosity and who is a dead goldfish.

Scientists have not been looking for this incentive, a curiosity gene, but when I asked, one of the leading orangutan researchers, Carel van Schaik, told me that something like it would have to exist. If not, there would be no incentive to leap and make advances beyond what is needed to satisfy basic impulses and needs. "There has to be an engine of innovation somewhere," van Schaik said. In the same way, Fouts says in his book *Next of Kin* that both chimpanzees and human beings are "endowed biologically" with curiosity and "biologically equipped" for learning. According to Fouts, a chimpanzee brain is not born programmed with instructions how to do things. Instead, a chimpanzee has to want to learn the rules, say, to crack open a nut and then be able to generalize what has been learned and apply it to other situations.

That's the kind of flexibility that lies behind real intelligence, and that "flexibility is the key to primate intelligence," Fouts said. Instruction applied rigidly in a forceful manner teaches the wrong thing. It produces rigid and limited results, a kind of mechanical repetition. It destroys the flexibility, curiosity, and play that drive learning and the ability to find new applications to what has been learned. Learning can't be forced or wheedled out of an individual. The learner needs a sense of free will, interest, and creativity to learn. Fouts gives an example from the zoologist Desmond Morris of chimpanzees who enjoyed drawing naturally and then were given a reward for drawing. The result was that the drawing changed to hasty, disinterested scribbles, or, as Morris said, "commercial art." It made the activity forced and utilitarian and it was not genuine anymore. Fouts said he learned from Washoe that apes, like human children, will do anything if it is a game and playful, but force it on them and they'll resist. "Learning emerges spontaneously," he said, and is "unpredictable."

And part of what nourishes that is the relationship. "The quality of the relationship is critical" in learning for both primates and human beings, Fouts said. He pointed to our common experience of this. "Isn't it interesting how often you hear people say, 'I was never any good at math or German because I hated the teacher. The teacher just rubbed me the wrong way, so I never learned anything.'" Fouts told me in an e-mail how he put that realization into practice: "I take the child or chimpanzee on their own terms and I adapt to them rather than expecting them to surrender to any pre-conceived 'empirical' training regime."

One time, Princess demonstrated how an experiment can fail with an orangutan when human beings failed to understand the need for a relationship. A student researcher was sent from Scotland to Camp Leakey to conduct an experiment that tried to get apes to imitate the researcher by opening a clear box latched with bolts and pins. The goal was to retrieve a small treat inside. None of the orangutans opened the box at Camp Leakey, except Princess. She did it once and quickly, and then wouldn't do it again, to demonstrate to the human beings that orangutans did indeed know how to do it. According to Galdikas, the reason why Princess showed a willingness to cooperate at the moment when she did, unlike the other orangutans, was because Galdikas was there and Galdikas was an old friend of hers. The orangutan didn't know the researcher from Scotland and so wasn't interested in a relationship where she performed for a stranger.

In a similar experiment by two American researchers, the orangutans didn't imitate human beings and the researchers simply concluded it was because the orangutans couldn't learn by imitation, exactly what the research of Anne Russon in the jungle demonstrated they can do. The social context, motivation, and dynamics of captivity weren't considered. "Lack of motivation" or a decision to "deliberately fail to solve the problem" may explain what happens with orangutans in experiments in captivity, according to Gisela Kaplan and Lesley Rogers. The orangutan has to decide to cooperate willingly. That's why Gary Shapiro and Princess were so successful in their experiment in education in the jungle.

Permisi, as they say in Indonesia. Excuse me. At this point I have to interrupt again. I have another question to ask. I had listened to what Shapiro said about teaching Princess and I had listened to what Fouts said about apes and learning. Fouts told me that our education system is "broken" because it is "not based on the natural way we learned as families and communities for millions of years." This made a lot of sense to me as an educator. I have seen broken students, but what about Fouts and Shapiro? Didn't they have a relationship as teacher and student? How well did that go? And does Fouts apply his own ideas in the classroom? I know that I have a lot of great ideas as a teacher that my students don't think are so great. Sometimes they look dumbfounded.

So I asked Shapiro and Fouts. There are obvious signs of a bond and kindred spirit between the two. It would have started with a shared interest in teaching primates sign language and the time the two spent together with Washoe, who Fouts says was a "sister" for him, like Princess was "an adopted daughter" for Shapiro. Shapiro was quick to write a tribute to Washoe for Fouts's website when Washoe died in October 2007 at forty-two. That tribute is likely in part a homage from Shapiro to his old teacher and the bonds they shared, including Washoe. Fouts, who was pained by the loss of Washoe, told me, "I appreciated the tribute very much. Only people who have shared these bonds with our fellow apes can truly understand what we feel during times of loss."

Shapiro told me that he remembers Fouts creating enthusiasm in "small, very informal groups of graduate students." That was "energizing." "There was a kind of casualness about the relationship and I think that was perhaps like the way chimpanzees learn, more of a free flow, less of the 'I'm-the-professor' attitude." But Fouts was Fouts. "He never let you forget that he was the professor, that he was the alpha chimp with regards to his students." Fouts went drinking with his students in the local tavern and invited them into his home to meet his family and created "a very intimate and flexible atmosphere for his students." That is the same intimacy and flexibility Fouts talks about in educating chimpanzees.

In all this, Shapiro said, Fouts "accepted me," a kind of blessing or personal anointing of student by teacher. There are also signs of the relationship in Shapiro's sense of Fouts's "faith" in him and a feeling between them that Shapiro was a kind of chosen son to continue the language research with orangutans. "He made it a challenge to me," Shapiro told me. Shapiro remembers Fouts saying to him as he set off for Borneo not to "disappoint" him. The thought of honoring his teacher's faith in him gave Shapiro an added sense of mission and responsibility. Shapiro told me that he still feels "warm" about the man, although Shapiro had to make it clear that "I don't always agree with some of his ideas." Fair enough. The student always needs to be independent. Mine are the same.

When I asked Fouts about all this, he said that he still used "the family model," but was careful to say about the old days in the tavern, "I don't drink anymore." He said that he tries to appeal to his students in ways other than words. That means avoiding the threatening and condescending behavior of some teachers that is "a defense against their own insecurities." He said, "I am comfortable with myself and accept them as well." Fouts sees a family structure in graduate studies in the way the student is absorbed into the family of the university as the "progeny" or surrogate child of the supervising professor. The professors "socialize" the graduate students into the academic culture.

I asked Shapiro, then in his late fifties, if after three decades he still feels emotionally like a student of Fouts's. I know I would. Even in asking questions of Fouts, with the respect I had for his accomplishments, I felt somewhat like his student. "I think you can't lose that," Shapiro said. "It's like your parents. You know you're always going to be their kid no matter how old you are. I would like to think that the best of Roger Fouts is something that I have taken in." And pass it on to others, he added.

With the orangutan Princess, Shapiro, the student of Fouts, assumed the role of teacher. He takes the pride that any teacher would feel in what his student Princess has accomplished. She has grown into a mature and respected orangutan. She has a reputation for being sensible, clever, even tempered and a good parent. The last time Shapiro saw her in the jungle it warmed his heart that she still recognized him over the years as they aged. She showed him her cuts and scars as a child would to a father. He asked her questions in sign language, partly to show that he still cared. He thinks she took pleasure that it was him who was asking her the questions.

"We created this classroom in the jungle," Shapiro said, thinking back to that time, "and Princess had all the hallmarks of a kid who wasn't that interested in schoolwork, but I think she picked up a lot. I think it was transferred to other aspects of her behavior. How would she be if she had not had this experience with me? She probably would be just another orangutan. I think there was something about going through this at her age that awakened some part of her cognitive ability and extended it beyond the normal orangutan's abilities." Now wouldn't you say that that's education?

Shapiro's life moved ahead after his time with Princess in the jungle. After two years at Camp Leakey, he finished his PhD and shaved his red jungle beard off and married a sweet, brown-eyed city woman from Surabaya on the island of Java. He works now as a scientist in the California Environmental Protection Agency in Los Angeles. To make the marriage work, he said that he compromised by abandoning the idea of working for long periods in Borneo, and his wife compromised by accepting the idea of having only one child. Shapiro has a son, Jason, and his other child, his older orangutan daughter, Princess, is a mother herself and still lives at Camp Leakey, where she greets visitors. Shapiro sees her when he makes short trips.

As for Rinnie, what happened to her in the jungle is a mystery. There was no farewell. "She disappeared after I left in 1980," said Shapiro. "I like to think she went into the wild and took up with a mate." Aazk died in the Fresno Zoo where she was born, susceptible to mortality like the rest of us. Shapiro felt bad about that. "Aazk was someone special to me," he said. "She got me hooked on orangutans and gave me the chance, through Fouts and Galdikas, to experience Indonesia, which gave me the edge in wooing my wife." A press release from the zoo said that Aazk, "a dominant personality" who nevertheless put trust in her keepers, had ovarian cancer and irreparable kidney disease. She was thirty-four years old when she died and had no children.

Shapiro and Galdikas parted ways. They had started the Orangutan Foundation International and managed it together for eighteen years, until Shapiro created his own organization, the Orang Utan Republik Education Initiative, to help the endangered Sumatran orangutan. Shapiro was there when Galdikas and Brindamour broke up after eight years in the jungle. Galdikas then married a Dayak two years later. Brindamour also remarried, a year after his breakup from Galdikas, and became a father, too, with three daughters born in Canada.

Shapiro married not long after his Borneo venture—a woman who would teach him in the years to come what it is like for an independent man to be married to an independent woman. He met his wife, Inggriani, the day he passed his PhD thesis on orangutans at Oklahoma

University. He was ready for the relationship. It was almost a supernatural moment in the rites of passage of a young academic, intense like the time he purged himself of all the pent-up information he'd been gathering at Camp Leakey. "I was ecstatic," he recalled. "I came to the door of my friend's house, knocked on it, a beautiful Indonesian girl appeared, and I greeted her in Bahasa Indonesian, *'Apa kabar?'*—How are you? I spent the night impressing her with my two years in Borneo, chattering with her in Indonesian until the wee hours of the evening. Ten days later, I proposed and she accepted. I never suffered from the post-PhD blues because of her. Had I not gone to Indonesia, I would have never learned the language and I would never have wooed her and proposed to her in ten days."

Still married after all these years, Shapiro, with a child of his own, works in the huge sprawling city-state of Los Angeles. The long tangled hair and the drooping hermit's beard of his early jungle phase have been replaced by a pate shaved smooth. His voice, perhaps slightly deeper, still has a clear, warm timbre. By now, his time in the jungle with Princess has grown remote, that part of his younger self distant. How has the passage of time affected the experiences that shaped him decades ago in the tropical forest? Is he missing a part of himself now? Does he regret what he has lost?

The nostalgia of his younger self is connected to the jungle swamp that he says was "magical." A decade after his original time there, he returned and met, in a shady place that pleased the orangutans, some of his old ape students. "Princess was there, and some of the larger orangutans, and we'd sit down. I could pass out the food and work with sign language. It was a special moment, just being surrounded by all these large orangutans and being able to spend some time with them. To me, just being with these orangutans is special, but, when you get a group of them around you, you can't duplicate that anywhere else. You feel secure, knowing you're not going to be harmed by them. You feel privileged. It could be dangerous, if you didn't know what you were doing.

They are no longer the sub-adult males they were when I first knew them. It was a moment that will never come again that was very special and I recognized it at that time.

"I know Princess remembers me, because she is an orangutan. Relationships are maintained over periods of years. When I come, she'll sit down with me; she'll go back and do the signs, like she did before. There'll be the food signs and then I'll try some of the non-food signs—leaf or pen or hat." He said that orangutans recognize people in a "gestalt consciousness" similar to recognizing a person by a combination of size, gait, and body language. "I think they have to recognize individuals at a distance in the forest."

"What did Princess bring into your life?" I asked.

"I think I gained the perspective of being a father. It accelerated my role as a father and now grandfather, although I don't feel the same connection to her children as I did to her. I still consider Princess my adopted daughter, literally. When you adopt somebody who's not your blood kin directly, when you raise that person as your daughter, even though it's not from your own genes directly, you still feel that connection as your child. I don't think one should deny it, even if it's a different species. Taking an orangutan as I did and raising her for two years, I felt heartened that she was becoming more and more independent. I felt good that she was learning how to climb trees and fending for herself, just like any human father would feel about his daughter. So I said to Jason my son, 'Want to go see your sister?'"

"What does he say about that?"

"He's perfectly comfortable with that. He loves seeing his sister."

"He understands that literally?" I imagined the boy trying to figure out how his orangutan sister was conceived.

"Well, he understands it. He understands that she's not my blood relative. He understands that when I'm saying it, I'm not saying it as a joke. I even said it in court once when the judge asked me, 'Are you married with children?' I said, 'Yes, sir, I'm married. I have two children, one human and one non-human.'" At the time Shapiro was being considered for jury duty. "They dismissed me," said Shapiro. "I don't know why. The judge asked me and I said that 'I raised an orangutan as my daughter in the jungles of Borneo, your honor.' I would even talk publicly like that about my orangutan daughter in a court of law."

"At the risk of people thinking you're a kook?"

"Sure."

"Because, if you denied it, how would you feel?"

"I would be denying something that meant something very significant to me, something that is the core of my being right now. I really do feel like I was her father. It just happens that her genes are slightly different than mine. Living and working with Princess taught me that I could be a responsible parent, be patient in my pursuit of science, love a child unconditionally, and see orangutans as unique individuals and as persons. I could be passionate about saving my primate relatives from extinction. I am proud to call Princess my adopted daughter and have come to realize that I am an honorary orangutan through her adoption of me as her father years ago. In that way, I feel compelled to save my people."

CHAPTER 8

Music to Their Ears

FOR A WHILE it seemed as though there was no pain or trouble in the whole of the world. I was riding on a klotok again and the jungle flowed past in a long cool green breeze against the flat brown river. First the short frilly Nipa palms that drink the salt-water from the sea were flowing past in the salty section of the river. Then, deeper into the jungle, it was the flow of leaf and palm and mangrove root in freshwater from upriver. You were never quite sure where saltwater became freshwater, so absorbing was the sweet unending momentum. Then the moment passed unawares and you wanted to catch it again and hold it a bit longer, like other things in your life, like your children. My thirteen-year-old son, Pearce, was scrambling around the boat like a gymnast trying to master a new piece of equipment. I knew that he was still young enough to need a father in the way that a father wants to be needed. Our captain, Nanang, wore a frayed straw hat that seemed to make him happy. He sat on the deck above the wheelhouse with his feet dangling through an open hatch, gripping the wheel with his spidery toes, just like an orangutan would. It felt like a family. In a klotok, you relax and enjoy the moment. You are strong, in control. It feels as though the boat has no destination, no schedule to keep, no purpose except motion. You cease to care about anything else. You lie on a pad in the shade of the canopy on deck, watch, listen, eat, talk to others feeling unhurried. There is a moment when you say to yourself, "I wish everything in life could feel this easy." Maybe this is the contentment that an orangutan feels in the jungle.

People come to the jungle for different reasons. For me, this time, most of the book was written and I could relax and just be happy to feel sensations rather than pursue knowledge. I was thinking about music. I didn't expect to hear symphonies playing in the tropical forest, but, when I think of the jungle, I think of music, maybe because all the films of the jungle that I love have music, like Wagner's "Ride of the Valkyries" in *Apocalypse Now*. I thought it was time to take a break from the seriousness of working on the book. I needed to give myself the freedom for a while of exploring the idea of culture in a quirky and unscientific way. And that was how I had the idea of inviting a classical musician from a symphony orchestra to travel with me by klotok into the jungles of Borneo. He would be my musical interpreter in a strange land. I knew from experience that the jungle played a music that I didn't understand. What sounded like a buzz saw was actually a cicada that lives under the ground for years. What sounded like a flute was a tree frog. The only sound that made sense to my ears was the sound of crickets, but then crickets speak a universal language and I've heard them around the world like old friends in the oddest places. I liked the rhythm of the clatter of the cheap diesel engine of the klotok. It was reassuring. The klotok beat its bass drum of ironwood and metal as it sliced through the brown river and echoed against the forest. The boat made the jungle feel real and substantial to me. It was music too.

The musician I invited to come into the jungle with me was a lean and reedy assistant principal French horn player for the symphony in Winnipeg, a bachelor and, as a bonus, a Zen Buddhist. His name is

Ken MacDonald. He played "Ride of the Valkyries" for us on the klotok as the mangrove trees floated past. His music almost lifted the boat out of the water and into the sky and made us soar, although when we reached the camp in the jungle his horn would have effects I hadn't anticipated. It would be more radical than I realized.

His choice of instrument, the French horn, was windy and brash. It didn't allow for the gentler mood of the flute, which is probably closer to the sense of "forest murmurs" and of contemplation in the life of orangutans. Orangutans like flute music, according to what I learned from a keeper at the St. Louis Zoo, and for me, that was one more reason to like orangutans.

MacDonald had his own reason for making the trip halfway around the world. He wanted to find his voice in the jungle. He intended to experiment by using his French horn to create a version of the long call that the male orangutan uses to establish his position in orangutan society. The male orangutan can broadcast his long call through the trees and catch the sounds from other orangutans partly because of large flaps called cheek pads that grow on the side of his head. The cheek pads are activated in the male by a hormone when he is ready to be a dominant male. Of course, MacDonald interpreted the cheek pads musically. The cheek pads inflate like a satellite dish, "the way I'd look if my horn was built into my face," he said. The male orangutan does not utter a long call to hear the brilliance of his own sound. His long call is an expression of power, confidence, and mastery. He calculates how it will be heard.

MacDonald told me that he wanted to give the orangutans "a real concert" and, in the interests of relations between our two species, to conduct "a cultural exchange." He noticed that, just as orangutans have a long call, Siegfried, the hero of Wagner's *Der Ring des Nibelungen* cycle, has a motif that is played on the horn each time he appears onstage, also named "the long call." His mind saw a connection, although when I mentioned the idea to scientists they seemed baffled and one applied the term "bullshit." "If your French horn player runs into a badly tempered male," a scientist told me, "he might get chased. It depends how the French horn sounds to the orangutan." I thought it would be interesting to experiment to see what kind of reaction the musician would provoke among both orangutans and scientists. It didn't seem that it would do any harm to bring a musician into the jungle, at least not at that point. And the musician had long legs and could run fast, if he needed, although running through the jungle with a French horn might slow him down.

Before he joined me in Borneo, MacDonald was in Toronto playing in an orchestra the entire cycle of Wagner's *Ring*. My admiration of him increased when I heard this. It takes four long nights to complete the epic of the Ring cycle in the most beautiful and damning combination of music in Western culture. This was exactly the kind of person I thought I needed with me in the jungle, and I hoped that he had none of the mad and prickly traits of some artists. My artist had tried his experiment twice of playing to orangutans at the Toronto Zoo. He played Bach's six Suites for Solo Cello, Wagner's Ring theme of the "long call" of Siegfried, the jazz of David Amram's "Blues and Variations for Monk," and some improvisations. The orangutans listened, hooted, and urinated, so it wasn't an easy crowd to please. But it was enough for me to ask him to come to the real jungle and play to orangutans in the wild. He said yes, although he barely made it to Pangkalan Bun the day before our departure up the Sekonyer River. A thief in Rome with no musical appreciation had drugged his drink after a visit to the Vatican. MacDonald's money, credit card, airline ticket, and passport were stolen. He wandered the streets of Rome in a dazed and tuneless state for two days. It was as though his identity and personality had been stolen, too. The whole episode was a moral allegory about how far to trust human beings in a holy city. Yet the musician still made it to Borneo in time and was able to change the tempo of our venture. He wasn't going to miss a performance.

To interpret the reaction of the orangutans to the French horn music,

I went to a musical ape keeper, Terri Hunnicutt, of the St. Louis Zoo. I explained that the French horn player had told me that Wagner got the strongest reaction from the orangutans. The musician thought the jazz disturbed the males, and one male even urinated to it, but the same jazz made a female flirtatious, which is worth keeping in mind. It seemed they all preferred Bach, which tranquilized them as it does human audiences because of the similarity of our brains. One of the females was excited and started hooting lowly in the same tempo as the music.

"I am not surprised," said Hunnicutt, "that the females in general were more interested in the music. Remember, a male orangutan is a universe unto himself. I think male orangutans either ignore something they feel isn't a threat—otherwise they are completely relaxed—or they challenge it overtly. Yes, I believe the defecation and urination were signals! Most males won't even look at someone unless they either love them or are thinking about hating them. I think most males like a lot of peace and quiet and predictability. Females are more open to things and female orangutans don't mate for life, either. Also the musician was entirely novel, something that males don't seem to care about and females enjoy much. I have played Wagner and Bach for the orangutans and while not noticing a significant reaction to Bach, I noticed that Wagner wakes the males up, young and old. Again, I think the horn player's ideas were correct: Wagner is more a call to battle and perhaps stirs up something in these old souls. Testosterone has been around for a long time! Anyway, I did also play some Mozart Nachtmusik and the effect was noticeably calming." If I were an orangutan, I'd want Mozart, too. These creatures have refined tastes.

The apes at the St. Louis Zoo also listen to music and show clear preferences, according to Hunnicutt, and I also heard that the chimpanzees at the Los Angeles Zoo sway to the rhythm of African drummers playing to them. "We have a beautiful Native American flute CD," said Hunnicutt, "which seems to cause everyone—orangutans, chimps, and gorillas—to sit and listen." The apes also listen to instrumental music and Buddhist chants. Popular music on the radio they ignore—as they should. "We often leave the radio on classical music at night, playing softly. I think it keeps everyone calm and drowns out the background noise of the heating and air-conditioning system. Orangutans pay attention, whereas other apes may or may not. It seems that once an orangutan is emotionally mature, he or she has an infinite attention span, an amazing ability to focus and concentrate."

Hunnicutt said the CD of Native American flute music got the strongest response from the orangutans. "The first time I played it, everyone was spellbound. When the flute CD started, everyone stopped what they were doing and came to the front of their cages, sitting quietly for the duration of the CD." Rachmaninoff also evokes the same "quiet behavior," she said, "particularly with the orangutans and gorillas." Otherwise, she noticed that the more social chimpanzees, and to a lesser degree, the gorillas, aren't as attentive to the music as orangutans. An African woman has been singing to the apes at the zoo her improvised songs, which sound "like African chants with a gospel twist." When she does that, a thirty-five-year-old female orangutan named Merah comes to the front to sit and watch. Merah has a son, Sugriwa, and a daughter, Rubih. Music that is played too loud makes her "irritable." I had the same issue with my teenage daughter and know how Merah feels.

To appreciate the experiment of the French horn with the long call of the orangutan, it's important to understand orangutan society and the role the long call plays in it. And so, before I went to Borneo, I went to see the Dutch American biological anthropologist Carel van Schaik, who was then at Duke University in North Carolina. A brisk, tall, lanky man at six-foot-two, he is a veteran of years in the jungle. "Lanky," he said, "I hate that word, but it's true." Of course, any Westerner looks tall in Borneo, but the photos of van Schaik in the field doing research show the trimmest of men thinning more on a diet of rice, tea, and sardines. I don't know if that's why our conversation often turned to food.

Van Schaik had assembled in San Francisco nine orangutan scientists from sites scattered across Borneo and Sumatra to confirm that orangutans have culture. The researchers were able to compile a list of twelve examples of variations in cultural behavior from six regions in Borneo and Sumatra and published the results in *Science* magazine in 2003. Since the orangutan field researchers all have strong individual personalities, in a discipline, science, which has its own culture and divisions like a nation unto itself, it was a diplomatic coup for van Schaik even to bring the group together. The group worked with the standard scientific criteria. It had to demonstrate documented observations that groups of orangutans living in different locations had significant and numerous differences of behavior that could only come from local initiative and group learning. It is similar to finding different dialects among speakers of a language, except that orangutans have to communicate without spoken language. The culture of the local groups had to be created and transmitted and couldn't be acquired biologically.

The most obvious signs of culture in primates are use of tools in some locations and not others. There could also be traits and characteristics of group behavior found only in some locations. All this would depend, van Schaik said, on the tolerance of social situations to overcome competition and ranking in hierarchies. These types of situations would interfere with the transmission of knowledge. Social tolerance is critical for culture, van Schaik said, and orangutans, who are traditionally seen as solitary as adults or, at least as less social than gorillas and chimpanzees, have a "tremendous capacity" for tolerating the presence of others. Species need that ability to be successful in creating culture, van Schaik said.

The examples of culture in orangutans cited by the researchers in van Schaik's gathering included the orangutans in the Kinabatangan bedding down in a nest with "a loud spluttering sound" described in *Science* magazine as a "cross between a hoot and a sigh." The sound, like much of human culture, has no practical function and orangutans don't use it elsewhere. In Tanjung Puting, orangutans enjoy "snag riding," or swinging on supple young trees like a spring, but not orangutans elsewhere. In Sumatra, some orangutans eat the neesia fruit while others in Borneo don't even know it is food. In some locations, orangutans build nests for social play or to nap, and not just to sleep at night. Some build sun covers over their nests, use a stick to scratch an itch, use a leaf like a napkin to wipe liquid off a chin, use a branch to swat bees, use a leaf like a glove to protect their hands from the sharp spines of fruit, use a branch with leaves to scoop and drink water, use a leaf like a towel to clean the body, or build a nest to connect trees with a bridge. All this behavior was created by innovation and then transmitted to the group and perpetuated. And that's culture.

It sounds simple now, although it took years for van Schaik to have the moment of revelation that culture could be demonstrated in orangutans. The breakthrough came when van Schaik was studying how two groups of orangutans on different sides of the Alas River in northern Sumatra used tools to get food. Van Schaik was investigating the way that his orangutans at Suaq used a stick as a tool to get honey out of bee nests and seeds out of the neesia fruit. The orangutan cracks open the neesia fruit to find the seeds—"lima-bean size, brownish, embedded in this matrix of stinging hairs, glasslike needles"—which stick into the fingers. The fruit was evolved for a bird called the hornbill to extract the seed with its long bill and disperse it. But the plant doesn't want an orangutan. A big male has the strength to open the fruit, but others don't, van Schaik said. "So, if you can't be strong, you've got to be smart, and that's what the orangutans found out in Sumatra."

The orangutans want the neesia seeds because of the high fat content. "It's very good to eat," said van Schaik. "It's extremely rich. You can see them getting fat."

"Have you eaten it?" I asked.

"Yeah, it's coconutty. They like fat foods. There's no cholesterol problem for orangutans. It's not quite peanut butter. It's a bit harder than that, but it tastes very fat, and it gets even better at the end of the season. It creates a little attachment to it that is like a ball of oil and, if you eat that, it's like you're getting a taste of cooking oil in your mouth. So, it's extremely rich in rewards."

"Have you eaten any of the other foods that orangutans eat?"

"Now I make a point of eating everything they eat, unless it's termites," he said. "The locals have a rule, 'If the orangutan can eat it, we can eat it.' It's not so much that it tastes awful or heavenly, it just is edible and it's good." The neesia fruit was so difficult for a human being to crack open that van Schaik broke several knives trying to do it.

Van Schaik had different groups of orangutans to compare in the similar terrain of large swamps, all using tools. The group across the Alas River from his Suaq group had plenty of neesia fruit on the ground, and it was obvious they were eating it, but van Schaik couldn't catch them using tools. "I was wondering what the hell's going on. And it finally dawned on me that there weren't any tools. I said, 'God, I'm such a fool. Why didn't I think of this before? They eat it in a different way.'"

"But you have to know what you're looking for," I said.

"Of course, and that is so interesting in a way. I felt like such a moron for a while and when the stories piece together it all makes such perfect sense and now when I go back, everything fits. In retrospect, I should have been more primed. I should have given more credit to Christophe Boesch because he was studying nut cracking in chimpanzees—and the chimp people have been on to culture longer than we have. He was studying the geographic distribution and he said, 'Look, there's this Sassandra River in the Ivory Coast, where everybody cracks nuts, but to the east they don't crack nuts, even though the nuts and the chimps are both there.' Why didn't I think of that before?" If this moment of science is ever put to music it will be called *The Nutcracker Suite*.

Culture and personality are both forces that play a role in someone like van Schaik becoming a scientist and not an artist. Scientists say that their tribe is notorious for its reluctance to talk to outsiders and those who haven't been initiated, like journalists and other rabble. They have their own societies, assemblies, publications, languages, politics, and social customs. Their behavior toward outsiders can range from friendly to cold and contemptuous. Once someone decides to be a scientist, they go through a period of testing, indoctrination, and initiation in a university, which also instills in them rules of speech and social behavior. That distinguishes them from others and allows the individuals to bond more in a group. All members of the intellectual class go through a process like this, according to Noam Chomsky. "Let's take Harvard for example," says Chomsky. "You don't just learn mathematics at Harvard. In addition, you also learn what is expected of you as a Harvard graduate in terms of behavior and the types of questions you never ask. You learn the nuances of cocktail parties, how to dress properly, how to develop a Harvard accent." Van Schaik survived the indoctrination unscathed and is now more approachable than some scientists. He seems to enjoy discussing science with non-scientists and gives people sour Chinese prune pits, which he explains later is a test of his. I flunked that test and rolled down the window of his car to spit the thing out. Sucking on a sour prune pit may demonstrate strength of mind. It probably makes a person lankier, too.

Van Schaik didn't come from a university family, which may partly explain his flexibility and openness. He was born in Rotterdam, Holland, into a working-class family with few books in the house and not much intellectual ferment. He described himself to me as a child with intense curiosity who took pleasure in feeding an intellect that was looking for "a natural outlet." He brought home "chunks of moss" from walks in the forest with questions about them. Those pieces of moss have stuck in his memory for some reason, while other events have been forgotten. The family moved out of Rotterdam to eastern Holland. It was suburban there, with "little pieces of forest and ditches with wildflowers. It was nice for a kid with a bicycle. Basically I was a naturalist without knowing what it meant." He joined a young naturalists group, which gave him the kind of cultural support for this activity found in countries like Great Britain, where children grow up collecting beetles and butterflies and pinning them on boards. The British scientists told me about their childhood mania for collecting bugs.

It was in the young naturalists group that van Schaik met Maria, his future human mate. He was eighteen, she was a year younger, and by the next year they were living together. "So, you two were really destined for each other," I said. The scientist in him shuddered at the word "destiny" and he said, "Maybe so. I don't know. I don't tend to think in those terms." The two Dutch teenagers shared a love of nature and an openness of mind—and Maria was smarter than him, van Schaik said. They went to Sumatra together for a year to do research for master's degrees on the long-tailed macaque mainly because of Maria. He was a twenty-three-year-old botanist helping his mate work on her science degree in Sumatra and there he saw the magnificence of the tropical rain forest—"I decided that in Europe we virtually had no real nature left." One of the reasons they went to Sumatra was history and culture—the Dutch connection with the former colony of Indonesia and the scientific links that went with it. He discovered that he wanted to work in ethology, or animal behavior, not botany. In the end, they returned to Sumatra for another three and a half years both to do PhDs on the macaque.

It was in Sumatra that van Schaik saw his first orangutan. He has strong memories of the moment three decades earlier of the humid smell of the jungle and the sense of power as the tall trees bent and swayed under the passage of a large orangutan like a storm passing through the forest. The isolation, the solitude, and the intense work in the jungle brought the two lovers together. It put them in situations where they could test the different sides of their personalities and see the stress points more clearly, as well as enjoy the pleasure of the freedom to follow their own inclinations in their studies.

"Together you form your little island," van Schaik said.

"You also found out if the marriage will work," I said. "There's no greater test for a marriage than spending a year together in Sumatra. If you can live together in Sumatra, you can live together anywhere for the rest of your life."

"Maybe that's good," he said.

The years passed, the van Schaiks had a boy and a girl, and van Schaik was working in mosquito-infested swamps ripe with malaria. He started going to Indonesia alone and was intrigued by "the deeper questions" that scientists weren't asking about orangutans, such as the role of the female in mating. The male only spends two weeks with the female to mate and then returns to his solitary pursuits. How the arrangements for this kind of a fling are made need more study. Van Schaik established his research site at Suaq in Sumatra to study the social organization of orangutans and "purely by chance" shifted to the use of tools and the creation of culture.

"The scientific method comes as child's play," van Schaik said. "You're asking questions and the questions hone your observations. Without knowing it, by the time I was eighteen, I was a real scientist. I just like being outdoors and I've always been a curious kind of fellow. I remember my grandfather wasn't very pleased with me because I was always asking him why and what and how. So I guess it is just a sort of a natural outlet, if you have this insatiable curiosity."

"It makes me wonder where curiosity comes from," I said. I asked van Schaik about the role of the questioner in society and in evolution. Socrates asked too many questions and look what happened to him. He was forced to drink hemlock.

"Most people do not like questions with no known answer, especially disturbing ones," he said. "I realize that I may annoy people—my grandfather certainly was annoyed—but, for science, it is a great way to proceed."

"Is curiosity an instinct?" I asked. "Is it a mental ability? And this applies to orangutans, who are intensely curious. Why are they curious?"

"Obviously because it's an adaptation," he said. "The whole innovation side of culture comes from that."

"What is curiosity?" I persisted. "Is it an instinct?"

"Oh, yeah," he said. "I wasn't stimulated at home into intellectual pursuits. So that must have come intrinsically from my own inner self."

"Is there a curiosity gene?"

"Oh, yeah, there must be lots of curiosity genes out there, because culture is, of course, innovation and transmission. But there has to be an engine of innovation somewhere. And look at those young orangutans we throw out in the forest, the orphans. They try all kinds of things."

"So, if you don't have a social structure where there is a lot of education, you need a curiosity gene?"

"Right. In fact, that's one of the puzzles we still have about the whole question of culture. If you look at young orangutans, they're incredibly conservative. They copy exactly what Mommy is doing. They tend to eat after Mommy starts to eat. Where's the curiosity there? Where's the innovation?"

"How do they break out of that?"

"The answer is, they tend not to, just like humans tend not to. The only situation where you have a strong urge to innovate is when nothing works, either because your mother isn't there to tell you how things work or because what Mother tells you is completely useless."

"If the condition for innovation is when the mother isn't there," I said, "that still doesn't have the spark of curiosity. You could just sit there and do nothing."

"If natural selection likes the end point of innovated behaviors that are going to be useful for you, then you need equipment to get there."

"And curiosity is the equipment," I said.

"Exploratory behavior. Fiddling."

"My mind gropes for something tangible in curiosity," I said. "The phenomena is there, but what's the physical basis of curiosity?"

"There is a neurobiological component to it, no doubt. It's a good question."

"As a species is it possible to have a stronger curiosity gene?"

"Oh, very much so. Yeah. Orangutans have this tremendous capacity for social tolerance and species that don't have that just aren't going to go very far on the road to culture."

"It would be fascinating to develop a test for curiosity," I said. "I'd like to give it to my students. If tolerance and curiosity are important, it would be interesting to find that early in children and in students to develop it and stimulate it."

Van Schaik explained how orangutan society operates. Orangutans are basically solitary creatures who live in the forest apart from each other, except when the lone female is raising a child. The separation of orangutans is necessary in a forest where there is not enough food in single locations to support groups. And yet, although orangutans are solitary, they are "not hermits," according to Gisela Kaplan and Lesley Rogers. They occasionally form a temporary group at a fruit tree, at which time some sense of rank and hierarchy may be observed among them. Where the density of fruit trees varies, such as between Sumatra and Borneo, says van Schaik, there can be different densities of orangutan populations. As a consequence, Sumatran orangutans are more social because their environment has more food. In turn, the density of the populations is a factor in the creation of culture among orangutans.

"Basically," van Schaik said, "we think there is something like a society in Sumatra where clusters of related females live together and they all seem to like the same dominant adult male who has a relatively small home range compared to other adult males. The reason for this strong preference is this male somehow offers protection. We have all kinds of evidence now of that because the females are orienting toward his long calls and staying."

"Is that part of the function of the long call?"

"Yeah," said van Schaik. "The other part is keeping the other flanged males away from his females, so it's purely selfish."

"It's a long-distance family," I said.

"You can call them 'exploded harems,'" he said.

"It doesn't seem to be a family structure, but orangutans can have relationships over space and time," I said.

"Exactly," he said. "You don't have to meet every day. There is a lot more structure than meets the eye."

"Don't they have the capacity to respond to novel sounds and novel situations?"

"Probably, but like you, they might first try to categorize it as something they know. So, you hear somebody speak, you first say, 'Is this a language I know, yes or no?' We can describe orangutan vocalizations and put them in a bunch of categories. The kiss-squeak, the long call, the lork, the grumph, the pig grunt. And those are specific sounds in a specific context with a specific meaning."

"But," I said, "if you take a specific sound with a specific function, whether it's a long call or not, there would have to be, I imagine, individual variations."

"Oh, of course."

"You could recognize so-and-so's long call."

"We know that. That's been shown."

"And within an individual, could there be individual variations? You could pick up that so-and-so's in a good mood or a relaxed mood?"

"Well, with long calls you know they vary the speed of the calling. So whether they go *oo, oo, oo, oo*"—he said, with a deep bass sound and then repeated the phrase with longer periods between each sound—"and that is clearly linked to their motivational state, how aroused they are, how mad they are."

"Is there any sense what that means when there's a longer period between—"

"Yeah, it's an arousal thing, so, when the males are really wound up, then they'll give a faster long call. There is that kind of variation, but, it's not entirely open ended. And, I'm also saying with culture, that we might actually see some of the first stirrings of symbolic communication. It's a long jump from that to music. In fact, it's one of those questions that people are now thinking about—how did music evolve? I don't think there is a satisfactory answer."

"What is the function of the long call?"

He responded as he often did by posing himself questions out loud, working to define those questions, and then working on an answer. He reasoned by creating dialogues with himself. "The function of the long call? Well, what's the message in the long call? That's the first question we can ask. The message in the long call is 'I am here' and, depending on where you are, it also says, 'I'm going that way,' because they give the long calls in a particular direction, and so, if you're behind the animal, he sounds farther away than if you're in front of the animal. The message is also, 'It's John calling. I'm here and, if you don't hear me very much, it's because I'm moving in the opposite direction of where you are.'"

"And this is to make sure that everybody respects the boundaries?"

"That's the function question. The question is, what do you do with that information? It depends on who you are. If you are a male, you say, 'Okay, there's John, he's sounding far away and it probably means he's going that way,' or, 'If he's coming my way, he's still very far away.' If I'm dominant to John, and if I know there are some females over there, I might go and chase him. If I'm subordinate to John, I might say, 'Okay, it's good to know. Let's keep my distance. Now I know where he is. Thank you very much.' If I'm a female, again depending on who John is, I can draw my conclusions. If John is the dominant male, I might decide that I want to stay closer to him, maybe reduce my distance to him."

"It does away with stealth," I said, "because, if you're not the dominant male and you could get beat up"—

"It's one of the mysteries, isn't it?"

"Or, if you're interested in sex, you're giving the females a chance to avoid sex. It may not be to your advantage to have a long call."

"But the alternative—and this is one of the mysteries I've often asked myself, why do these old guys continue to give long calls when it exposes them to a considerable social risk?—and the answer I have is it's the best they can do, because if they didn't call, they would never attract any females. And a male isn't necessarily calling to other males to beat him up, of course. The male is calling to try to attract females. And we did see that, when the locally dominant male is completely absent, females might respond to the second-best guy. There's always the second-best guy somewhere. So the subordinate males maybe go and call in an area where there's maybe one female off living on her own and the dominant male isn't around and she might still find him relatively attractive."

"Doesn't the long call really give the choice to the person who is not doing the calling?"

"Absolutely. To stay away."

"Or to decide what to do?"

"Of course. But again what's the alternative for a male? If you're an orangutan female and you don't like the male, you can hide. And they do. We see them doing that, try to be very still and hide and not attract a particular kind of male, because they don't want him."

"And they're not in a social group, and, when you move in a group—"

"You can't avoid each other, right? So this is a very interesting question. It remains an interesting question, why do these males call? Well, like I said, I think they have nothing else that works better, because if you're the dominant male, it's obvious why you call. You tell all your rivals to stay away, because they might get a serious dressing down if they come too close and you tell the females where you are and the females use that information. They're really interested in it."

"But," I said, "if you are a male who has been dominant and your power is fading and your ability to withstand fights is fading, or you are an up-and-coming male and you've been losing a few battles, it really isn't to your advantage. In human beings, we'd say that is just ego—"

"Right."

"When you won't admit you're weaker."

"But, in animals you call that maladaptive."

"So all meetings are prearranged with orangutans?"

"Yes," he said. "They advertise and say, 'Meet me, if you feel like it.'"

"Is the power in the person who makes the long call or in the person who has the choice to avoid or have a meeting?"

"You're answering your own question."

"It gives a lot of power to the female."

"To the audience," he said, "because the audience has information the male doesn't have. The audience knows where the male is, but the male doesn't necessarily know where his audience is."

Fortified with rudimentary knowledge about culture and the long call of the male, it was time to put it to the test with my own foray up the Sekonyer River to the camp of the scientist Biruté Galdikas in Tanjung Puting park. After four hours on the slow, brown river our klotok arrived, French horn blaring, father, son, and Zen Buddhist. The musician had spent hours learning the Indonesian national anthem from Nanang on our klotok, and now he played it as we pulled into the camp. Those standing on the dock and lounging on the other klotoks turned to us, made large grins, and waved. We had arrived. It was as though we were part of one big family. Galdikas was not there, although she'd promised me that she would be and a film crew was waiting for her, too. This tardiness of Galdikas is so well known that it has created its own social ritual of gathering to speculate where Galdikas is and how late she will arrive. Some say the delays of Galdikas are a way she exerts power and authority. I argued that her mind works according to its own schedule, which sounded so feeble once the words were out that I wished I hadn't said it.

The others at camp told us how much Galdikas disliked the disruption of the quiet at Camp Leakey, so my musician began blowing his horn to announce himself. It was a way of asserting his voice, as a male orangutan would do. It also seemed to join people to him. The camp sits inside a national park and so the authority of Galdikas is tenuous, based on the loyalty of her Dayak employees. The camp is a society unto itself, with its own history, memories, and ranking by power and prestige. One of the things that binds this society together is its interest in the orangutans, who are as familiar to the Dayaks as members of their own family, and so when I returned to the camp this time I carried photos of the orangutans to show them and that got me past the language barrier. As for MacDonald, I saw that he was able to enter the culture quickly and make friends easily with his music. Even the orangutans reached out to him. He was grabbed on the ankle by the flirty orangutan Siswi while she was lying in ambush at the camp mess hall. It is a trick of hers to initiate newcomers.

When Galdikas arrived late at night and heard the musician playing, she asked about it and her assistants claimed they didn't know what the music was, although I doubt that anybody at camp didn't know MacDonald and his horn by then. That would be a social lie to protect the peace or at least not expose the messenger to the unpleasantness of controversy. The assistants told Nanang later that they were nervous what *Ibu Professor* would think. MacDonald walked around the camp in the day and played music like Benjamin Britten's *Serenade for Tenor, Horn and Strings,* which is a gloomy, prickly little piece written during the Second World War.

As soon as MacDonald blew the horn one of the assistants came to him and said, "It's too loud for the orangutans." MacDonald asked which orangutans had said that. None had, of course, and the assistant retreated. Another assistant said that *Ibu Professor* must have said the music was too loud, because she was the only person who could tell a white person what to do. But that was pure speculation. And yet I saw that Galdikas was aware of the effect the French horn was having in her camp. I was walking with her when she stopped to break up a group of her Dayak assistants who had gathered to play music and were neglecting their work. I admit that I felt a bit guilty as the person responsible for bringing a musician into the camp, but I also liked the new spirit of liberation from the control in the place.

One afternoon, I was sitting on the dock talking to Galdikas when MacDonald walked past. Galdikas said, "Hello, Mr. MacDonald. Did I hear your French horn last night or was I imagining things?" The whole camp would have liked to hear the exchange between the two at that moment.

"You heard a short call," said MacDonald with a nice parry. He had been challenging the dominance of Kusasi with his French horn calls.

"You did one," she said.

"I did a short call," he said.

"I thought so."

"I feel one coming on right now," said MacDonald a bit pertly. And he left to climb on our klotok.

"Well," said Galdikas, "some would say he's mad; some would say he's a genius." We'd been discussing the opinion that she was mad.

"He has been a lot of fun to travel with," I said.

"Madness and genius are not that far apart," she said. She said there was a connection between genius and bipolar disease in artists but not scientists. I wondered what made scientists more sane than artists.

I could hear MacDonald's horn in the background while we talked. We stopped talking several times and listened to the slow, wistful melody. It was reassuring, because I knew that MacDonald was with my son Pearce and that as long as he was playing the French horn my son was safe. At one point we clapped at the end of a song.

"Very nice," she said to MacDonald, raising her voice to carry to the klotok. He had played the opening call from Britten's *Serenade* again. "Actually, it suits the mood here, too, doesn't it?" Galdikas said to me.

"Yes, it does," I said firmly. I continued, "He has been talking about the resonance of the jungle, trying to translate things into musical terms and trying to cross cultural barriers with music, which he did brilliantly with the Indonesian anthem. He won some instantaneous friends. In fact, now when we go around somebody will be humming that song, to greet us or to try to get him to play it again."

"Well, that's progress," she said, a little obscurely. "Indonesians, of course, love to strum their guitars. They love music." We could still hear the music as MacDonald played Indonesian songs for the Indonesians on the klotoks.

"Do you think it would be upsetting," Galdikas said, "if we asked him to stop for a minute or two." Apparently a good mood has its limits.

I didn't think the music was hurting anything and felt like saying so. "I think those people are enjoying it," I said.

So the musician played on until he was satisfied and then stopped. Galdikas called out politely, "Thank you, Mr. MacDonald."

That summer in the camp in the jungle by the brown river there were two series of long calls, one from the orangutans and one from a lone human being. I heard Kusasi call one night and then again just after five in the morning. I was half awake in the klotok at the time while my son slumbered undisturbed in the big mosquito net beside me on deck. I let my son sleep. The heat and the jungle had tired him and there would be time enough later for the world to hear his voice.

I heard Kusasi call two other times, at two and three in the morning, and was amazed that I could recognize him now. "They were fight calls," Galdikas told me later. "He was chasing somebody." Kusasi had put so much fear into a male orangutan that the other male had scrambled over the roof of a building at the camp and woke the human beings sleeping inside by the sound of the pounding. I was talking to Galdikas in her cabin at night when we heard the long call of Kusasi just after eleven and stopped to listen. It had a kind of low, slow whoop. The call made Kusasi feel close.

"It means that he's announcing his presence to the world," Galdikas said. It didn't have "the intensity" or "fast pace" of a fight call, she said, which starts more abruptly, is shorter in length, and doesn't have "the long tapering sighs" of the long call. "That was a strong long call," she said.

As for the man with the French horn, I remember that he made the experiment of his long call at night. At the klotok under the stars, we heard him clearly, sounding a little more distant than he actually was. The whole camp heard him and the whole camp knew who he was. It was a pure and windy blast on a horn that filled the immensity of the night. The other sounds in the forest ceased, then returned one by one. I was worried that he might get lost in the dark walking alone back to the klotok. I imagined his skeleton would be found years later slumped under a tree still clutching the antique horn in long, bony fingers.

But he survived. And he had performed something that was deep and personal to him. I thought he was a lonely man and he didn't have the comfort I had with my son there. Some day my son will leave home to seek his independence like an orangutan. That may be part of the meaning of the long call, too. The musician had made good use of culture. He had spread the spirit of liberty through the camp by playing concerts for the orangutans he found sitting on paths through the trees. He played a Bach cello suite for Princess and her son Percy, who sat and listened. The males gave him askew glances. One time it almost seemed as though an orangutan responded in the distance. For the orangutan Pan, he played a bright little minuet and gigue from Bach's Cello Suite One. It was a better choice than the prickly Britten tunes. Pan sat politely, listened, and then drank MacDonald's sweet tea in one swift final lip-smacking swig and walked away. Now that's an orangutan who appreciates culture.

CHAPTER 9

The Heartfelt Man

It is MORNING in the jungle. Still cool, or at least cool for the tropics. The sunlight seems to fall with a gentler touch. The air is milder. It is the old, sweet, fleeting moment of disengagement before the demands of the jungle return like the crash of a big wave. A four-year-old orangutan named Joshua has swung down from a tree in the tropical forest at Meratus in East Kalimantan. Joshua, you should know, is a good-natured orangutan, the type who might blunder into an array of trouble he does not deserve. When he was younger, human beings took him captive, killing his mother and yanking him out of the forest where he belongs, holding him against his will, against the law. The contact with human beings changed him. He no longer was careful to keep a safe distance from those who could harm him. He trusted human beings in a way that a wild orangutan wouldn't.

Eventually, Joshua got a reprieve from captivity, thanks to an eight-year-old boy who heard in school that it is wrong to keep an orangutan as a pet. The boy felt bad. He was too young to know differently. The boy whispered into the ear of an official that his family had an orangutan at home. The orangutan was confiscated. The boy was given school books as a reward, and Joshua was taken to the tropical forest at Meratus to live like an orangutan should be allowed to live.

There, in spite of his time with human beings, he was affable, charming. He made friends easily with other orphan orangutans, like Alf. An orangutan named Maya saw qualities in Joshua that she liked and let him hold her infant. She wouldn't do that with just any orangutan. But with Joshua she knew she could. So that morning in the jungle when the sunlight was gentle once more and the moment was sweet for a time, Joshua ambled toward the man who was calling his name, the man who was sitting on a log waiting for him to come. The man was the Dutchman Willie Smits. I watched that happen.

I traveled with Willie Smits across Kalimantan to see what it was that orangutans have come to trust in him. I realize that he may be the most intense person I have ever met. And when I use the word "intense," I am not fooling. He is so intense that he makes everything else seem narcoleptic by comparison. We look like we are in a coma next to this man. Willie Smits lives in a world that is larger than mine and yours. It is a world he has partly made, too. In a few years Smits has helped to build the largest organization in the world for protecting orangutans and for rehabilitating them for the wild after they have been kept illegally. He says that he has employed between six hundred and a thousand people at a hundred sites. He talks about the large and revolutionary enclosure he designed for primates as a separate facility inside the Jakarta zoo. He has built a miraculous new forest for orangutans and people out of a wasteland in Kalimantan near Samboja. And that is just the beginning of his accomplishments.

I might have suspected a wee bit of exaggeration and embellishment in all this, but I traveled with him from orangutan quarantine stations, to release sites in the jungle, to wildlife confiscation centers, to plant nurseries, to experimental farms, to Dayak villages, through airports, through cities, down dusty roads, across rivers without bridges, into the

forests at night. It was continuous movement. It was so much movement I wondered why he wasn't a blur. One time a journalist and I were
waiting for him on board an aircraft in Jakarta, and he just flew in the
doorway at the last moment with only a change of clothes in a small
briefcase.

I never knew what he'd do. Volcanoes and hurricanes are more predictable. He'd rage. He'd be sweet. He'd overwhelm you with a burst
of passion like the sudden onset of the monsoons on the equator. This
is a man who feels strongly, makes sharp distinctions, speaks his mind.
All this very much like the Dutch, maybe more Dutch than the Dutch,
although Willie Smits says that he is now a naturalized Indonesian and
so a "former Dutchman." He has liberated himself from his country, his
origins, like a little country unto himself. In the end, I admire and trust
him. I just don't feel like we are living in the same world. I don't think
we could.

Smits lives in a world that is darker and harsher than the one many
of us know. One time, when we were driving through the streets of Jakarta, Smits showed me one of the death threats he says he gets all the
time, this one by text message on his cell phone. This man is perilous,
I thought, and wondered how close I should be sitting to him. Maybe
a car would pull alongside us in the traffic and riddle him with gunfire.
A colleague of his explained to me later that Smits is the type of person
who sees the world in the extremes of good and evil, which may sound
bizarre unless you are the former Dutchman and have seen what he has
seen, the brutality committed against individual orangutans, the insane
destruction of the rain forest. That's not good. That doesn't suggest that
the world is being managed by the saintly and the angelic. Maybe a little
more intensity is actually required.

Smits found his mission in life in opposing the destructiveness of
the world, and he tries to pull you into that mission. And sometimes
you just don't feel you have the strength that he does. I spent endless
hours with him on endless, dusty, rutted roads in the jungle and saw the

orangutans he has helped. It was like they are a procession passing, one by one, individual by individual, pouring out of some miraculous place that has created them as thinking and feeling creatures. I remember being with him one night on a road in the jungle. We were forced to stop at an outpost built just days before by military officers to extort money from illegal loggers. Smits told my young son and me to keep out of sight and then went for a conversation with the officers in the dark. I never saw him flinch. Not with an orangutan. Not with a corrupt army officer. Farther down the same road we had to stop again, this time at a Dayak outpost built to extort a toll for crossing what was once Dayak land. More talk in the dark. The unofficial outposts were sprouting like thistles out of the ground when nobody was looking.

It never ended. Coming back from the forest where Joshua lives, Smits had to stop once more at a restaurant to chat with the local people to investigate the source of the illegal loggers. I watched how skillful his questions were, how he got the information he wanted. It seemed that the local people were not pleased with the devastation of their forests by people they didn't know. They felt his concern, his passion. Then Smits arranged a dinner of wild boar meat at night for my son and me. The meal was at the home of the man who Smits said was the greatest wild boar hunter in all of Borneo. The fresh meat was washed down with a big glass of thick, milky palm wine or *tuak*. I read that it was traditional that, after the Dayaks had drunken *tuak,* to take their weapons from them to avoid accidents. I remember that bright night of wild boar meat because two civet cats were fighting in a palm tree under a full moon. That was a great meal. Down the lane from the boar hunter's house we saw the truck of an illegal logger stop to hand a bribe to a police officer. The boar hunter said that he had paid to have his son join the forest ministry, a good job, although the staff is as corrupt as everybody else, he said. This is the world that Willie Smits inhabits. This is the world he knows. Cruel, corrupt, inhuman. And yet that morning in the Meratus forest the orangutan Joshua made him a different person. The orangutans always do. He does not buy their affections with the ripe mangoes the way that I saw others do. The orangutans come to see him because they want to be with him.

I saw it again elsewhere. It's like there is a nation of orangutans with their hands out to Smits. You can feel their interest in him. At the Nyaru Menteng orangutan station, near Palangkaraya, in Central Kalimantan, I saw him touching orangutans and communing with them. It was quite a sight to witness. Maybe I even got more out of watching Smits and orangutans than I would being with orangutans by myself. He used gentle, orangutan-like grunts and hoots. It made you laugh to see such joy. He conversed with orangutans, spoke the mute language of touch and embrace, like a lover would. He had no fear of them and told me that he had never been harmed by an orangutan, aside from the bites that are a normal part of their rough play. Orangutans have a tough skin for this kind of affection.

The orangutan keeper Leo Hulsker told me later in a conversation in the Netherlands that he has seen Smits commune instantly with a strange orangutan many times. One time Hulsker said that he was having trouble establishing a rapport with a large male orangutan named Karl in the Apenheul Zoo in the Netherlands. "I just couldn't make the connection," Hulsker said. "It's like you want to have a connection with an individual and it doesn't seem to work. He was getting frustrated and I was getting frustrated and I didn't know what to do and then Willie came along and he sat down with Karl and in two or three seconds he had a connection. I could just see them talking to each other. If an orangutan gets a little bit excited, you can see on the cheek pads the goose bumps. With Karl I could see the goose bumps and within two or three seconds Willie was talking in a really soft voice to him and I could see him relaxing. Karl was getting more and more interested in Willie. I've seen Willie do that a lot of times."

Hulsker has been to Kalimantan several times with Smits and seen him rage and cry about the treatment of orangutans. He remembered the time that a pair of burly Indonesian construction workers confiscated two small orangutans from a dealer they had beaten. The men drove nine hours through the night to bring the orangutans to Smits at the Wanariset station north of Balikpapan. "It's bullshit to say Indonesian people don't care," Hulsker said. "We opened the crate and there were these two tiny babies with the two pot bellies and the eyes deep in the sockets because of dehydration and malnourishment, and they were really sick. Willie took out one of these babies and I took out the other. I looked at Willie and he was holding his baby and he started screaming and cursing. He walked away. He kicked against a rock. He was shouting, 'Why are people still doing this? What is wrong with them?' He has seen some pretty nasty things over the years and he still gets emotional."

There is an uncanny side to Smits, too. He seems to understand the minds of orangutans and to be able to read their moods. I watched him sitting on the grass one evening mauled by affectionate young orangutans as the sun slid toward the horizon. For about two hours he bathed himself in that glory. The Smits at this moment was different from the one I'd traveled with across Kalimantan, sometimes tense and raging and volatile. You had to love the person he was with orangutans at that moment. In the orangutans, he finds a pure and simple delight, without pretense or affectation or feelings of superiority. That may be one reason why orangutans are so open to him. It may be why I saw Joshua come to him that morning in the forest.

So what is it in a difficult man like Smits that an orangutan feels it can trust? Do they sense a goodness in him? If I were an orangutan, why would I be drawn to him? Actually, when you think about it, it's not so far-fetched to ask how we would feel as an orangutan. There is great similarity between the way that apes and human beings react to each other. Smits told me he was able to read me better because he'd spent so much time trying to understand orangutans. I may be a lot more obvious to orangutans than I think. I remember one time, at his orangutan station at Wanariset, I watched Smits, as he often does, slip at night into the nursery to see the infant orangutans sleeping in the dark. The small orangutans made gentle rasping sounds as they breathed in their dreams, their dim forms barely visible. Two orangutans were cuddled together in sleep. It was wonderful to watch the way Smits took pleasure in the sight of the sleeping orangutans.

And yet Smits is a volatile man who burns hot like a flame. Those who know him talk about "the flaring of the passion" in him, a fire that sometimes singes those who get too close. They told me that he has a bit of ego—actually, more than a bit—and yet, as one person also told me, you learn to appreciate him "for his virtues and forget his flaws." I wondered why his friends could be so critical of him without fear when I'd seen the frightened hush that surrounds some other scientists, the feverish efforts to protect them from anything that might tarnish their idealistic public image. It seems that this is a man who is larger than whatever human flaws he has, that you can trust that larger part of him, that part of him committed to orangutans. Lone Dröscher-Nielsen told me what those who know him say, "Anybody hurts an orangutan and he just totally blows up." And maybe in the end Willie Smits will be consumed by the flame of his passion and by the flame of his commitment. And maybe that will be a good end for a man like him. But not yet.

The Smits that we have now was reborn in the early 1990s after he had come to the Indonesia that would become his home country. The story he tells about his rebirth at that time begins with an incident with a small female orangutan named Uce. It has become a kind of personal legend for Smits. He tells it over and over again. What happened resembles a conversion experience where the life of an individual is changed radically with some kind of enlightenment and change of purpose. Smits refers to that orangutan sweetly—"my Uce," he calls her, the name pronounced as Uy-chay—as transforming his existence.

The orangutan was an orphan when Smits found her, which may be an emotional connection with his own life since he also described himself to me as an intelligent but lonely child, an "orphan" suffering hardship and abuse at an early age, "locked in a dark cellar and forgotten for almost a day and beaten." He described his family in Holland as poor but hardworking, never owning a home or a farm of their own, without food, catching pigeons to eat. He also talked of a deep loneliness and vulnerability in himself. "People can easily hurt me," he told me, "and it takes me some time to overcome those feelings." What does it take to hurt you? I asked. "To doubt my sincerity," he said.

Of the loneliness in his childhood, his sense of distance from others, he said, "But now I'm trying to compensate, I think, for what I've lost over all these years." So it was in this Smits, at the age of thirty-two, that the orangutan Uce kindled the desire to rescue orphan orangutans and return them to the wild. Smits found Uce in Balikpapan, a sick orangutan in a local market, and simply walked past her the first time. It meant nothing initially. Then, something worked itself deeper into his brain and what he had seen started to disturb him. He felt compelled to return to look for the orangutan. He found her gasping for breath on a garbage dump where she had been abandoned to die. He took her home and cared for her. Then he was given a second baby orangutan, Dodoy. He nursed the two back to health.

The well-known Dutch orangutan scientist Herman Rijksen remembers Smits at the time showing him Uce in a cage on his back porch among some exotic caged birds. At the time, Smits was the local manager working for Rijksen under a Dutch rain forest conservation program. Rijksen told me that he convinced Smits to release Uce into the jungle, and from that moment Smits realized the importance of returning orangutans to the wild. It was difficult for Smits to detach himself from the orangutan and let her return to the forest, but he did. "He saw an enormous opportunity," said Rijksen. "In no time he set up the most fantastic oversized quarantine facility, better than any hospital in the whole area, because that's typical of Willie. He wants to do it very, very good."

Up to that point, Smits had been a plant biologist and forester working in Indonesia. After that, he was fighting the wealthy and the powerful to protect orangutans. There is an intense moral idealism in Smits and that may be why he also sees goodness in orangutans, too. Orangutans have a basic sense of fairness and morality. Smits says they can also be unselfish and altruistic. It is an interesting point of view and one supported by a lifetime of observation of apes by another scientist who is also originally a Dutchman, Frans de Waal. De Waal believes that morality originates in both human beings and apes in "social instincts" and moral emotions such as empathy, rather than in what we call the rational faculties. If that is true, then the experience of Smits with Uce may also be a moral awakening.

The experience with the orangutan Uce climaxed in 1991 when Smits released her in Sungai Wain, two years after he first found her, to live in the jungle again. Years later, Smits returned to Sungai Wain. Uce had mated with the orangutan Charlie, from the controversial group of orangutan refugees known as the Taiwan Ten—ten orangutans repatriated from Taiwan to Indonesia in an incident that caused a political furor both internationally and inside Indonesia—and the two had produced a son, Bintang, a word that means star in Indonesian, and, by extension, fate or destiny. Smits was anxious about finding Uce and her son Bintang in the jungle. He found them, but the second orangutan he had originally nurtured, Dodoy, now a full-grown male at fourteen, asserted himself against Smits, preventing Uce from coming to Smits. Ironically, his own goodness made this possible.

In front of Smits, Dodoy raped the orangutan he cared so much about. For orangutans, that is also a display of power. "I feel sad for Uce," Smits wrote later, describing what happened in the present tense, as though it were happening again and again, "but this is how it has to be. She lives in her own orangutan world and our love must bend to that." Smits tore himself away. "She cries when I pass them and stretches her arm out to me, trying to follow me, but Dodoy resolutely pulls her back." The episode ended that day in a sinister way as Smits tried to find the man who called on the phone to say that Smits's throat would be cut. The man had phoned from a telephone shop and left without a trace.

During the next visit Smits made to Sungai Wain, the orangutans Dodoy and Uce returned. By this time Dodoy had a new consort, Siti, who was pregnant with the seventh orangutan to be born in the release area of Sungai Wain, after surviving a period of drought and fires that led to the deaths of thousands of orangutans. Smits said that the orangutans were surviving because his group had followed the advice of Herman Rijksen to return orangutans to the wild as soon as possible without the contact with human beings that would habituate them to human beings and human settlements. Later Rijksen would say that he didn't agree with the approach that Smits was taking of preparing orangutans for the wild and not releasing them immediately after a six-week quarantine period. Uce, Smits's first jungle romance, emerged from the jungle at Sungai Wain and Smits was overwhelmed emotionally in the reunion with the orangutan he had saved from the garbage heap. He wrote this account:

> She first just looked intensely at me from high above in the
> distance, as if she was not sure. My heart beat so fast while
> I was just standing still looking at her high up there. Then I
> called her name and immediately she started crying and came
> down close to the ground, while stretching out her arm to
> me. She had not forgotten me. I climbed and stumbled over
> all the dead wood of the drought-stricken trees on the forest
> floor towards her and we touched each other on the back of
> each other's heads. She just gazed intensely into my eyes and
> her lips and soft shrieks showed how happy she was. Then she
> pulled me over to the back, away from the technicians and
> almost out of sight. She gave me her three-month-old baby
> son. The little one was very afraid, never having seen a human,

but she assured him with short soft grunts. I felt completely overwhelmed at the trust she put in me after all those years. My first little orangutan was a mother. She had given birth all by herself in the forest where I had released her. It must be Charlie, an orangutan from Taiwan, that is the father of the baby. He had been passing through that area for the last few years and I saw him several times trying to catch and rape Uce.

Uce kept showing me her baby and . . . seized my arm. She came out of the tree and wandered off some twenty metres towards a Licuala repens palm. She bit off a young leaf and shared it with me. With a shock I realized what she was trying to tell me. May 23, 1991, the day I released Uce in the Sungai Wain forest, she did not immediately follow the others. She always was a bit of a loner. Instead, she looked warily around, frightened, with her arms crossed around her upper body. I went over to her, pulling her gently by the arm towards a Licuala repens palm near the release cage and, trying to reassure her, I shared a leaf with her. She remembered! It is not scientific, but I just know this was her way to say thank you.

"She showed me," he told me, continuing the story in Palangkaraya, "that what I did was the right thing. The fact that she realized she could put herself in my mind. It was a beautiful"—he elongated the word "beautiful" as though he were caressing it—"meeting we had in the forest and she loved me there and she gave me her baby, but she was telling me more. She was not just telling me that she still loved me. No, no, she really said, 'What you did was a good thing.' When she took me to that tree, that leaf, she told me 'what you did on May 23, 1991 was the right thing. Thank you for it.' To be told that—just the goodness."

One afternoon, I sat with Smits in one of his dark, sparse rooms in a government facility. The room had a cloistered feel. The darkness felt conspiratorial. The story he told me of his origins in that moment of trust was painful to hear at times. I felt grateful for his confidence in me, fleeting as it would be.

Willie Smits was born in 1957 in a small village near the city of Nijmegen in the Netherlands where his father was a farmer working small plots of land. His father and mother were from poor farm families that went back three hundred years. "Both my parents did not finish elementary school, for they had to work on the farm to help the families." His father had "a horrible life," he said, and his voice grew softer and softer the more he talked. "He was always exploited, by his own family, by the places where he worked. He never had owned a farm. He died not ever having had a house. He died so poor. But he was still always happy, always proud, always passionate." The animals on the farm were a comfort to Smits, a sensitive child. "I have always been very close to all kinds of animals, dogs and birds, but also the cows at the farm," he said. "When I was one and a half years old I ran away from home and they found me after five hours, sleeping on the belly of the meanest dog in the neighborhood, who let nobody come close to me. He was chained and I had gone in his dog house to play with him."

In 1980, Smits came to Indonesia as a tropical forest ecologist to work on material for a PhD thesis about the symbiotic relationship of trees and fungi. He was following the old route of the Dutch to the Far East, where the Netherlands had established colonies and found itself fighting in the late 1940s against the Indonesians who wanted their independence. In his first year in Indonesia, Smits met in the forest a woman named Syennie from the north of the island of Sulawesi, who was later chosen to be queen of the Toumbulu tribe on that part of the island. The history of her family extends back fifty generations. They married a few months later, to have three sons, and Smits would become a naturalized Indonesian.

Two years after his initial encounter with Uce, Smits started the Wanariset orangutan reintroduction program, which grew so fast, with so many orangutans, that at times it almost ran out of money. Now, in addition to the Wanariset facility north of Balikpapan, operated jointly with the Indonesian Ministry of Forests at Samboja, there is the Nyaru Menteng facility near Palangkaraya in Central Kalimantan, and the foundation Smits created is helping set up a sanctuary for releasing orangutans at the new Meratus National Park.

In 1991, Smits founded what is now called the Borneo Orangutan Survival Foundation. In the first decade of its existence, the organization released more than three hundred orangutans into places in the jungle empty and bereft of the creature. Between the orangutan stations at Samboja and Nyaru Menteng in Kalimantan, the organization cares for between five hundred and eight hundred ailing or orphaned orangutans at any time, besides other wildlife such as sun bears, birds, and snakes. The head native at Nyaru Menteng is a local Dayak named Odom who worked for Biruté Galdikas for twelve years at Tanjung Puting. The founder and manager of Nyaru Menteng, Lone Dröscher-Nielsen, also worked at Camp Leakey with Galdikas.

Smits is an aggressive conservationist. With a team made of foundation staff and forestry officers, he confiscates orangutans kept illegally as pets. The numbers of orangutans have been declining for years as human beings cut down the trees of the rain forest to grow rice to feed their families and to make palm oil and rubber tree plantations. Some of the palm oil is used for products in the West like chocolate, ice cream, toothpaste, and cosmetics. Orangutans are killed to protect the crops and plantations and to acquire infants to sell as illegal pets. The trade of illegal orangutans sold as pets is profitable by Indonesian standards. An infant orangutan sells for five U.S. dollars in Borneo, five hundred dollars in Jakarta, ten thousand dollars in Japan or Taiwan, and thirty thousand dollars in the United States. Tourists buy their skulls as souvenirs. Sometimes the mother is killed and the infant kept for the money to be made by selling it. At other times a male or female orangutan may be killed for raiding a plantation or a village garden.

When an animal is confiscated from a home by Smits and officials, the family is given medicine to fight the parasites they may have contracted from the orangutans. The fear of being infected by parasites is used to deter Indonesians from keeping orangutans as pets, but the threat is real in this part of the world, as Smits knows personally.

"With a cold shiver over my back," says Smits, "I remember my three days on chemotherapy in hospital abroad to kill the lungworms that were eating me from the inside, together with a number of other parasite species that almost killed me."

The memory of the parasites came to him at the scene of a confiscation of an orangutan at the home of an old man. The house was suspended on stilts over water, but, because of the drought, the ground below was dry and collecting the garbage and feces normally washed away. Smits found a baby orangutan on the verge of death from dehydration and parasites. He saw "from the silvery patches on his forehead and the dirty yellow stripes in his eyes" that the creature was full of parasites. "The moment an orangutan stops taking food, the parasites in its intestines get hungry and, after two days, start migrating out of the intestines into other vital organs like the heart and lungs. This can kill a baby in a matter of days."

Other orangutans are in bad shape—a fractured skull, an arm hacked off, *parang* slashes. Once the papers of the confiscation are signed, there is a procedure to give the animal medication, make a record of its condition, and take information to identify it in the future: "Blood samples are taken, parasite treatments applied, a chip is implanted under the skin, fingerprints are taken, hair and nail samples collected, weight, temperature, pulse and blood pressure are recorded, photographs are taken, feces samples collected." Then Smits tries to catch some sleep before the next day, in this instance, five hours' worth.

*   *   *

The confiscations are a perilous activity. There have been threats against Smits and the others, and attacks. One time a team trying to confiscate primates at the Barito market in Jakarta on the island of Java was attacked by a mob hurling stones. The police fired their guns into the air to deter the mob and then tried to flee in taxis, which refused to take them because the cars would be set on fire by the mob. The leader of the team, with a broken arm, broken ribs, and bleeding from his head, took cover in a police station. Only when the last of the mob had left after midnight was it safe to take him to the hospital.

And yet, whatever the tension, Smits recognizes that the people also bond emotionally with the orangutans in their homes and are sorry to see them gone. Smits described the scene at one confiscation: "The lady cries and hugs and kisses her baby for the last time, tears rolling over her cheeks all the time. It is easy to understand why people want these little orangutans so much. They just want love and give love so easy themselves."

People see orangutans as surrogate children, said Smits. "We've found orangutans that were shaven bald, wearing rings, sleeping with the owners in their bed. A couple of times we confiscated orangutans where we had to physically pull them from the breasts of women who were feeding them with their own milk."

The route to the confiscations is often through muddy roads and down jungle rivers. The mosquitoes are thick in the swamp forests and leave the skin a mass of bites. The people in some of the Dayak villages along the way still eat orangutan meat. Smits recalled one confiscation at the Dayak village of Miau Baru. He gave the name Pur to the infant orangutan found there. "A terrified little baby under a rattan chicken cage stood shrieking with hollow eyes on a wet floor—a floor wet with body fluids of the half-eaten corpse of his mother next to him. His mother was the third orangutan eaten by the family that year."

During the drought and forest fires that decimated Borneo in 1997 and

1998, travel was particularly hard. The rivers were covered with smoke from the fires. "We see the red glow of fires all along the river banks for hours and hours of travel through the night. On the way to Sebulu," wrote Smits, "we pass through a blackened brownish landscape. There is hardly any green left to see. The wind blows up dust, as do the passing cars with water tanks. Along the road near Sebulu we see the burned houses and fruit trees. In the trees we see the remains of orangutan nests. These timid animals looked for respite from the fires along the main road next to a villager's house. How desperate they must have been."

Along the road there were people with bags of turtles burned black by the fire. The people and the animals were hungry because of the destruction. The orangutans who had lost their forest to people were reduced to eating the bitter bark of acacia magnum trees planted in plantations. Smits reflected on the hellish pall cast by the destruction. The jungle is mute. Even the insects are gone. Smits and the others tried to catch an orphan orangutan to take it out of the plantation. "A green slurry of excrement rains on us standing ready with the net. It even still smells like the bitter acacia bark."

One time Smits found a jungle village threatened by smoke and flames. "For months they could not even see the edge of the water less than ten meters away and once they ran into the river when they felt the heat of the flames coming from behind." Then the villagers told Smits a preposterous story about a tiger coming out of the burning forest to attack a boat with a child in it. It didn't seem possible because there are no tigers in Borneo. The villagers took the skeptical Smits to show him the skin of an enormous clouded leopard.

At one jungle village upriver, Smits found an orangutan orphaned by the fire. "The fire came to the water's edge and the orangutan and its mother were completely surrounded and locked in between the fire and the river. The little orangutan dropped itself in the water when the flames touched it. It almost drowned when [a villager] managed to pull it out of the water into the boat with which he rushed to the scene. When he rescued the little one, the mother burned alive without making a sound. The body is still there at the place where she died in the flames."

Smits recalled the condition of an orangutan he came to confiscate. The creature was in a jackfruit tree at the back of a house, "blood and saliva dripping from his mouth with a broken jaw and a harpoon sticking through his right arm. His throat pouch had a deep hole just under his chin and a disgusting smell of rotten meat overwhelmed anyone coming near. Using an old saw and under a light anaesthetic, I managed to remove the hooks of the harpoon and pulled them out through the other side of the arm."

Another time, Smits wrote, "Some ten orangutans are spotted nearby an oil company office, after the nearby forest got burned and the people were giving the orangutans water and food to prevent them from going in the other direction of the village, where they might be killed by upset villagers if they would raid the few remaining fruit trees."

Smits and his organization are trying to save orangutans by teaching villagers to avoid burning and destroying forests by switching to agriculture combining rattan, sugar palms, and fruits and vegetables. He showed me a model farm built near Samboja to educate the people in better techniques for farming. In the next few years, the bare land that had been devastated by alang-alang grass, which secretes cyanide, became forest again. The trees like one I planted there created a microclimate that lowered the average temperature by between three and five degrees Celsius, increased cloud cover by twelve percent, and improved rainfall by twenty percent. By 2009, there were twelve hundred species of trees, one hundred thirty-seven species of birds, and nine species of primates. And an Indonesian community was being established that could support itself on the land.

Meanwhile, for the next generation, Smits's organization goes into the schools to educate children about their responsibility, which, in turn, leads to tips about illegal pets. One nine-year-old girl wrote to the project, "I think it is perhaps better that you come to my house and take the orangutan in the back to your station so he can later live free. But please don't tell my daddy." The police told the father and the girl was badly punished. When Smits's organization heard that, they returned to the village with journalists and gave the girl an award. Her father repented and identified the location of seven other baby orangutans, which were also rescued.

Smits wanted to show me the success of his Schmutzer Primate Centre at the Jakarta Zoo, which meant flying southwest from the island of Borneo to the island of Java. Jakarta is where the Prussian lady of the orangutans, Ulrike Freifrau von Mengden, lives. At the center, Smits stopped to spend some time with the chimpanzees, and I watched one of them groom Smits like another chimpanzee, which shows the respect of the creature toward him. There were gorillas there, too, and Smits described being in a cage with a gorilla one time. Smits said that the gorilla had "a giant face" and "warm breath, him smelling like plants and then he pulled me on the arm. I must have been thrown eight meters through the straw there. Then he quietly sat away and started chewing on some fruit and paid no more attention to me."

The primate section has an ingenious design that Smits created to give creatures like orangutans freedom and privacy in a habitat with a wide variety of real trees and plants. There are waterfalls, water with turtles and fish, artificial rock formations, and small animals like porcupines and deer mice. A thick, dark glass allows human beings to see the orangutans, but the orangutans can't see them. "I never wanted to be involved with a zoo," he told me, "but, this is not a zoo. I only keep the victims here, like a sanctuary." He takes primates for the zoo that have been confiscated as illegal pets. The healthy ones go through quarantine and rehabilitation at the sites of the Borneo Orangutan Survival Foundation, to be released again into the forest. The sick, the badly injured, the blind, stay at the zoo to have "a wonderful life," he said. They live "without being bothered by people, because there's no way anybody can interact with them unless they want to interact with the people. And this is what I want a zoo to be, a place to help animals survive."

Another side of Smits emerged in the forest of Meratus in Kalimantan, down the dusty road where the army officers were collecting bribes from illegal loggers. "Here it is the army and the police that are cutting the trees," Smits said. He talked about protecting the forest in Meratus by giving local people jobs guiding tourists. By changing the economy, there would be an incentive to save the forest, and all the attention from tourists would also make it harder to do what is illegal. In Meratus, Smits showed me one of the release sites for orangutans, on the other side of the Bongan River, crossed by a small open cable car. This was the same river the orangutan Joshua had found his own way across to eat fruit from the trees on the other side. I noticed that Smits was more relaxed among the trees. He is a man of the forest. Walking through a jungle with him is like taking a lesson in a biology class. His knowledge is boundless. He showed me two plants growing side by side that looked similar, although he could see the difference. One was medicine for malaria and the other was poisonous.

"One seed is enough to kill a cow," he said.

"It's not poisonous to touch?" I said, too late. I'd already touched it.

"It has to be eaten," he said. "Look at this. This is a beautiful fern, a species I have never seen before in twenty-five years. That is the wonderful thing here. Every time I go into the forest, I will see something new."

He made my son and I stuff a plant under our shirts. He said it would mix with our sweat to produce a chemical to keep the mosquitoes away for the day. Then Smits found an orchid with tiny white flowers and I found a leech on me. "Is that a leech?" I said, even though I knew what it was. That was all the invitation Smits needed to deliver a long-winded lesson on the science of leeches, while our group picked the spindly creatures off their legs. The leeches that Smits said had been exterminated completely from the area by a dry spell in the burned forests were stuck to my legs like black rubbery spit. It was a miracle of life and rebirth.

"Yeah, give them a bit of blood," Smits said. "Let's help the population."

"I got one, too," said my son, Pearce. Before long Pearce had a small leech dangling on a stick like a trophy. Give a boy a pet leech and he can be happy for hours.

"They do have some parasites, though," Smits said. The word "parasites" didn't sound good.

At one of the old release sites for orangutans, Smits explained that the orangutans, after spending time at a quarantine station to cure ailments and help them learn how to socialize, are brought into the jungle. They are kept in cages a few days and released slowly to give them time to adjust to a strange forest they don't know. Sometimes, if there is trouble, said Smits, the orangutans return to the release site, or "halfway house," or to the camp, for help, like the time somebody hacked with a machete the big, bold orangutan named Bento, the one who made friends with the Canadian researcher Anne Russon. Bento had been cut badly. "He came back to the camp," said Smits, "and showed his wound and asked to be taken to the doctor. We did not need to tranquilize this giant." In the jungle Smits said that Bento was able to rekindle a romance that started at the quarantine station, where he and a female orangutan named Isabelle gazed at each other across the space between their cages. It was a jailhouse romance. They had "fallen in love," said Smits. Four years later, when Isabelle was taken to a release site, Bento came out of the trees to greet her and take her back into the forest with him. A deep love never dies.

Smits takes a strong delight in the forest and in orangutans. One time, riding in a car in Jakarta, he pulled out an artifact to show me that had special meaning for him, a gift an orangutan had made for him. It was a disk about the size of a silver dollar, meticulously wrapped in strands.

An orangutan he had met only once two years earlier had bitten pieces of an orange peel to make it into a disk, unraveled a burlap bag to get the string, and then wound the string all around the disk. Orangutans are known to be skillful in untying knots. One orangutan, Junior, a forty-four-year-old male at the St. Louis Zoo and a father of two, likes to tie knots and creates "long knotted strips that look like elaborate braiding." After the orangutan created the disk for Smits, the orangutan gave it to him and closed the man's fingers around it. It seemed that the orangutan had found a way to communicate symbolically through a gesture, like Uce had done by giving Smits the leaf of the Licuala repens palm. I discussed the incident later with a scientist who was a friend of Smits's and he was skeptical of the meaning Smits saw in it. I persisted, though, and said, "That doesn't seem to represent anything in the natural world or to be part of an orangutan's experience. It looks purely symbolic. I would say it is a sign of love or affection." That's what happens when you spend too much time with Smits. You start to sound like him.

I met Willie Smits the first time in Jakarta in 2001. I would not say that it was a mild experience. It never is with Willie. That is just not his world. He raged, he fumed, he pleaded, he prodded, all with such intensity that it seemed as though he would ravage anything in his path. He over-whelmed you if you got too close, like a big wind blowing out your little flame. I was in an untrusting mood at that time because another scientist had broken promises to me that threatened to end my book project and I wasn't sure who this Smits was, maybe more of the same madness. Who knew? Were all these scientists insane? I left Jakarta without accomplishing much except meeting Smits, and then a year or two later a person who knew him in a peripheral way started a nasty e-mail campaign against me. That once again threatened to damage the book project. I felt battered. I may not have been in a trusting mood. But I tried to keep in touch with Smits. There were some difficult exchanges.

Then, three years later, he relented and it was sweet, like the aftermath of a storm. He let me spend time traveling with him and I appreciated that, although there were some prickly moments again. One time he stormed away from me in the jungle because he thought I was not respecting the Dayak belief in the spirits of the trees. He told me a few years later that he doesn't believe in the spirits any more than I do—although he says now that he wishes he did, which is an interesting contradiction—but he thought at the time that I should show a little more respect to the beliefs of the Dayaks. I had a different sense of what was happening. I thought that he wanted me to embrace the idea of spirits in the trees, but maybe something was "lost in translation" between two people living in different worlds. After all, this is a man who spent four days participating in the grueling Dayak blood ceremony of Manyanggar just to show respect to the old traditions. He was bitten by ants, watched ghosts appear and take over the bodies of some people, was covered in the blood of a dying pig, and then buried the head of a butchered cow, all to bless an island to become a new release site for orangutans. It was an epic effort on the part of Smits to respect the traditions and save a few orangutans that way. And yet, as Smits knows well, the slaughter of orangutans as a species continues quietly on a massive scale with no ceremony to mark it.

I continued to learn about this man and came to respect him. I heard that in 2004 at forty-seven years of age he had achieved prodigious things. He was a master of languages, of different sciences, of enormous feats of memory. He was knighted in the Netherlands. He became a senior adviser to the Ministry of Forests in Indonesia. He consumed gigantic amounts of information and his brain worked at a feverish pitch. Smits told me that he'd read "so many thousands and thousands of books on all kinds of subjects, that I can always make connections, that I can link things. If I am given a problem, I can formulate fifty hypotheses within seconds. It's just there, and that linking is something not many people can do." He said that his mind seized on a solution to a problem instantaneously. From anyone else, all this might be hard to believe, but Smits lives in a larger world, of emotional connections, of spiritual values, and he forces you to think that way, too.

We talked about his life and his involvement with orangutans in his room at the Wanariset orangutan station near Balikpapan. In his life this room is as close as he comes to permanence, outside of the home he shares with his wife in Tomohon, on the island of Sulawesi. "I normally sleep in the zoo close to the orangutans in Jakarta," he said. But that room in the zoo in Jakarta holds little trace of his transitory existence. I'd seen it when I slept there. His room at Wanariset consists of a chamber with a bed, a desk, a small coffee table and chairs, and a wardrobe cabinet. There is the gloom of thick curtains in the room to preserve the coolness inside. He was very trusting with me at that moment. I wasn't sure why after the tension between us. At that moment I asked him simple questions about orangutans that awakened a sense of pain and loneliness and emotional vulnerability in him. I persisted because I wanted to know what kind of human being it takes to unlock the intimate life of an orangutan. And here was the person who had done that. Smits talked about how disturbed he was by the destructiveness of human beings toward orangutans and life on the planet. It was as though he took it personally.

"If other people could see, could understand, what I know, in my mind, in my heart, about the orangutans, they should feel ashamed. If you look at the intelligence, if you see their culture, mathematics, accept that they have Grandma, that they have this phenomenal learning and planning skill, the capability to put themselves in the minds of others even across the species boundary, maybe people will realize what they are doing and be ashamed."

I asked about Lone Dröscher-Nielsen, the project manager of the orangutan station at Nyaru Menteng. The bond between Smits and Dröscher-Nielsen was apparent, almost like a shared state of mind.

"She has the same source of energy as I do," he said. "She's a fighter, just like me." She had also gone through the four days of the grueling Dayak blood ceremony of Manyanggar with Smits.

"She has good empathy with the orangutans," I said.

"Oh, yes. She is sacrificing everything. If she doesn't sleep, it doesn't matter, because she gives it all. If there is a sick orangutan, you won't be able to keep her away."

"Why do the small orangutans accept her so easily?"

"She has it. She has it in her eyes. The deepest, sincerest love for those babies. Absolutely. It's love. She also, like me, must feel a little bit like an outsider. Alone." A slight huskiness crept into his voice.

I remembered him rubbing his temples in pain as we drove through the streets of Jakarta. He was cursing then and didn't want to stop to eat or to sleep. Wasn't that a hard way to live? I asked.

"Yeah," he said softly. "It sure is. I've got death threats. I don't sleep at night. I just keep traveling, having to face all the injustice. It is not an easy thing if you are an idealist."

That idealist in Smits believes that there is goodness in orangutans. Like Frans de Waal and others, Smits thinks there is a natural morality and sense of fairness in them and the other apes. It is a revolutionary idea. The world is a different place if morality is a natural thing and we share it with the other apes. We have less to excuse our own immorality. Smits told me a story about two orangutans named Buddha and Romanis.

"These two were such good buddies," he said, "and they always shared a nest when they went into the forest. They were out quite a while after their release in the Sungai Wain forest and had adapted wonderfully, but then one day, Zainal Arafin, one of my technicians, made a note in his book, 'I've seen Romanis all by himself on a branch and he was whining. He was only a hundred meters away from the release cage. We had provided food, but he didn't want to come.' The next day Zainal walked by and smelled a horrible smell underneath the tree where Romanis had sat and there was the body of Buddha. He had been ripped open by a wild boar. That's how he died. He had broken a shoulder. He had some wounds. And, with one arm, he had pulled himself all the way to the path. And his friend in the tree did not go to the food. He did not leave his dying friend alone. He was actually asking Zainal, 'Please help my friend. He needs help.' He was doing anything he could for another orangutan. He did not leave him alone in a weak moment."

"Do you think that orangutans have a sense of right and wrong?" I asked.

"Yes," he said. "I'll give you an example, one that shows both altruism and a sense of what's right and wrong." He said that a woman named Suci, the vice chairwoman of his foundation, had been following a large adult male for six months to study him. "One day two wood thieves tried to rape Suci in the forest, and this big orangutan who had nothing to do with Suci decided he had to come down and chase those bastards away. Why would he care for a human being? Why would he understand that she was being forced into sex against her will? He might have the same urge. Still, he thought, it's not right. He helped her."

I mentioned accounts of male orangutans forcing themselves sexually on female orangutans and the signs of distress in the female, that she doesn't like it and doesn't want it.

"You know how I witnessed the rape of Uce," he said.

"Yes," I said, startled, sensing something that was coming. "In the female orangutan's mind this is not right. This is unjust," I said.

"Uce was very angry with me when I met her next time. She sat back and she slapped me. She turned around as if saying, 'I don't want to see you. You could have helped me the last time when I was being raped.' She told me that. And gradually made up with me again."

"Is that true that you could have helped her and didn't?" I said.

"Yes," he said softly, describing the dilemma he had at that time. "But I felt I could no longer be part of her world if I had wanted to give her freedom."

"Even if it means that she suffers for it?"

"Yes," he said. He seemed upset.

I'd learned to tolerate his rages, to wait until they finished, to understand what was deeper, the unusual intelligence, the affection, the sincerity, the morality, the sensitivity, the vulnerability, the loneliness, the pain. I liked this man. The idea of him grew the more I thought about him. Here was a man who set himself impossible tasks in a world that spun in a different direction. It seemed so impossible at times that anyone would struggle against the odds to save orangutans. I remembered the vehemence of Dian Fossey trying to save gorillas, and she was murdered in the end. Fossey also seemed to be fighting the world. Some people thought she was going mad. That's a thought. Do people go mad within the jungle like in Conrad's novel *Heart of Darkness*? I had a number of conversations with orangutan scientists who would point to one of their own and say that person was mad, and they didn't mean it in a joking way. It seemed like the moment to ask Smits about that, that I could no longer avoid the question, but I wasn't sure if he would see it as an attack. I could never predict how he would react. Do people go mad here? I asked.

"I think there's some truth to it," he said. "Yes. There's a lot of people who start living in their own world. And many of them have been here too long, in this place too long."

"Is that a risk in coming here and immersing yourself and staying too long? That you can go mad, that you can lose your moral bearing?"

"I see it happen with quite a few people. Yes."

"What if somebody said you're mad?"

"They're probably right."

That surprised me. I had to ask, "Why aren't they wrong?"

"Because I'm not like other people."

"Does just not being like other people make you mad?"

"A lot of people would think so."

"It doesn't matter what they think," I said, surprising myself with my own vehemence. "What matters is what the truth is. What if the life they're leading is an illusion? How sane is it to destroy your planet?"

That thought turned him. "Indeed," he said. "So, for me, they're mad, what they are doing. Some people see me as mad." He was very soft spoken now. Milder, different.

"So, truly, although some people think you are mad, you know you are not mad," I said.

"I am not mad," he said.

CHAPTER 10

Our Lady of the Forests

IT WAS HOT. The day was hot. The air was hot. I was hot. From the end of the long ironwood dock at Camp Leakey I could see a sign where the words had faded in the sun and the rain. I thought that I might fade, too, if I stood here long enough in the sun. It takes some effort to endure. The woman standing beside me on the dock, Biruté Galdikas, knew that. It felt like I'd drifted mentally through the years as I made the slow trip up the river to Camp Leakey in the klotok to see her. I knew her story by heart now. Maybe I could even quote her back bits she had forgotten. The same river, the Sekonyer, meant an even slower, contemplative half-day trip for her in the 1970s from her camp in the jungle to the closest sea town of Kumai. I'd seen the same endless succession of trees that she had along the river with the same distraction of a few quick bright birds. My mind may even have drifted the same way hers did. But something had happened here to this woman that had not happened to others. Galdikas had penetrated the inner life of orangutans. Not everyone could do that. Not everyone would want to do that. You could accumulate all the information in the world about orangutans and really know very little about how they think and feel.

The difference is sensibility. And that was what I ultimately sought in Galdikas, that sensibility in her, in the only place in the world that made sense to know it, here in the jungle where the exotic happened to her every day. For her, this was a place of birth and death, of joy and sorrow, of romance and betrayal, everything that could possibly be packed into the small space of a few trees in a tropical rain forest in a faraway land. She had lived it all here. I doubt if anybody has sacrificed more for a longer period of time for the sake of a few scraggly apes in an obscure patch of jungle. But I also hoped that she had not faded in the sun and the rain like the sign. We want people to be as they are in the beginning. We want someone to persevere and endure and stay pure.

A klotok had brought me to Camp Leakey once again, and now the boat sat moored and motionless. It was as though the klotok had always been rooted in that spot on a river in the jungle like some kind of floating water plant. I knew that Galdikas had once paddled across the water here to feed orangutans on the far shore. Now it was mainly occupied by the macaque rabble, by the monkey parents and monkey children that I'd seen in the morning. From the dock I could see that a gray boat without an engine had been pulled up on the other side. The last time I'd been here three years earlier the boat had had an engine and a purpose. Now it seemed to exist separately from everything else. A dugout canoe was tied to poles in the center of the river to protect it from the orangutans. In the early days, Galdikas had paddled a dugout like that, once with her husband lying feverishly in the bottom with malaria, at other times with her young son Binti and orangutans.

To the side of the dock were the remains of a tower that was still standing when I was here before. The boards of the dock had had three more years to grow worn, although they still sounded the same under the pad of feet. Like a keyboard on a piano, each board gave a different modulation of weather and warp. "I half suspect the orangutans can tell who is walking across them by the sound," I said to Galdikas, grasping for something to interest her, to bring her into the moment with me. Sometimes you could feel her mind probing you. Sometimes you could feel her mind detached. This time it felt that she was not really there with me on that dock. I wondered why. She answered my question in a perfunctory way whether orangutans know a person by the sound they make on the dock. "They can probably tell a Westerner, as opposed to an Indonesian," she said. "We walk more aggressively." The dock was aging. "Even though it's ironwood," she said, "the ironwood is of uneven quality, so the boards crack."

This is where Galdikas entered the jungle when she was twenty-five. The night of her arrival in 1971 a male orangutan made that distinctive long guttural cry in the dark to remind the other males and the forest that this was his kingdom. My son and I heard the same calls, too, as we slid in and out of sleep on the klotok. Human beings will probably never understand all the individual inflections that a male orangutan puts into his call, but we understand the basics. At a distance he wields power; in his absence he asserts his sex; in his solitude he stays connected. Galdikas has described the long call of the orangutan as "a series of low grumbles that peak into loud bellowing, then subside into more grumbles and sighs."

It was into this jungle that Galdikas came when she was young, a jungle different from what she had imagined and yet a place that fit her spirit perfectly. The forest was the right place for a woman like this who knew the pagan mysticism of forests as a child and who loved to go into the dark trees by herself when she was young and who would eventually marry a forest Dayak in Borneo. She made a commitment to the jungle and out of that she would find fulfillment through the forest and through its creature, the orangutan. Like that moment with Akmad that made it all worthwhile. The orangutan had let Galdikas pull a fern out of the hair of her child, and Galdikas knew that the orangutan had accepted her as a fellow creature. That gave meaning to the life of Galdikas.

Galdikas had cared for Akmad. The orangutan had been confiscated as an illegal pet and then released into the jungle again when it was time. There was such a bond between them that the orangutan returned out of the jungle to be with Galdikas. It was a moment when it no longer mattered if the ape and the woman belonged to different species. "She came straight over to me, sat down, and leaned into me as she ate," Galdikas remembered. "She stayed there, leaning slightly against my side, for more than fifteen minutes. When she finished eating, her dark brown eyes flickered over my face, as if I held only momentary interest for her." Galdikas understood what had happened in the mind of the orangutan. It is a creature that communicates by sparse, subtle, discriminating gestures. It might seem as though little happened. The orangutan sat, leaned, ate, glanced, and was gone. But it meant that the orangutan had accepted Galdikas again as another living creature and had given her a message. It was why she said one time, "I was born to study orangutans." Galdikas knew where she belonged, but belonging to this place would have a price.

In the early days she was isolated with her husband Rod Brindamour and the orangutans in the primitive conditions of the camp, in a world where only orangutans and the forest mattered. And that's what she wanted. Barbara Harrisson had told me that she was "aghast" by the conditions of the camp when she visited it in the early days, but then Galdikas was "crazy" to study orangutans, said Harrisson, and her husband came with her to the jungle out of love. "They were in love," Harrisson said, laughing in delight. "That is quite natural. It was a kind of huge adventure."

Galdikas described herself falling in love with Brindamour to me as the sort of intense and instantaneous passion that is typical of her. She is quiet on the surface, intense underneath. She saw Brindamour as a rebel on a motorcycle who would uproot himself and travel halfway around the world with her. In the jungle, he grew into that image by letting his beard and his hair grow long. "Sexuality is the edge of defining what a species is," Galdikas told me another time, when we were discussing orangutans, but the idea applies to us, too. "Who you want to mate with defines you." Galdikas chose the rebel who would come to the jungle with her. "It all seemed risky and dangerous," she told me.

"We had to walk through the mud in waste-deep water because sometimes the water gets as high as this bridge. I'd have to walk on slippery logs." Galdikas said that the two-hundred-meter dock was built in 1975 over the mud and the rise and fall of the river from the wet to the dry season, a symbol of early support from Indonesians. That support was important to her. Galdikas's three children by two husbands played on the boards. The orangutans had clustered on the dock for food, for sex, for the view, for the simple pleasure of being ornery. It was here that her son Binti fought a young macaque and won with a sense of triumph. "He was very happy," she said. It was here that a large and quarrelsome stork chased officials and lay in wait for the boys coming to barter fish in exchange for sugar and rice. The boys brought a sacrificial fish to throw to the stork and distract him. When this dock was built, it was a relief for Brindamour. He told me that he no longer had to struggle through the mud with huge sacks of rice or the engine of the boat.

"Can you see your past here?" I asked Galdikas, standing on the dock. Every rock and tree must have a memory for her.

"I've been up and down it many times," she said. "I used to spend a lot of time here." It sounded strangely unemotional, noncommittal, as though she were reading from a script. She said that what she originally liked about life at Camp Leakey was "the power" of a small, intimate circle of orangutans and people. "Life was so familiar and at the same time so intense," she wrote in her book about these years. A few of the orangutans from those days are still at Camp Leakey—Princess, Siswi, Unyuk—older, making the negotiation of the dock difficult, like the tension on the border zone between two countries.

"What's the etiquette if you meet an orangutan on the bridge?" I asked her, hoping to find an idea that would inspire her.

"Well," she said, "it depends on the orangutan. It's mainly different by size, and males tend to be much, much bigger and much more aggressive than females. So, the etiquette, basically, is like with human beings. You walk past each other respectfully without touching each other. Now, if it's a male, and he's in the middle, well, then, you wait until he passes. You really don't want to get into an antagonistic encounter with him. I have a lot of pleasant memories here," she said, pausing for a moment and then resuming, "of sitting at the end of the bridge." She spoke in the kind of soft forest murmur she has and seemed detached.

In those days the peace in camp was preserved by feeding the wild-born ex-captives on the other side of the river. The orangutans hadn't learned yet how to use a log like a bridge to cross the water. That came as a revolutionary breakthrough on their part, like Hannibal crossing the Alps into Italy. "Yeah, they learned to use logs and they learned to use boats, to steal our boats. We'd go by a boat over there and while we were there, an orangutan would take the boat and go across, even in feeding. In the seventies, Sugito would do it. He was our first infant. My first infant." That was a provocative reference by itself and even more so if you knew her story. It was Sugito who was the catalyst of one of the biggest betrayals in her life. Sugito was an orangutan who Galdikas loved like a mother despite a mean and vicious streak in him that made Galdikas's husband a target. Brindamour released the vandal of the camp into the jungle while his wife was absent. Galdikas felt betrayed, but didn't see this incident at the time as a sign of the rift developing between her and her husband. For a woman who could understand the secrets of another species, she could be blind to the people close to her. Her mind was elsewhere.

"He would have canoed around with you," I said of Sugito. "He would have seen you—"

"Yes. Absolutely. He would have seen me canoeing. He was in the canoe with me. In the first year or two we did a lot of canoeing."

From the long ironwood dock the indecipherable words on the faded sign beckoned again. I knew that my week in Camp Leakey with Galdikas was coming to an end, and that awareness brought a finality to my questions. Maybe I would never speak to her again like this. I had resisted the way her presence could absorb people until they either succumbed or rebelled. I had my own life. What did the faded sign say? I asked.

"That sign," Galdikas said, ignoring the question, "shows you the effects of deterioration of"—pausing as she often does when she thinks about what she wants to say—"wood and paint."

"What do the words say?" I persisted.

"'No swimming. Crocodiles.' I think we put up the sign two years ago and look at it now."

A faded sign in a foreign language may not be the best way to warn people about crocodiles. I knew the stories and wouldn't let my son swim in that water. I started to say to her, "About two years ago there was a British tourist—"

"Yes, an English tourist who was swimming and you can't see what's underneath, the water is so black, and—"

"Like madness," I said, which we'd been discussing a moment ago, "which is hard to see."

"Is madness black?" she asked.

"I don't know. Can you see what is underneath in madness?"

"My guess is that you probably can't to some degree," she said. "So what happened was, one of the assistants was in the water and he felt something brush by his leg and he yelled 'crocodile.'"

The native staff swam quickly to the dock, but not the tourist. "There was a scream and he was pulled under and that was it. They found his body, I think, the same day. The assistants were quite brave. They hit the crocodile with their paddles and he—or she—let go of the body."

"Wasn't a policeman killed, too, by a crocodile?"

"I think two years before," she said. "More towards the mouth of the river." Galdikas heard later what happened. It was the sort of thing she would remember. "He had a dreamy look in his face as he was pulled under and there was no scream."

After walking along the dock and through the years, we wandered into Camp Leakey, past the worn green buildings and the slow vigilant orangutans and the hungry wild pigs, across the bald sandy stretches where her three children from two marriages played, into the jungle by trails that felt packed as solid as cement now. A short distance down the main path, it splits into two directions, into the two past lives of Galdikas. The left fork goes to a house built in the Indonesian style on stilts where Galdikas lived with Brindamour and Binti.

"Can you still see Binti running around here?" I asked.

"It was too long ago and so much else has happened in his life," she said, but it shook loose another memory for her. "Binti was energetic in the womb. There was a lot of movement. A lot of kicking, kicking in the stomach while I was sitting during a follow"—of watching orangutans. "It really reminds you how mortal you are and how you're part of nature. You can't control it. You really are a part of nature. When you're pregnant, things happen without your control."

For the delivery, Galdikas went to a hospital in Jakarta. "It hurt. It hurt like anything," she said. She refused to give the infant to a nurse, afraid he would be mixed and lost in the swarm of other babies. From the hospital, she spent the next month in a friend's house in Jakarta. The child screamed through the nights in the strange city. The sound of the traffic in the streets was fierce, the fumes as suffocating as a forest fire. When he was brought to the camp in the jungle, he fell asleep in an instant and slept through the night. He had found peace.

At Camp Leakey, the right fork in the path goes to the mess hall, the staff and volunteer quarters, and the house where Galdikas lived with her second husband Bohop and their children Fred and Jane. This is the cabin where she stays now when she comes to camp. At both houses she talked to me about the changes in the ways the trees have grown or disappeared, the way that sun and shade have shifted, which is the sort of thing she notices. Paths have appeared that look as though they have existed since the beginning of time. We took the path to the mess hall, past a sign that said "Don't litter" in Indonesian and what looked like a lone marker for an orangutan grave. It was carved by the Dayak Bohop. Is an orangutan buried there? "No," she said. "That was my husband's idea of a joke. My husband noticed that the white people like funerary statues."

Galdikas stopped to talk to someone in Indonesian and I could see a large dark form approaching out of the shadow of the trees. It was the huge male Kusasi. Time to stay cool and look unaffected. Galdikas diplomatically allowed Kusasi to pass and then we walked farther. "And then we have a little graveyard," she said. It was a graveyard for orang-utans, sought by forestry officials in one of her battles with her enemies in the bureaucracy. It seems that human beings have a need to fight even over such things as orangutans, even when they are dead. "This was established in the eighties," she said. "These are mainly infants who died. There was a nursery here. And they came to my husband's house and tried to find the graves of orangutans—because we also had graves there of infants who had died." Some people whisper about a graveyard of orangutans downriver in the village of Pasir Pajang kept secret by her Dayaks out of their traditional sense of decorum.

"A couple of these have heads carved in them," I said. I liked the spirit of this graveyard, where things poked at different angles, instead of standing stiff and regimented through all of eternity.

"That's what the traditional Dayaks do," she said. "The assistants carved them."

"How many orangutans are buried there?"

"Maybe six or seven."

"Why do you think it's important to have a graveyard for them?"

"Oh, just to remember. Just to remind ourselves of who they were. And what the toll is"—I could see tears were starting to gather in her eyes—"It's not just these. It's all of them. These are representative, probably, of hundreds of thousands. It's a memorial to them all. Thinking of all the infants who died through no fault of their own, it's too hard for me. Those infants didn't deserve to die."

Later that night, I talked to Galdikas in the cabin she has occupied for decades in the forest of Tanjung Puting. I'd been there during the day when an orangutan pressed his face against the window to stare inside at us. The rubbery dark face of the orangutan seemed even more massive than it was, as if the whole forest were staring at us inside. I felt as though I were in a cage with the wild animals outside. It was quieter at night and the orangutans had gone to sleep in their nests high in the trees closer to the stars. If you listen carefully, you can sometimes hear an orangutan snore, even the little ones. I listened to the crickets outside and heard the occasional strange hoot or thrum. I wondered what it would be like walking through that darkness alone to return to my klotok in the river. My son Pearce would be asleep on the boat now. Neither the heat nor the cool of the jungle night bothered him. He slept like an orangutan would sleep. Deep. Untroubled.

My mind returned to the cabin where I was. Inside, it was bare, unpainted, rough, like the inside of a wooden crate. There was a box of plump, yellowish mangoes on the floor to feed the orangutans. I'd heard the orangutans use their teeth to rip open the mangoes with a sharp tearing sound. Galdikas showed me the cabinet where a mirror on the door had been smashed by Kusasi. It had never been replaced. She didn't need mirrors, she said. Interesting, I thought. No mirrors. She showed me the door to the outside that had been repaired after Kusasi burst through it, leaving his outline etched in it like a cartoon figure. His shape is still visible in the repairs. Kusasi had certainly left his imprint on things. So had Galdikas.

On the wall in the cabin hung the lute of her second husband, Bohop. He had lived in this cabin in the forest with her and their two children, Fred and Jane. It seemed to make sense that someone like Galdikas who loved the forest so much would be attracted to a forest Dayak like Bohop. They share a sensibility that is important for her. I remember Lone Dröscher-Nielsen had told me that she was attracted to the Dayak Odom, the nephew of Bohop, for the same reason. The Danish woman had grown disenchanted with the Dayak when he lost the part of him that she said "lived with the spirits and lived with the traditions." I talked to Bohop once through a translator and heard how he learned the wisdom of the forest as a boy. He told me that his mother wouldn't let him put poison on his blowgun darts until he proved himself a man at fourteen. His father had died when he was seven.

Galdikas had been too much on my mind over the years. I had talked to people who loved her and people who hated her. I had to struggle against the desire of different people to convert me to their particular image of Galdikas and suffered the storm when I wouldn't. Something in her seemed to inspire that in others. I knew that some people theorized that there was a radical change in Galdikas in the 1990s and yet, in conversations and in her writings from the 1970s, her thought is consistent from the beginning. Whatever an apologetic Galdikas says about her "unpredictability," her lapses in keeping to a schedule, to other people's time, she talks of a single-minded, snail-like consistency of direction and purpose in her life.

Galdikas was following her own path even before she wrote the cover stories for *National Geographic* magazine that established her image, before she even went to Borneo in 1971. She told me that she prepared herself for the lengthy study of the elusive and little-studied orangutan in Borneo by spending six months with the orangutans at the Los Angeles Zoo. It was at that time that she established a link with the red apes and learned that a relationship was possible across the gulf between the species. She shared coffee and sandwiches with the orangutans. She didn't force a relationship on them. It was their desire to be with her that allowed her to glimpse into their inner lives. This was radical thinking in the 1970s in the way it violated basic premises of the Western intellectual tradition about objectivity and detachment and relationships with other species.

The same attitudes would persist in her when she went to Borneo in 1971. But these attitudes weren't as visible then, when Galdikas was an obscure scientist in the jungle studying an obscure ape. The first article that Galdikas wrote as the cover story for *National Geographic* in 1975 established her as an icon in the historical sequence of Goodall, Fossey, and Galdikas. Galdikas was the image of the surrogate mother and rehabilitator of captive orangutans. It was her image from the beginning and didn't change over the years as the world changed around her. Galdikas was pictured on the cover of the magazine walking hand in hand with the orangutan Akmad and carrying Sobiarso on her hip like a child. By that time she had amassed an unthinkable five thousand hours of observations of orangutans in the jungle. She intended to be a mother to orangutans and not to have children of her own, although her pregnancy in the jungle in 1976 came not "totally" as an accident, she told me. She thought at first that she was dying from "some obscure disease."

"I remember the heat when I was pregnant, the feeling it was interminable. It was a funny year. Dry when it shouldn't have been dry. It was the first time I saw orangutans eating caterpillars. The caterpillars were infesting the trees, thousands of them, reddish black with yellow stripes. The pupaes were like raw eggs and were roasted by locals." She ate them and they tasted like egg and shrimp.

By the time that she was pregnant with her son Binti, she believed that being a mother of small orangutans like Sugito had prepared her to be the mother of a human child. "I said, if I love Sugito so much now, how much more am I going to love my child."

At the camp in the jungle that she and her husband Rod Brindamour established, the pair lived with orangutans and let them play havoc with their lives. Nothing was safe from the apes. No inconvenience to the human beings mattered. The orangutans ate the candles and drank the shampoo. Galdikas held infants through the day drenched in their urine. She never worried about the illnesses she suffered, the poor food, the humiliating conditions, the isolation of years in the tropical forest. She and Brindamour were young then, she said. "When you're young, you believe you're invulnerable."

In that first article the young Galdikas observed, "Humans who were bitten or wounded had invariably provoked the apes," a remarkable statement that was the beginning of her radical position in defense of orangutans that would disturb others and lead to rifts, defections, and controversy over the years. Some would come to see the behavior of orangutans as the action of "thugs" that Galdikas let loose in the jungle to injure people and then blame the victims. It seemed to some that she cared more for the welfare of apes than her own species.

In one notorious instance an orangutan named Gundul raped the longtime native cook Bariah at the camp. Gundul was one of the more peaceful, milder orangutans, confiscated from a gentlemanly military officer in Jakarta, and not a threat like a full-grown Sugito would be, Brindamour told me. The orangutan had been in the care of a man with "a genuine affection for him" and was not abused like some orangutans are in captivity. The day of the rape, Galdikas told me that she fought the creature while it was attacking Bariah. She hit the orangutan on the back with the flat of the blade of a paddle, which had no effect, then rammed her fist down the throat of the creature with its large canine teeth, which cut her and left her bleeding. "I was fighting Gundul with all my might and I was having absolutely no effect on him." Brindamour told me that Galdikas was upset by the incident and shocked by the behavior of an orangutan she thought she knew and trusted. "She didn't know Gundul as well as she should," Brindamour said. "It showed that she couldn't influence him. After that, Gundul was feared more than he was before."

Life at Camp Leakey was an ordeal from the beginning, and there was violence at times, but Galdikas was doing what she wanted to do and nothing else mattered. For the next eight years, she and her husband Brindamour ignored their own comfort and well-being to study orangutans in the harsh conditions of the jungle. They isolated themselves, survived on basic rations, endured leeches, disease, and the hostility of loggers trying to cut down trees in the park. It was their choice, and the solitary life with a solitary animal suited them. From a distance it was easy to romanticize what was happening after reading an article in *National Geographic* or watching a documentary on television.

Galdikas had stamina and ignored discomfort. John MacKinnon told me that he remembers the young Galdikas had "enormous determination" and was "fairly aggressive," especially for someone studying orangutans and not the more volatile chimpanzees. "Women get into a level of intensity that men rarely do," he said. "I think that's what Leakey recognized." Galdikas, said MacKinnon, is "still very serious— and more human. In 1974, she was stunning, but she didn't smile. She has humanized a lot. She is more fun to talk to now. It was very difficult to tell her anything then."

The first refugee orangutan brought to the week-old camp in 1971 was Sugito, rescued from the illegal pet trade. He was being held in a crate downriver in the seafaring town of Kumai. Galdikas told me that she remembered her first sight of him as an "awkward fledgling with downy hair, almost birdlike. He was slightly bald on the top of his head and had a big belly button. The moment I met him I knew we had to get him. I grew to love him. He became my child, my son. I became his mother."

As a girl she had dreamed of intellectual pursuits and exotic places. As a woman she found both in the intelligence in the eyes of infant orangutans like Sugito, who she described in the cerebral way she likes as "little Einsteins." Sugito played a crucial role in Galdikas's life, and the relationship with him changed her sense of herself and her work.

Sugito spent the day attached to Galdikas as she followed the orang-utans in the trees and made notes. Sometimes he'd groom her hair. "I would climb into the branches with Sugito and stay there virtually all day." At night, he slept on her body. They were so inseparable that "it was like having an orange tumor on your body."

Galdikas was entering the world of another species, in the phrase she used for herself in 1975, as "Sugito's mother." "He was a very strong character," she said of the orangutan. "Assertive, very sweet. He knew what he wanted. He was also very jealous of Rod. Sugito would bite him. We had an unspoken rule: once Sugito was on my body, he was home free." At night, Sugito slept clutched to her. "Rod disliked him. Sugito would pee and get the bed cold and wet. Sugito was a real source of tension between Rod and me because Rod felt I had chosen Sugito and the orangutans over him, and I guess I had."

And yet Brindamour told me that he saw Sugito in a different way. He saw a young orangutan disturbed both by his captivity and by the time he spent in Camp Leakey with human beings. "He spent an awful lot of time with Biruté," Brindamour said. "I think he was bright and devious. I think he perceived himself to be more connected to the human community than any of the other orangutans did. Almost in a way Sugito viewed himself as more human than orangutan. I felt that really he ought to be encouraged to fend for himself more." Sugito helped to determine the relationship of Galdikas and Brindamour in a way that Galdikas condoned and, in the opinion of the writer Carole Jahme, that did more harm to the marriage than an affair would.

From Galdikas's point of view, the relationship of Sugito and Brindamour eventually became locked in "a vendetta" between two unyielding males. The objects around camp that Brindamour showed an interest in, Sugito would deliberately attack and demolish. Sugito understood that Brindamour had an affinity for the electrical generator at camp, so Sugito would attack the generator as a way to injure Brindamour. The presence of Brindamour was abnormal in orangutan society, Galdikas tried to explain. "Baby orangutans normally have the female all to themselves," she said. But Brindamour told me, "I think what happened with Sugito was that he was with Biruté all the time. In a wild orangutan situation an adult male will often have to put up with the bites or the annoyance of a young orangutan during mating."

Five years after the first *National Geographic* article and eight years after arriving in Borneo, Galdikas wrote a second cover article, with an idyllic photo taken by Brindamour of their son, one-year-old Binti, bathing with an infant orangutan in a tub in the jungle. The young orangutan was Princess, who learned sign language at Camp Leakey from Gary Shapiro. Galdikas and Brindamour had separated a year before the article was published and by that time Binti was living with his father in Canada, although the article did not mention that. Readers had a Galdikas who was still in the jungle with husband and son, as far as they knew. The article opened from the point of view of Galdikas in 1976 eight months pregnant with her son and facing a crisis in her belief that orangutans embody an innocence that Western culture has apparently lost. The situation recalls Goodall discovering that the chimpanzees she thought represented a peaceful and benevolent primate society were capable of wanton murder and violence. Sugito, the orangutan who was Galdikas's first wild child, was a devil of an ape.

Sugito's fragile state of mind seemed to become even more diabolical when he was suspected of drowning orangutans out of jealousy for the attention Galdikas was giving them and also of killing cats. There were two murders and another attempted murder by the guilty-looking Sugito. In one incident Sugito held the head of a kitten under water. Galdikas thought that he was experimenting with life and death. He seemed to understand that death was "a very different state," she said. He performed "a weird fluttering of the hands" by the dead orangutan. "I've never seen that before," Galdikas told me. "It was almost ritualistic, almost as though he was willing the second orangutan to get up." Galdikas had to consider the personal moral dilemma of a mother whose child kills another creature out of spite. It was as though there were a demon in him where there should have been innocence.

Sugito was a shock to the idealism that inspired and guided Galdikas. The violence of him, she said—senseless, wasteful of life, unnatural— still troubles her today. "It was a horror," she said. "It was anguish. We hadn't known to stop it. There was never a case of infanticide among wild orangutans. I wondered what there was that was different with my relationship with Sugito."

Was there corruption even in the attempt to repair the damaged soul of the orangutan? In her autobiography, she wrote, "The eyes of the male orangutan remind us of the awkward combination of angel and beast that characterizes the human soul." There is some violence among orangutans. Orangutans rape females, but the sort of conflict that leads them to murder each other in the wild, like chimpanzees, is rare. For one thing, the solitary male orangutan spends his energy keeping his distance from other males, without the social structure that leads to conflict. But Sugito was not a normal wild orangutan. He had been taken from his mother, his normal development disrupted, and human beings had contaminated him. He was the lost soul and jungle bad boy. Just what human beings love.

Nevertheless, by 1980, Galdikas was convinced of her radical position that if orangutan surrogate mothers weren't available, human surrogate mothers needed to be used for a long period of time. That was the only hope in her mind that dysfunctional orangutans could be returned to the wild. It was this concept that led to a serious rift with others working with orangutans and more separation from others. Some say it is wrong to use human surrogates because, aside from the issue of catching diseases from human beings, it contaminates the wild mentality of orangutans. Kaplan and Rogers say that studies show that orangutans raised by human beings have a much worse chance of surviving than orangutans raised in captivity by a mother orangutan. That would make human beings a poor substitute, although maybe it's better than nothing. Still others, like Goodall, say it is simply impossible to rehabilitate any primates who have been kept as pets.

By 1980, the preeminent orangutan researchers in the world were Biruté Galdikas and Herman Rijksen, although Galdikas was more famous. No one was close to matching the twelve thousand hours of observation in the wild of Galdikas and Brindamour. She calculates that eighty percent of her findings would remain unpublished in the decades to come as her energy shifted from a focus primarily on science. Orangutans came first for her, then science. Galdikas was the surrogate mother of orangutans who would see her son grow up with them with all the joys and fears that involved. She saw her son Binti start to behave like an orangutan. He could climb trees and communicate with orangutans in sign language, although he was still very much a human child.

The years leading up to 1980 were also full of unique revelations that were part of the glory of the work for her. Galdikas slept at night under the tree where an orangutan nested, to be the first Westerner to witness the birth of a wild orangutan. She was the first to see the rare combat between wild male orangutans in the forest. Life with orangutans was giving Galdikas what she wanted—a sense of strength and independence and insight into nature. She was where she wanted to be. She wrote in her autobiography about these qualities of life in the natural world, saying, "In modern, Western societies we yearn to be like orangutans." She had also found again in the forest the serenity that she had cherished since she was a child. She had a large life and she even seemed to have her own personal cosmology. But sometimes the things that make us unique draw us deeper into them where they have power over us.

The years after the 1980 *National Geographic* article brought difficulties, too. Brindamour had reached his limit and the marriage had fallen apart. Brindamour felt that living with orangutans in the jungle was his wife's passion, suiting her life, not his, and Galdikas was clear, on reflection later, that orangutans had been her priority at the time ahead of her relationship with her husband. In her autobiography, Galdikas made comments in retrospect about the way that a spouse becomes "peripheral" in the "obsession of working on a PhD thesis" as she was. "One's whole life revolves around it," she said. And the larger world of orangutans revolved around the thesis, too, not a dry intellectual exercise for Galdikas, but a commitment and a way of life that relegated everything else to a lesser status.

Galdikas was developing a strong and idealistic sense of individuality and of the rights of the individual that seemed subversive to other people, and she saw orangutans as individuals with rights. That was satisfying for her and yet also led to conflict with others. Brindamour said, "She lived in a world of fulfillment and disappointment." The orangutans were her sustenance, yet she rarely smiled and there was a brooding sense from her family history that, as Brindamour told me, "a good day is when nothing bad happens." And yet, "Things did not deter her," said Brindamour. Her attitude was stoical, he said: "Life is hard. You just get on with it. You simply persevere and expect no joy." The difference of opinion between Galdikas, her husband, and others about Sugito was a pattern that would be repeated in her life. The essential larger question was how many rights did an orangutan have when it interfered with human beings?

For Galdikas, Sugito was an individual and had rights whatever he did. For Brindamour and the researcher Gary Shapiro, Sugito was a threat to the order and safety of the camp. The situation became intolerable when the orangutan broke into the quarters of Galdikas and Brindamour and destroyed the medical and chemical locker. Shapiro recalls the incident, since one of the reasons Galdikas wanted him at Camp Leakey was to teach Sugito sign language in the hope of unraveling the mystery of the killings of the other orangutans. It didn't work, because Sugito refused to have a relationship with Shapiro.

"My memory of Sugito," Shapiro told me, "was of a very clever and wily orangutan who would plot break-ins and cause mayhem. He would sit up in the trees and kiss squeak at me—an indication of his dislike of me."

The second day that Shapiro was in the camp, Sugito was on the roof of his cabin trying to pry loose the ironwood shingles. "He was conniving," said Shapiro. "He'd be sitting in the trees and you could see the cogs in his head turning." Sugito was a typical orangutan with a taste for "retribution," says Shapiro, and he had marked Brindamour for his animosity.

Galdikas's willingness to endure Sugito as one more indignity of the jungle was beyond the limits of Brindamour and Shapiro. Similar situations would also lead to the defections of others from Camp Leakey in later years. Brindamour said from his home in British Columbia that he thought Sugito was a threat to others and he took the responsibility to remove him. The orangutan was between the ages of eight and ten at the time, and was becoming stronger and more destructive. "My feeling was that, if we didn't remove him, then somebody might get seriously hurt," Brindamour told me. It was "unfortunate timing" with Galdikas absent, Brindamour said, but necessary to take action while she was gone and couldn't argue and delay what needed to be done. "It would have required a catastrophic incident before she'd do anything," Brindamour said.

The two men took Sugito far into the jungle and let him go. The result was that the exile of Sugito wounded Galdikas in a way that only she could be wounded. "Biruté never quite forgave Rod for that," says Shapiro. He believes that the incident with Sugito finally destroyed the marriage for Galdikas. "It was a great betrayal," Galdikas admitted to me. "I was fond of Sugito." She notes that both men thought they were doing what was logical and neither felt guilty, although an element of revenge toward both Galdikas and Sugito hung in the air. "It was a very complicated emotional thing," Galdikas said. Otherwise, with Sugito gone, "It was much more pleasant in camp," Brindamour said.

But there were other problems, too. Galdikas described in her book *Reflections of Eden* how she was oblivious to the affair her husband was having with Yuni, the teenage Indonesian nanny of their son Binti, although she also recounted in her book the glaring signs of what was happening. Galdikas was formal and distant with her husband in a way that others could see, but that is also typical of how she behaves with people. She treats a person with a respectful social formality in front of others. "There was a definite coldness," Gary Shapiro says. At that time, unknown to Galdikas, Brindamour had been in Jakarta with his new love, what Indonesians call the *madu* or second wife, literally "honey." Meanwhile Galdikas was angry that her husband had delayed his return to camp and hadn't photographed the birth of the orangutan Siswi, the daughter of the orangutan favored by Galdikas, Siswoyo. For Galdikas, Brindamour had essentially missed the birth of the couple's wild orangutan granddaughter. She rationalized her husband's behavior in her book in an anthropological way as the simple hormonal desire of the male of the species for "a young, slim, adoring wife." But by the time her book was published Galdikas did not mention that the hormonal urge of Brindamour had lasted through fifteen years of marriage and two children.

By the time I talked to Brindamour, he had been married to Yuni for twenty-four years with a third child being born. He said that there are limits to the sensitivity and perceptiveness of Galdikas toward people. "I'd like to see her develop a bit more empathy for others," he told me. The circumstances of the breakup of the marriage were "hurtful," he admitted, but ultimately beneficial. "The greatest gift I have gotten out of the whole orangutan venture," he said, "was meeting and marrying Yuni."

At that time Galdikas made a painful choice. She decided to stay with the orangutans at Camp Leakey and to agree that three-year-old Binti would live with her ex-husband in British Columbia to attend school and grow up. Galdikas's biographer Sy Montgomery describes the decision as necessary and sympathizes with Galdikas for being in the position of "losing" a child. Galdikas reasoned that she'd have at least four months a year with Binti when she took a seasonal teaching position at Simon Fraser University in British Columbia. But essentially, it meant that she had chosen orangutans again as a crucial part of her existence. Orangutans and the forest filled the place of almost everything in her life.

Orangutans were like her, which may be part of her insight into them. Most of the time, like her, orangutans are always thinking and watching and absorbing, as though they are another part of the forest. "I really, really like orangutans," Galdikas said in a conversation with me. "I like being in their company. I find a serenity with them, because they're not demanding. They are very calm and serene, seemingly to the point of passivity. Orangutans were my sole companions," she said.

"Just your simple company is enough to satisfy them. It's very humbling. They don't impose themselves on you. All that is needed is your presence. That's why it's very calming and reassuring. I got lonely following an orangutan for twelve hours from dawn to dusk and maybe that orangutan will look at me once, twice, maybe never. I'd wonder if they were lonely. They don't need anything. They are universes unto themselves. That's why they are less hostile."

She got a similar satisfaction from the natural world. "The river ran pure, translucent, black," she said one time, sitting with me in her orangutan clinic in the village of Pasir Panjang. "You could look at yourself and the trees by looking down into the river. It was eerie, black and clear." When she said that, she looked down at the white tile floor as though seeing through it like water.

So, Galdikas took her son to Canada and returned to Camp Leakey to work with orangutans. When she caught sight of the plastic toys left behind by Binti, she told me, "I was overwhelmed with the emptiness of him not being there." After eight years in the jungle, the marriage was dissolved. Then, two years later, in 1981, at thirty-five years of age, Galdikas married Bohop, one of the Dayaks working for her at Camp Leakey, and had two children with him, Fred and Jane.

When I talked to Brindamour, he enjoyed reminiscing about the orangutans and the days with Galdikas at Camp Leakey, without a tone of conspiracy or scandal or bitterness in all our hours of conversation. "She has only been able to accomplish what she has because of who she is," he told me. "I admire her for who she is and what she has accomplished."

As for Binti Brindamour, he spends time at Camp Leakey, although years ago he found it dull to be there as a teenager. Sitting with me at the orangutan clinic in Pasir Pajang, he said of Camp Leakey, "It's dirty. It's grimy. But there are more realities of life here." He also married a young Indonesian woman.

Time stops for no one. In the 1980s, Galdikas came out of the protection of the jungle and into the political maelstrom. For a person who valued peace and the respect of others, there were issues of power, dominance, and violence. Galdikas continued to fight illegal logging and told me that she was kidnapped and punched in the face by "thugs associated with loggers" in the early 1990s. Two of her teeth were chipped. A British woman with the Environmental Investigation Agency who came to investigate illegal logging in the same park where Galdikas had her facility was also beaten, and the camp of the American researcher Carey Yeager on the edge of Tanjung Puting park was stormed by loggers with machetes. Yeager abandoned the camp.

Galdikas told me that she could never be sure who to trust. Her home in Pasir Panjang was raided by forestry officials with guns. They came to inspect the treatment of orangutans kept there as refugees after fires had swept the jungle and killed thousands of orangutans. The inspection of her property was a political ploy during a corrupt regime to try to discredit her, according to Galdikas. "It was Suharto's Indonesia," she said in an even tone. "You can imagine the terror." Others interpret the incident as an attempt to clamp down on a renegade scientist.

By this time Biruté Galdikas had spent so many years with orangutans that she was in a unique position to see the entire life and development of an orangutan, not just loose and unconnected parts of a life. She even saw the unbroken succession of the generations from birth to death. Part of this was an orangutan named Siswoyo who she'd brought from Jakarta in a plane she had to charter for the purpose with three other orangutans who had been confiscated by officials. Siswoyo, then about ten years old, had been kept illegally as a pet and looked "dazed" during the flight. Her muscles were weak and lean after years in a small cage. She had trouble walking. Galdikas nursed her back to health at Camp Leakey and let her wander into the jungle. Later Galdikas rescued Siswoyo when she had difficulty adjusting to the forest. Galdikas found her in a swamp. "She seemed to be in a state of shock, her eyes glazed over." Galdikas thought that Siswoyo bonded with her during the time Galdikas cared for her. "She was my best friend," said Galdikas, although she gave Galdikas a deep "love bite." Siswoyo grew up, had an infant that died soon after birth, then had three orangutan children in succession, Siswi, Simon, and Sugarjito.

Siswoyo was free to roam the jungle around Camp Leakey and yet she came back from time to time to visit Galdikas. She'd bang on the door with her "sloppy" knock and "come and sit beside me, put her hand on my knee. She'd just sit with me. She just liked being with me and would put a hand around me," Galdikas said, and then turned away as her eyes grew watery from the memory. "Sorry, I'm getting emotional about her," she said. "We'd sometimes walk into the forest. She'd do her orangutan things." In the world of orangutans Galdikas learned that intimacy is expressed by sitting together in peace without displays. The absence of action is significant for creatures like orangutans who have conflicts if they are too close together. Orangutans normally spread out in a forest of meager, scattered food. Galdikas explained that silence can be a form of intimacy in the same way between human beings where there is "no void to fill." It's the communication that comes from knowing what another is not saying.

Galdikas has a supply of memories of Siswjojo that she treasures.

"Siswoyo was quite a character," she says. In a picture frame at her office at Simon Fraser University she has the scrawls Siswoyo made with a pen on paper. "She and I were friends. She was very much my equal. Orangutans do not establish relationships easily, but, once they do, they seem to be true to it."

Siswoyo died after childbirth in 1991. "The last time that I left Camp Leakey before she died, she put her arms around my legs and wouldn't let me leave. She'd never done that before." Siswoyo was buried in a coffin under a small wooden cross at Camp Leakey, where other orangutans are given simple markers. It is the graveyard mentioned earlier where Galdikas stopped and wept. But then there was a struggle over the corpse of this orangutan. The primatologist learned that the head of the park whom she was battling had dug up Siswoyo's body and brought it to town to put on display as an orangutan skeleton. That would obviously disturb Galdikas. She recovered the corpse of Siswoyo from the official and buried it again in the original grave. It was another instance of the strange and cruel battles for power between human beings over orangutans. And the orangutans have no say in that.

In the late 1990s, stories circulated about Galdikas as a renegade who battled officials in Indonesia over orangutans and the rain forest, who fought with scientists who disagreed with her style of science and rehabilitation. Whether she liked it or not personally, Galdikas had acquired power and influence and needed to make decisions that affected others. And where there is power and influence, there is disagreement, conflict, and animosity. Galdikas's operation had grown in size. She had maintained more independence than scientists attached to universities, but realized that she needed an independent source of publicity and funding, such as her own foundation, to protect and support the orangutans, her work, and her philosophy.

In 1986, she and Shapiro created the Orangutan Foundation International. She was spending more time by then on political issues of protecting the rain forest and orangutans and less time on a daily basis with an increasing number of individual orangutans. She told me that the result is that she has saved the patch of forest of Tanjung Puting and that the population of orangutans has increased there to six thousand. She said that this accomplishment ensures the survival of orangutans as a species.

Aside from the politics of saving primates in the 1980s and 1990s, the mythic dimension of the life of Galdikas was growing larger and she could not control it the way she wanted. It produced two extreme and contradictory images in the minds of others, one an idealistic Galdikas, the other a demonic Galdikas. There were significant defections from people who worked closely with her. Bizarre stories and rumors started to circulate. Those people closest to Galdikas say that there is sometimes a glimmer of truth in the stories, however much the information is darkened and distorted. "We know she's a very complex person," said a fellow researcher and longtime supporter who has ceased to be a friend. I talked to some of the defectors, and it made me feel uncomfortable, like being in the midst of a family quarrel about the children, the orangutans.

The most radical part of the behavior of Galdikas is the power she gives to orangutans to make decisions about their own lives as individuals and to wander without the kind of restraint that human beings would prefer. Galdikas lets the twenty or so orangutans at Camp Leakey wander freely and make their own choices, while the majority of the other orangutans are released in the wild in different locations.

Sometimes the results at Camp Leakey are harsh for human beings. People break the rules that orangutans live by and they get bitten. At the time of my last visit to Camp Leakey, one of the favorite orangutans of Galdikas, Princess, bit a woman badly on the ankle over an incident with a paint brush. The person tried to take the paint brush from Princess. I saw the people close to Galdikas work to hide the incident from Galdikas.

There are instances of excess in Galdikas with individual orangutans that are typical of her thinking, like keeping the paralyzed orangutan alive in her clinic in Pasir Panjang or, the most blatant one, rescuing the refugee orangutan Rusti on the island of Hawaii. Half a million dollars was raised to build a new home for Rusti. Is the life of one orangutan worth that much? For some people, who'd instead put the money toward a larger number of orangutans, maybe no, but for Galdikas, it is. She values the life of the individual orangutan like others do the life of an individual human being. It's the old dilemma of what is worth more, one life or many lives. What is practical and what is humane?

Scientists like Herman Rijksen told me that orangutans should be given the same rights as human beings, which he calls "existential rights," on land where they are protected. "I don't think we have the right, as an ape, to say to another ape, you shouldn't be here," he said in a conversation with me in the Netherlands. But Galdikas goes further than Rijksen. She says that she believes that orangutans should be allowed to make some basic choices in their lives. One of the rights of choice that Galdikas thinks orangutans should have is whether they want to return to the wild or stay in a sanctuary without walls like Camp Leakey. "We have never forced them to go back," Galdikas told me. "Why should an animal have to go back to the wild? We have to deal with the great apes as people. It should be up to them to make the decision, if they want to go back or not. To give the orangutans a choice is very important for me." That's as radical as you can get as a human being.

My own history with Galdikas was what we writers call "frustrating at times but still illuminating." I admit that I like a little radical thought now and then to jolt us out of our complacency, and there is a gentle wisdom to Galdikas at times. I learned a lot from her. But after three years of dealing with a person who seemed to live by her own inner logic, I was growing a bit weary of her behavior. Nevertheless, in spite of it all I was finally able to have one of those conversations with her one night at Camp Leakey that makes you forget a lot.

How do you make sense of Galdikas? This is a woman who says she is known as "the pale ghost of the forest" and is believed to have the mystical power to command wild animals. She may not believe that herself literally, but she knows the power of what others believe and she tends her image. She is also as good sometimes at not answering questions as she is at answering them. There is a consistency in her life from the time she was a child as someone who is private, independent, persistent, curious, and connected to the natural world. She has been able to embrace the contradictions in life, cope with years of isolation in the jungle, and live in a foreign native culture, all of which would alone distinguish her.

The forest is a consistent theme in her life. I remember what she had told me about her love of the forest from the time she was a child. She started kindergarten in Canada speaking only Lithuanian, after being brought to Canada at age two by two refugees from Lithuania after the Second World War. As a young child in Toronto, she wandered by herself in a large park where there was a pond and big trees. Her father took her fishing in the woods in northern Ontario when she was nine and ten. She told me how she enjoyed being among the dark trees there and remembers, among the natural sanctity of the forest, a church where people kissed relics of dead Jesuits in a glass case.

The influences of childhood are always important, even if you outgrow them, and her consciousness of nature grew as a child in Toronto's Roman Catholic Lithuanian community with its beliefs from the old country. She told me that the community she knew as a child was a "Lithuanian Baltic culture, with a very strong undercurrent of druidism. The first poem that I read in the Lithuanian language talked about the forest. It was about the beauty of the forest and the fact that without the forest the Lithuanians could not survive." As a child, she remembers that for eight years she went every Saturday to a religious school, long enough and early enough to have made some impression. "The Lithuanians are also very heavily steeped in pagan mysticism," she said. "The Lithuanians were the last people in Europe to convert to Christianity."

Her use of the word "mystical" and the association she has of it are also revealing, although with a person like this you have to be careful that she may be using the word her own way. I found her using the word at the crucial moment in her autobiography when she decides to study orangutans. She makes a reference to a "strange mystical incident" she had at UCLA when she was nineteen and became "obsessed with the idea" of a woman like Jane Goodall living in the jungle with animals. She had the sensation at the time of a chime ringing and a chill in her bones, and she had similar sensations at other moments in her life that were important, sometimes associated with death or a dramatic change.

In a conversation with me at her orangutan clinic in Pasir Panjang, she described a mystical sensation in the forest when she was pregnant with Binti. "I could actually feel," she said, "my molecules flowing out of me and merging with the forest." Like Fossey, Galdikas had entered a world where birth, death, and the natural world became strange, and Fossey and Galdikas had discussed it. Before her death, Dian Fossey hinted one time to Galdikas about her own entry into this uncanny world. "Oh, Biruté," she said, "if you only knew what I've done and all the things I've seen." The two women talked about witchcraft and mystical experiences. Galdikas enjoys any sort of conversation like this, and there are stories of her having conversations on the subject of religion and mysticism late into the night. It is certainly a topic that fascinates her.

Galdikas has suggested that communication between species is "mystic." "Communicating with a wild animal of another species means glimpsing another reality," she said. "Things move very slowly in the forest," she told me. "Most trees ripen over one to two months. Every day a little, but they will ripen. Nothing in the environment presses orangutans to be fast movers. Over long periods of time they just slowed down. Orangutans think, ponder, and plan. They're very deliberate. Orangutans live in the moment, to a certain degree in the past. They're Buddhists. They enjoy the moment. I think they're slow thinkers, but

deep thinkers. We misinterpreted the intelligence of orangutans because of their slowness. We see quickness as intelligence. They don't
waste their energy. Their universe evolved in solitude." Maybe the life
of Galdikas did, too.

That night in her cabin in the jungle was the time to pursue the ideas
I had come halfway around the world to understand. I'd brought my
battered copy of *Heart of Darkness* to discuss with her how the jungle
affects the minds of Westerners, but set it aside on her table. We talked
for a while about how "the ghost of the forest" thinks and what mysticism is and how she believes that Western culture is "totally alienated
from its roots in nature." She said that the pleasure of being in a forest is
mystical and changes people, but it felt as though she kept what she was
really thinking elusive. It seemed to be held dangling just out of sight. I
wanted to know if she experienced mysticism.

"I think the forest has its reality," she said at one point. "The forest has
its power and that power is overwhelming. That's a spiritual power."

"If somebody described you as a pagan mystic—"

"Oh, I'm not a pagan mystic. I don't think so."

"Are you a mystic?"

"I'm not sure."

"Do you believe in a mystical reality?"

"I believe that sometimes it's appropriate to believe in a mystical reality. I don't necessarily believe in it all the time. When we have intense
pleasure it becomes a mystical experience. It's the way our brains work
as human beings."

She told me that she hears voices in the jungle and thinks that hal-
lucinations from such things as the fever of malaria can be a revelation, like Indians using the natural drug peyote. We talked about these
things and then our conversation was interrupted by a tremulous hooting sound outside, bleating like sonar. It was a reminder of the forces
we were talking about. The forest wanted to join the conversation. "That

sounded like it was coming through a pipe," I said. "That might be the Pan pipes."

"That's a frog," she said, being more practical.

"I wonder if people originally thought that's what Pan was, listening to the sound," I said.

"I've heard people say that it's a singing snake. I've heard people say that it's a singing snail. I once asked my husband and we had an argument about it. He went out and found it. But who would think that it was a singing frog?"

A gecko chirped loudly in her cabin while she talked, and outside there was the rhythm of the cicadas in the trees. I love crickets and warm to anyone who does, too. That made me ask why she talked about cicadas so much in her autobiography.

"Because they're overwhelming and they're also the sounds that the orangutans hear and have been hearing for two million years. It has been a part of their history. The cicadas have been here a long time and orangutans have been around much longer than human beings."

"So when you hear cicadas, you're listening through orangutan ears?"

"I'm listening to orangutan evolution and adaptation. It's the adult males I'm thinking of, because for the adult males it's very important to listen for long calls and fight calls. For them, it could be a matter of life and death. So they must listen at night because they call in the night."

"They must wake up in the night then."

"Kusasi called three times in the night," she said.

"And he's not going to call if nobody's listening."

"That's right."

The moon was full that night. The nests of the orangutans were high in the trees. I was thinking what it would be like to be an orangutan at this moment. It would be brighter up there. An orangutan in the trees must see the moonlight fall through the layers of leaves until it is extinguished in the darkness at the roots. It would feel good to see all that and hear the sounds. It feeds the sensibility.

"You can almost see color on a bright moonlit night," she said. "The reds start emerging."

"And since the orangutans are red, they'd be able to see each other in moonlight."

"Maybe," she said.

It was getting late, near midnight. We were tired. It would be a good time to sleep after the heat and fatigue of the day. I needed time to think about what I'd heard. I had a lot to absorb. I was also wondering if the big snake I'd seen during the day would be awake somewhere in the dark as I was going along the path back to the klotok. My eyes and ears would adjust to the dark, though, and the old primitive hunter instinct would probably come out. I remember Galdikas telling me about the luminescence of the fungus lighting the dark bottom of the forest. "I've seen that," she said, "but you have to be walking in the dark. It is astounding. It's a whole ghost forest out there."

CHAPTER 11

Requiem for an Ape

SHE WAS BORN in captivity and she died in captivity thirty-four years later a few feet from the spot where she was born, and in between that time she had to teach herself to be an individual. Nobody else would.

Her hair was lighter in color than the others and her heritage may have been Sumatran. The records were sketchy after that. She never climbed a real tree or swung through the rain forest or knew the land of her ancestors. She had no children.

Yet she had dignity, and confidence in her solitary manner, although later in life she could not resist making a few friends, if reluctantly, as though it were a secret she was keeping from others, maybe even from herself. She didn't defer to a male just because he was male. Whatever the laws of the jungle are for the sexes, they did not have to be her laws, if she did not want them to be.

In her isolation from her kind, she had to create her own existence out of what she could scrounge and patch together, which she did. She developed her own style in the way she walked, in the way she moved her eyes and reacted. She refused to be manipulated. She learned how to exert her power over those who managed the cages at the zoo and reversed their positions. She persevered and changed and took what pleasure she could out of her existence.

I heard about her death from a scientist who knew her three decades earlier when she was young. The scientist had used her in an experiment to test the ability of orangutans to communicate. He said her death more than twenty years later affected him deeply.

She had affected the keepers at the zoo and the volunteers who worked there, too. It was a story repeated by different people who know orangutans in different parts of the world. They said they'd looked into the eyes of an orangutan like this and seen a glimpse of a world beyond that is larger than we can ever know. It is a place of clarity and peace without the doubt and hesitation and uncertainty that troubles us. An orangutan knows its own mind.

Few people have had the opportunity to observe an orangutan close enough over a long enough period of time to know them beyond our faint grasp of what we imagine they might be. Science only gives us patchy, abstract, clinical impressions of the creature. There is more than that.

On my way to Sumatra and Borneo I flew to Fresno, to talk to the people at the Chaffee Zoological Gardens who knew this orangutan. I cleaned the cages with a shovel and a hose and chopped fruit and vegetables for the orangutans' lunch. The steel of the shovel scraped against the cement, and the force of the water from the hose washed it smooth again. The orangutans must have noticed how thorough the human being was. One attractive female orangutan was noticeably drawn to the anthropoid with the graying beard.

At the zoo, my son painted scenes on large rolls of paper to entertain one of the orangutans. If orangutans are left alone in cages, without stimulation, without a challenge for their brains, like the fat and joyless one we saw later in the zoo in Manila, they become listless and depressed. Without the exercise and stimulation they get in a tropical forest, they merely fatten on food.

That night we heard the stories about this one orangutan and tried to piece together an impression of her as a single being, which wasn't easy. "There are so many sides to her," one of the keepers, Lyn Myers, said, "and you can interpret all those different sides. Everybody's opinion of her was she was this, she was that, because they only knew one tiny part of her. But as soon as you started experiencing all the different sides, your opinion of her changes drastically. And there are so many interpretations and that's what's so great. Everybody's interpretation may just have a little bit of difference in it."

A single personality is large and contains contradictions, multitudes, said the human poet Walt Whitman. He would have liked orangutans.

Her name was Aazk. The researcher Gary Shapiro still remembers her, after the eighteen months he spent with her at the zoo in Fresno when he was a young biologist in the 1970s. Shapiro was studying the ability of this orangutan to communicate with human beings through sign language. The venture would change his life and lead to lifelong involvement with orangutans. It made it possible for him to spend two years in the jungles of Borneo raising a young orangutan female to see how well she could learn to communicate. Aazk was his first orangutan and she taught him.

"Her hair," said Shapiro, "was reddish-brown and her big toes lacked a thumbnail—not uncommon in the species." Shapiro went inside the cage and came to see her as "a friend," he said. "It was not unlike working with a child. You develop an affection—and patience."

Working with Shapiro, the orangutan was able to place symbols on a board to name things and to make sentences. She was about three years old at the time. "I was a bit uncertain the first time I entered the cage with her," Shapiro said, but the orangutan quickly became interested in playing with the human being and the games he brought into the cage. She was playful and cute and loved to swing and get tickled. "This is when I first learned that orangutans can laugh." She would give the researcher the hand signal to tickle her. She liked being tickled under her chin and laughed in hoarse little bursts. "I learned that most young orangutans enjoy being tickled on the neck under the chin."

The orangutan came to expect the visits of the man in the morning. He formed a relationship with the young ape partly so that their experiences together would be part of the understanding and vocabulary they could use to communicate. From that, the experiment with language and symbols got its personal meaning and reference points. "Over time, she became close to me and appeared to look forward to my visits. She would play with me between learning trials," he said. "She liked me to swing her hanging by her toes." When it was time for him to leave, he saw that she looked "disappointed" and "resentful." He watched the change in her from outside the cage and tried to understand what was happening. "She would look at me and then go into the night house and not leave until I left the area. I would get stares from visitors who wondered why the ape acted that way in my presence."

The young orangutan learned to communicate with the researcher by symbols and gestures and behavior. She understood that the plastic symbols referred to other things and she used them individually and combined them in sequences. Their activities together were a kind of conversation. "She would entice me to play with her," he said. "She enjoyed being an orangutan—climbing on the chain link caging or performing acrobatics on the swings in the cage.

"I didn't mind being in the cage. In fact, it gave me a better perspective what it might be like to be locked up like a zoo animal. Yet, perhaps she understood that my time in the cage was temporary while she had to stay in the cage."

When the research ended, Shapiro discovered that he missed the time spent with the orangutan. "It is hard not to have feelings after developing such a special relationship with an animal like her. I remember how she treated me only a few years after I stopped working with her. She would take a mouthful of water and spit at me. I don't know whether it was resentment. Orangutans like to torment humans." But then maybe we deserve it.

The four people in the world who knew Aazk the best are the ape keepers in Fresno, Lyn Myers and Nannette Driver-Ruiz, and two volunteers, Trish and Bruce Campbell. I sat down with the four of them to have a group session about Aazk. Normally, I like to talk to people alone because being in a group can suppress the willingness of some individuals to talk, but this time I thought it was important for them to hear what each other said about Aazk. The result was interesting. At first, they listened to what each person said. Then more and more they started to add details, to elaborate, until it became a conversation between them about an orangutan who had affected their lives in a way that only they could appreciate fully. The orangutan was a bond between them even after her death.

"I met Aazk in the late 1990s when I started at Fresno Zoo," said Lyn Myers, a senior keeper at the zoo, "although I was aware of her when I was a volunteer back in the early 1980s. The person who was taking care of her was having difficulties with the orangutans. There were two orangutans. Aazk was the older female, in her late twenties. She was in a backholding area adjacent to an exhibit, a very small, old exhibit. Out in the exhibit was a young male, Busar, in his midteens, and he was a fairly new orangutan, and once when they kept him out in the exhibit he refused to be locked back inside. Aazk was very aggressive toward him. She was very dominant. They tried to do an introduction of her to him and she actually beat him up several times. She punched him in the face and bit him to the point where they had to be separated. He occupied the exhibit and they wanted to alternate their time out in the exhibit, but he refused to be locked down. He didn't trust the keepers. He was very frightened. There was no way he was going to let them shut a door behind him."

The keeper came to Myers for help. She started to spend time in the holding area with the orangutans, to develop a relationship. Others had simply expected the orangutans to cede to their dominance, to recognize the control of human beings. The orangutans seemed passive, although the recent intransigence was troubling, even rebellious. And this was a female, who should recognize the dominance of males, shouldn't she? But then Aazk had had lots of time to think.

"She had not been in the same space with a human for fifteen, twenty years at least," said Myers. "She basically, was very accepting to new people—but, it had to be on her terms. And her terms are the way that she wants it. She was very set in her ways. She was very sure of herself. She ruled the roost. And if you were a keeper that came in with inexperience, lack of respect, she was quickly going to teach you respect. She was famous for teaching respect by regurgitating on people. It was a huge volume and she would aim it at you."

"Did she do that to you?"

"Often."

"How did you feel about that?"

"I was okay," Myers said brusquely. "That was part of being with her in the beginning. She did this to keepers and to Busar because she knew she would get a response. I could look at my shirt and I knew exactly what she had for lunch. I just hosed myself off and didn't let her get any gratification from it."

"Why did you want to put yourself through that?"

"She was worth it."

"Why?"

The keeper took a long pause. I could see the emotion gathering under the surface. "She was worth it," Myers repeated. "They're all worth it, because there's an inner spirit to them, something that you can't quite grasp. There's an inner being to each of them that is so different that you look into their eyes and you know that you're only getting a tiny glimpse of what's inside and you want more."

I asked what she was getting back from them. There was another pause. She thought deeply. She tried to find the words. "I'm getting back a glimpse into a world that I'm not familiar with, a glimpse into a world that's way beyond my world. It's exciting. It's something almost intangible. It's almost a world that I'm jealous I can't be a part of but yet they allow you to have a small part of. With an orangutan, there is a peace. They're very sure of themselves. There's such a subtlety about them. You look at them and you know that there is so much going on inside their brains, but yet they are so subtle about their body movements, about their body posturing. Everything is very small. Everything is very controlled. And so, oftentimes I look at them and I want to reach inside them and I want to open their brain to know just what it is to be an orangutan for one minute, one hour, one day, what it would feel like, because it is so far beyond my understanding."

"Have you ever had a moment when you thought you were getting close to that?"

"Never," she said. She repeated the word for emphasis.

"But it's there?"

"It's there. I remember Aazk training me. She taught me how to be an ape keeper and I messed up big time. And the nice thing is that she always gave me second chances."

"What did you learn?"

"You have to let them be in control. You have to let them have control of their environment. And that's part of the respect you give them. When I shift Aazk, I ask Aazk to go through the door. I ask her to allow me to shut the door. If you don't, you're not going to get anywhere with her. You don't have to ask for permission all the time. In the beginning, everything that you do, it has to be approved through her and, if you don't approve it through her, she will stop you dead in your tracks. What you're trying to achieve will take you fifty times longer to get it done, because she will make it very difficult for you. So, I think if anything, she taught me how to respect an animal and how to give them the control that they need for self-satisfaction. I don't think you can have an ego and work with an ape. I think you have to have a personality that is patient. I think you need patience. I think you need to let someone else make decisions—the apes."

Myers continued, "I'm sure I've gotten more patient with years and that's simply maturity. I know I used to be a perfectionist and I still am, but I've also got to the point where I just have to slack up. Life is too short. I think, in my human relationships, I still have more of a domineering personality. But with the apes you have just got to give in. You've got to work together with them. You can't always be in charge."

I asked Myers how she would describe Aazk.

"Confident, extremely confident. In everything that she does, body posturing. She's always got a confident personality. The way that she carries herself, that she walks. The way that she looks at you. The way that she looks at other apes. She's very sure of herself."

"How do the other apes respond to her?"

"They pick up on it. They're cautious. I think she's giving a message with her body posture. She will kick your butt if you don't respect her. And she has shown that many times. She is tough. She is dominant. Around the males she is very much dominant. She will light into them. I remember one time she beat Busar up. She went to Busar and you could tell she was angry that he was in the enclosure. She was fine as long as he was up high, because she couldn't climb. Her muscles were not built in her chest because the previous enclosure did not allow her much climbing. And Busar was a good climber. So he always stayed up high and she was down low and that seemed to work for a while. But she would stand underneath him and she would put her hand on her head and she would just look at him. You could tell she was planning. And there were days he would come down because it was shady down below.

"I remember the day she walked up and she just kept walking past him and her body posture was very footballish. Offensive. Just puffed out. She just kept walking by him and she'd yank hair. She kept going. And Busar wouldn't even look at her. She'd do that a couple of times. He didn't look at her. Then she'd go by and she'd haul off and she'd really pull a huge handful of hair. He was patient. He didn't react. She'd come around again and she'd just sock him. She had a great upper cut. Sock him in the back, though. He had his back to her. He was in her space. She didn't like him. She did not want to share space with him.

"The next time she came by him, Busar jumped on her; there was a big rolling red mess going along the ground and she got some bites. We pulled her back into the building, separated them. It was difficult to see how wounded she was, but the next day she was showing us her wounds. She had big punctures in her forearm. She had a really stiff neck. She had a limp in her hip on the other side. She was walking all scrunched up and she was dragging her leg. She was a mess. She looked terrible. And yet she punched at the door at the other side of Busar. She wanted to get at him and go after him, and she could hardly walk."

Others saw changes in the orangutan over time. She had an ability to reach unspoken relationships with a species that was not her own. She wanted more than just battles over dominance.

"When I started working with her," Nannette Driver-Ruiz said, "she was very standoffish to me and she would do a lot of spitting and regurgitating at me. Over time, that lessened, unless she was just in a mood, but she stopped doing that and she got soft. She really softened a lot. She had the relationship with Busar where she wanted to punch him all the time, but, at the same time, Busar would always stop by her door and sometimes they would pass food back and forth through the door or she would pull hair out. I think she liked him a little bit, but only liked him on her terms. She never did accept that the male was supposed to be dominant. But for all the displays that they did at each other, every night that Busar came into the building from the exhibit, he would always go over to her room, sit by her door and watch her."

With time and patience her attitude changed to Driver-Ruiz, too. "I think it helped just being around her and letting her tell you how to operate the door and how she liked her bedding and making her room special for her."

"Can orangutans see through people and their façades?"

"Definitely. I see it all the time. If I come to work and I'm in a bad mood, every ape knows it. They either do exactly what I need them to do with very little asking or they want to have fun with my mood and do not cooperate in any way at all. I think it really delights them to be able to pick up on my feelings and show that they can frustrate me but that I'm not going to get completely frustrated with them."

"Have you seen people have trouble with orangutans because of the way the orangutan was reading them?"

"I definitely saw that when any new people came into the area and Aazk would take advantage of the situation and make sure that that person knows who is in control. Orangutans have certain ways that things get done and you have to meet their expectations. We need them to shift from room to room or to the outside enclosure and they have the choice to decide not to do that. Apes know that we have a time schedule. They don't. And, if you let on at all that you're looking at your watch, they pick up on that. Or urine gathering. Like today, Siabu decided to withhold her urine because she knew it was very important to get it today. And so she withheld until two forty-five. I think she picked up from the very beginning of my day that I was in a hurry because I was expecting company. And you came, and now was another excuse that she could show that she could do that."

"You were trying to force her to fit your schedule?"

"I guess you could say that. I asked her twice in a row and that instantly told her that I was hurrying."

"Have you seen them laugh?"

"Yes," said Driver-Ruiz. "It's mostly Sara that I've seen laugh. I remember Aazk laughing. Siabu jumped on her belly and Aazk just lay there laughing and laughing. But Sara will just get silly on her own. She starts clapping and hangs her mouth open with her tongue down."

"You can tickle Sara, too," said Myers. "You can get a stick and tickle her. That was way beneath the dignity of Aazk. If you tried to tickle her, she would sit there and let you tickle her, but for a short time, and she'd walk away abruptly, like you had really insulted her. Yet, for a split second, you could tell that she liked it. I think she felt that she owned the situation by her stopping it and her walking away with disdain."

"Once," said Driver-Ruiz, "I remember when I was doing a tickle session on Aazk and she was giving me that you-had-better-stop look and I looked at her belly button and I touched it with the stick. She walked away from me and would not look at me for the rest of the day. I think I offended her that she was telling me to stop by the look she'd been giving me. I just pushed my luck too far and so she wanted me to know that."

The people who see past the shaggy red fur and past the apparent detachment of the creature see intelligence in the eyes of an orangutan. It's clear that orangutans can read the intentions of others by their behavior and their eyes and can use their own eyes to send messages. Bruce Campbell has seen that.

"You could not put on a mask," he said. "Aazk knew. She could see through any of the façades you put in front of you. It's a wonderful experience to realize that there are these beings out there that are so closely matched to us in DNA, and sometimes I think in their own way they may be smarter than we are. Yeah, they cannot do quantum physics, so what? They're very, very special beings. Somebody that can turn a truck tire inside out. I can't even bend the sidewall on a tire like that and they can bend anything like it's a rag doll."

"Did you talk to her?"

"Oh, yeah. I'd say, 'Hi.' I talk to the orangutans just like they're another human being. I think they fully knew a lot more about what was going on than most people would think. I'd say, 'Zakkie, how's it going today?' You're just a fine-looking orangutan.' She would come over to the wire and sit there as close as she could get to you so that she could be as personable with you as she could be. She would stare at you. Sometimes she would look away, but a surprising amount of eye contact. They would do a lot of staring at us. That's the superior being in them looking at the inferior human on the outside of the wire. All of the face around the eyes would change. The wrinkles would change a little bit. A furrowing of the brow. They've got lots of muscles in their head and face to give different expressions."

The more time the human beings spent with Aazk, the more they began to see subtleties in the way she expressed herself. Driver-Ruiz described a gesture of Aazk's where she put a fist with a thumb next to her eye. "It was like her trademark position when she was thinking. When you were asking her to do something and you'd look at her, she'd get in that pose. She was very expressive, especially with her eyes. She had these long slow eyeblinks that she would do when we would ask her to do something that really didn't interest her. I learned that the sideways glance that she had shown me years earlier was her way of saying, 'I'm interested in what you are doing, but not enough that I want you to *really* know that I'm watching.'"

"Did she have any other gestures?"

"When she got tired of what you were doing," said Myers, "she'd make a sound," and Myers mimicked a short spit of breath and a turning-away action. "It was a bugger-off gesture. 'You're annoying me. Buzz off.'"

"Sometimes she'd do her little shrug," Driver-Ruiz added.

"She did it when she was silly," said Myers.

"Yeah, silly," said Driver-Ruiz, "and she did it when she wouldn't do quite what you were asking but she didn't want to completely turn away from you. She'd just do this little bouncy shrug."

"Which was not the same," said Myers, "as her shrug when she would get mad at you. That was a different shrug."

"She wouldn't hesitate," Trish Campbell added, "if she was disgusted with you, to turn her back and walk away, because she knew you could not resist coming back."

"She was also very particular about the hair on her head," said Driver-Ruiz. "If I ever messed it up—and I loved doing it to her because I think she liked it when I did it—but she liked acting like it bothered her. I would mess up her hair with a brush and then she would take so long smoothing her hair down and looking at me like how could you touch the hair?"

"She liked her forehead touched," said Myers.

"She liked the tops of her fingers touched," said Trish Campbell. "But you had to be careful. If she was crabby and you touched the tops of her fingers, you had better be able to read that, because she gave you a quick grab."

"Yeah," said Myers, "Trish brought in a vegetable brush and started brushing her through the mesh and she always liked that."

"She loved having her lips touched and caressed, the bottom lip," said Campbell. "'Make hose mouth' is what I called it. The water had to be not too hard and not too soft, so you got to know exactly how she wanted it. That's another example of showing respect. You'd do it the way she wanted you to do it."

Trish Campbell met Aazk in the late 1990s in the infamous "old grotto exhibit." Campbell had a warm, playful attitude to which the orangutan responded, although Aazk also tried to keep her dignity intact at the same time. After all, she wasn't a young orangutan anymore. She had an image to maintain. And yet this human being was quick to learn her preferences. "The first time I spent with her was back in the bedroom area of the concrete grotto. It was a very closed, very old, very unstimulating environment."

"Were you frightened?"

"No," she said. "You know how sometimes when you meet someone you know your spirits connect right away? I felt that way with her right away."

"What sort of things didn't please her?"

"If you didn't respect her. If you didn't remember that she was the matriarch."

"When did that happen?"

"If I gave a drink of tea to someone else before I gave it to her and then also didn't give her the last drink of tea. I make tea for them. It's always decaffeinated, because the veterinarian doesn't want them to have any caffeine. Mango tea, orange, lemon, you name it, and I also add other flavors to it like cinnamon or ginger. I also make Jell-O for Aazk and I would put lots of interesting things in it. She does not like nuts in her Jell-O. We made jokes about how I put string beans in the Jell-O. I put anything in their Jell-O I could think of, but when I put nuts in their Jell-O, she gave me a very disdainful look and she would carefully separate the nuts out and drop them on the ground. That was not acceptable. She liked kidney beans, rice, sweet pickle juice, pickles. Bruce says he won't eat Jell-O from our refrigerator because he has no idea what's in it. I just used my imagination because I wanted her to have in her Jell-O what she didn't expect."

"Did she like surprises?"

"It depended on the surprise. We didn't surprise her very much. She knew us better than we knew her."

"One of the things," said Driver-Ruiz, "that would really tick her off is we would walk into the building first in the morning and say 'good morning' to anyone other than her first."

"She watched," said Myers, "when I enriched her room. The boughs, the paper, the scents, whatever I would put in her room, a container of tea, maybe a bucket of water."

"Was she comparing what the others got?"

"I'm sure she was. If you bring branches in to another room, you give some to her. It wasn't any of those things so much as you get down on one knee and talk to her. That's what mattered to her was paying attention to her. I never faked anything in front of her because she would see right through me and I wanted nothing more than to keep that connection with her. She was one of the best friends I have ever had. And I think she knew that."

"What kind of faking did she understand?"

"I didn't do it, but if I went in and said, 'Hi, how are you today?' and used a tone of voice that wasn't sincere."

"I think Trish is really different than Nannette and I," said Myers, "because Trish is very silly with the apes. She tends to really let down her guard with the apes. I remember Trish dancing in the hallway in front of Aazk with a stuffed orangutan that she had just put nipples on so that we could use it for teaching a baby to drink. So Trish is doing the waltz down the hallway with the stuffed orangutan and I remember Aazk turning her back on Trish. If she were a human, she'd be sitting there shaking her head wondering what this crazy woman was doing. But, after she turned her back, you would catch her out of the corner of her eye watching Trish go up and down the aisle. If you made eye contact with her, she'd quickly look away and shrug her shoulders."

"She knew she had a child in her," said Trish Campbell. "She never got to let that child out of her. She lived for thirty years in a concrete grotto, but once she moved to the new enclosure, a whole new side of her developed. That child got to come out. The day that the Sunda Forest opened, she marched"—her voice was starting to waver with emotion now and the group was listening intently—"across the grass like she owned the place. I was sitting next to the tower so she could come and sit next to me if she wanted. She marched across the grass. And she got into the pool and she scooped up drinks of water and she drank drinks of water out of her hand and she was perfect that day. She never subsequently put a toe in the pool that I know of. She never drank out of her hand in the pool. As a matter of fact, she didn't want to go out in the enclosure for quite a while after that. But that day she was a shining star. I think she realized from us how important it was. She was touching grass for the first time."

"You have a sense of humor," I said to Trish Campbell. "Do you think the orangutans respond to that?"

"I think they're a little more sophisticated than I am, although, yes, they respond, because I sing and dance and play while I'm in the building with them."

"How does Sara respond?"

"She pounds her chest against the wire and she jerks her head up and down and she hangs her tongue out of her mouth and she's very focused on whatever silliness is happening."

"That's showing delight."

"Oh, yes, and participation. This is her way to be part of it, part of the dance. One of the things Aazk loved to do—because she saw us cleaning so much with our buckets—if we gave her a bucket and a brush, she would clean inside her enclosure while we were cleaning on the outside."

The day that the orangutan was moved out of the old concrete bunker to a new enclosure was an important moment. It was moving from the known to the unknown and it could be intimidating. Over the years a cage can come to represent a measure of security and comfort, like the cell to which a prisoner becomes accustomed. There are mental adjustments to make. "When we moved into the Sunda Forest enclosure," said Driver-Ruiz, "we were really nervous about how Aazk was going to feel, because all she'd known was such a tiny space, and so that first night that she spent there, Lyn and I spent the night with her in the building. We slept in the building in a bedroom across the hall from her. She could see us the whole time. We did that because we needed her to know that we were there for her. We didn't want her to be alone and scared."

"Did she acknowledge that you were there?"

"She slept right next to the wire, as close as she could to the wire."

"Every time that I would look at her," said Myers, "she was looking at us. When she was in the enclosure, she couldn't climb. She didn't know how to climb, because her muscles had atrophied and she wanted to do it badly"—her voice was breaking with emotion while she said this—"and she would climb up a little way"—and now the tears that had been building started to flow with nothing to stop them—"because after thirty-one years of living in concrete without trees her muscles had atrophied and she couldn't climb in the beautiful new enclosure. She did not get much exercise in her old enclosure and lacked climbing experience, but that did not stop her. She gallantly reached for one of the vines hanging low and pulled herself up. Hanging on for dear life she swung, six inches off the ground, looking over her shoulder to make sure we saw this accomplishment. She always looked at us to make sure we were watching."

"Why is this so emotional?"

"I think it was because it was such a shame that she was in such a horrible enclosure for so long. It was like an injustice that was done to her. I came at a perfect time to meet her because, if I had to be with Aazk in the enclosure where she was for any long amount of time, it would have killed me inside. It was really an injustice to any ape. So, I came at a really nice time, because I got to be with her for the move. She hadn't been moved in thirty years. And to bring her to this brand-new enclosure and help her make that transition and then to see her actually touch grass for the first time, was wonderful."

The orangutan had a reputation in the zoo for being a very obstinate, stubborn, and even nasty ape who threw up on people. "No one had the confidence in her, other than the people she worked with, that she would make the transition well. They all put their hopes on Busar. And Busar, when we moved him, actually shut down. Most male apes do. He sat with a paper bag over his head for two weeks and refused to do anything. He didn't move. He didn't like change. With the public opening coming up, we were saying, 'Aazk will do it.' We knew she could do it. We moved Busar the day after her. We would pass spoons of yogurt tied to a piece of bamboo underneath the paper bag and his lips would take it. So he was getting some nourishment."

"Twenty-four hours a day he had the bag over his head? Slept with the bag?"

"Yep." When Busar had moved to the Fresno zoo he had also kept his head in a paper bag, too.

"He sat on top of his tree and wouldn't come in," said Myers.

Then three years later Aazk was dead at thirty-four. Orangutans can live longer than that, even in a zoo. An orangutan named Mawas from the zoo in Perth, Australia, lived to be fifty-six. Biruté Galdikas suspects that some orangutans live in the forest as long as eighty years. In spite of her captivity, Aazk should still have had more years. She had earned it. But she had ovarian cancer and kidney disease.

"What happened?"

"It was a gradual change in her," said Myers. "She was less interested in doing things. Staying in the enclosure. Less active. Her taste in food started changing rapidly. Things that she had loved forever, suddenly she no longer liked them. There was something, that, for her, was abnormal. It was just really subtle."

"I think," said Driver-Ruiz, "it actually started in November, the year before she died. Just her mood being a little off."

"That's right," said Myers, "because we started asking questions about menopause. We starting saying could something hormonal be changing with her. We often thought she had a headache. She'd hold her head. But we weren't really sure. We'd give her ibuprofen and it seemed to make her feel better for that short period."

"In January," said Driver-Ruiz, "it started getting worse. Remember we had that bad fire and we thought that was affecting her? She started coughing just a little bit. Congested."

"We all were," said Myers, "because we had a bad dump fire really close to the zoo. The air was so awful for so long. It burned for a month."

"She died on the operating table," said Myers. It was the spring of the year, three years after Aazk had moved to the Sunda Forest enclosure.

"Her desire to go out to the exhibit was so little at the end," said Driver-Ruiz. "It was really hard to get her to want to go out. But we wanted her to have sunshine and be with the siamangs because she was very close to Bunyi, who was the youngest siamang, and her last day that she went out to the enclosure"—her voice was breaking with emotion and she said, "This is going to be hard to say—Bunyi ran across the exhibit to see her and pumped on her chest and embraced her"—and she couldn't stop the tears now so she just let them flow—"in the longest hug and then he stayed near her and then, after a little while, she didn't want to be out in the enclosure anymore and we brought her in. It was like a final good-bye."

"Did Bunyi know that something was happening?"

"I don't know. He just ran up to her with such enthusiasm. But I think the neat thing about her, too, was she had a reputation for being a loner, because she was alone for thirty years, an obstinate orangutan; and yet the changes that we saw in her when we moved her to this enclosure were just extraordinary because she opened herself up to become the matriarch of this group. She and our siamang—who was a young boy at that time, a very naïve siamang—made contact with her, the first contact with her. I remember him sitting out in the grass and they would sit a couple of feet away from each other and Aazk would put her hand out, palm up, and the siamang would touch it really quickly and then pull away and she would never move her hand. She would just sit there. And the siamang, the young boy, would soon get the nerve up to touch her. She always was inviting to him to give him confidence that she was safe to be near. And just to see her start from hand touching and finger touching to, in the end, carrying him around walking upright on two feet with one hand bracing her and the other wrapped around this siamang while he had his little arms around her neck, was amazing, because everybody said she'd be a lousy mom because of her personality. And she was none of those.

"One sunny warmer day, she headed out toward the exhibit and sat quietly on the grass. Bunyi spotted her from across the exhibit and raced in her direction. At about fifteen feet from her, he dropped on the grass and somersaulted the rest of the way to her, then he reached up and put his face against hers in a long embrace. She developed more relationships. She was the boss over Sara. She tolerated Sara in the enclosure, but did not encourage interaction. Siabu, who is very pushy and somewhat naïve, was determined to interact with Aazk. She followed her endlessly until Aazk relented and let her approach without becoming aggressive. Less than a month after their introduction, they could be seen sitting on the ground, tickling each other with open mouth grins."

"And she never had any children of her own?"

"No."

Trish Campbell said that she and the others still see the differences in behavior at the zoo because of the influence of the intractable old female orangutan who had hidden her emotions and slugged her friend Busar to put him in his place. Campbell told a story about Lottie, a female siamang who had to be raised by humans when her mother was unable to raise her. As a result, when Lottie had her first baby, Bunyi, she didn't know how to raise him. The keepers had to care for Bunyi. When a second child was born, "Lottie didn't know what to do with the baby," said Campbell. "She set it down repeatedly, until the baby got too cold and we had to hold it so that it could survive. But Aazk had a lot of contact with Lottie's son Bunyi. They would hide under a sheet and play together. And this time Lottie has been the most wonderful mother. It feels like Aazk knew and Lottie got another chance. I think it was Lyn who first said this, 'It's just like Aazk was behind this somehow.' Her spirit was behind the fact that here was Lottie being a really good mother now. I know this probably sounds pretty crazy, but I believe it. I think it's something almost spiritual. I just see her hand in the things that happened. She is not gone spiritually. I believe this about her.

"May I say, as mystical as this is going to sound," Trish Campbell continued, "I saw her once after she died. Nannette was with me. We were in the building. Busar was outside. The two girls Siabu and Sara were in the bedrooms inside and, as I looked out through a door to the outside play yard, I saw what I knew was her—just her back; I didn't see her face. I saw her back walk by and I looked from there to see where Sara and Siabu were, because I thought it's got to have been Sara and Siabu, but Nannette saw that Sara and Siabu were somewhere else. And it was Aazk. Talk about wishful thinking. You can tell we had a really spiritual connection with her."

Myers said, "I remember seeing what Trish saw. Trish said, 'Who was that?' I said, 'Oh, it's Aazk,' and I remember looking at Trish. It took us a minute to register what I had just said. And I could swear that I've seen her a couple of times since. I've walked into the building when I know it's just Busar and yet I thought I saw her passing through one of the inside tunnels."

CHAPTER 12

Fare Thee Well, Orangutan

I WROTE THIS BOOK hoping that changes might come, and I saw during the years that it took to write the words changes in myself and the world around me. I returned from my first trip to the jungles of Borneo and Sumatra in August of 2001, flying halfway around the world to come home to the funeral of my father, standing in the sun at his grave in a loose and borrowed suit. His last years had been difficult. His mind grew dark and confused in the end. In my luggage I had a Dayak machete that Biruté Galdikas had given me. With my luggage was a six-foot-long Dayak blowgun tipped with a spear that she had also given me. I wondered if there was a hidden symbolism in giving a writer a machete and a blowgun. The customs officials considered these Dayak artifacts to be dangerous weapons, and it was a struggle to get them into the country. A few weeks after I brought these old death-dealers home, terrorists struck the World Trade Center in New York City and life was different after that. There were other changes as well from that time, the succession of triumphs and tragedies in the world that make history lurch forward. New beginnings. New ends. New reference points.

For me, there were difficult personal changes as I wrote this book. Time stops for no one. By the time I finished this book I had divorced my wife of twenty-three years. It wasn't as though my marriage ended because I'd become obsessed with orangutans and the jungle. Nothing so dramatic. Another change is that my children grew up. But at least I got to take them with me and share some of my adventures with them, and that changed the experience for me. I wonder how much they will remember as they grow older. I'll say to my daughter, Caitlin, do you remember the advice that Barbara Harrisson gave you in the Netherlands about men? Harrisson said stay away from men who are without "hope." Or I'll say to my son, Pearce, do you remember the elephants charging us in the Kinabatangan? The twitchy little tails?

There were some difficult times in writing this book, too. Some people broke their promises or did nasty things or the circumstances just took the joy and optimism out of my life for a while. I learned from those moments more about human nature than I thought I would. I learned, too, that I couldn't write then. I was a journalist before I was a university teacher, and as a journalist you learn to write no matter what the conditions. But I needed a sense of buoyancy to write this book the way that it deserved to be written. If I didn't have that, the words just came out dull and lifeless and I felt defeated. One thing I learned again in writing this book is how much depends on the hope and support that the right people give you at the right moment.

And two other things supported me, as well—the jungle and its creatures. Isn't that interesting? The jungle gave me a quiet, safe place to think outside the familiar things that affect our thoughts. There were times when I could return to that memory of the jungle and take strength from it. And most of all, orangutans gave me an idea of something good in life worth saving. How many times in your life do you have a thought as pure as that? That this is good and that this ought to be saved? But against all the changes in the world and all the changes in my life, the situation with orangutans is basically the same, maybe even worse. I am sorry to have to say that, orangutans.

Here's another thought I have about my friends, the orangutans. Even after the little time that I spent with them, I wouldn't consider eating one. It wouldn't feel right. What a person eats in part defines who that person is, and eating an orangutan would not be a good way to define us. The Dayaks once ate orangutan meat and, some people say, occasionally still do. The Dutch scientist Herman Rijksen cites reports that orangutans are still eaten "irrespective of traditional background" and that their meat is available outside Borneo and Sumatra. A guide and translator I used in the jungles of south Kalimantan told me that a Dayak from the village of Lubuk Hijau said that he had eaten orangutan meat. The orangutan meat was dried and made into a meal called *gegarai* with bamboo shoots. The Dayaks say that gegarai is "delicious." A Dayak told one scientist that he'd been threatened by a group of Dayaks who were roasting an orangutan "on a spit like fish." They said they'd roast the man too if he didn't eat the meat with them. And on it goes. The question is, is eating an orangutan in some way cannibalistic? The answer would indicate how close you see an orangutan to a human being.

In one of my conversations with the scientist Carel van Schaik I raised the issue. "In large parts of Borneo," van Schaik said, "there's still a culture where it's traditional to eat orangutans. It's not straightforward because, within the Iban there are particular groups that say, 'We cannot eat orangutans. It's taboo.' Whereas everybody else does. But, by and large, the Dayaks as a group have a history of eating orangutans. The Melayu, the people living nearer to the coast, tend not to. It goes along with religious differences and major cultural differences."

"Have you ever been offered it?" I asked.

"No," van Schaik said with a laugh, "so I never had the opportunity."

"What would happen if you were?"

"I don't know. It's like asking what would you have done if Hitler had invaded your country. Would you have fought? Would you have stood up? I certainly wouldn't eat it, that's for sure, but I tend to be a cultural relativist," he said.

"Why not?" I said, prodding him, playing the devil's advocate. "Isn't it just an animal?"

"No," he said with a trace of annoyance. "It's an orangutan and, after you've studied them for a while, it's like eating family."

There are some precedents in eating family, I thought.

"But," he said unprompted, "I'm not sure I would denounce in the strongest of terms what these people are doing. Of course, we should face the fact that, if everybody decided it's okay to eat orangutans, they're going to be extinct very quickly. I mean, it's not like pigs that—"

"Which are a highly intelligent animal," I insisted, "and pets for some people—"

"Absolutely," he interjected.

"In parts of the Caribbean—"

"Wonderful. I know."

"As much as a dog."

"Pigs are relatively intelligent," he said. "They're not super intelligent like a great ape, but, yeah. I try to stay away from these kinds of arguments, because the alternative is that you can only eat sunflowers and maybe not even those. Is it okay to eat fish?" he said. "Yep? Then is it okay to eat reptiles? Probably. So where do you draw the line? Most people draw the line somewhere between pigs and orangutans. But most people, in the West at least, if offered orangutan meat, would refuse to eat it. Just like most people on the farm wouldn't want to eat the meat of a pet they raised."

"Well, actually they do," I said. "Farm kids have no compunction about that."

"Maybe they develop a hard skin after a while."

"I've talked to natives in Canada about eating wild meat like muskrat and they talk about reverence for the animal. They say they have reverence for the animal and still eat it."

"Sure."

"In fact, they say that is part of the reverence, eating the animal."

"But, like a moral attitude, it's something that needs to be learned, because of the natural human tendency to bond, especially with animals that give you something back, like a dog or a cat or even a rabbit."

"Which are eaten."

"Right. And the areas where people eat orangutans, they also tend to eat dogs. Those are issues I normally don't address."

"So a nice fat orangutan steak doesn't appeal to you?"

"No, but that's probably because I tend not to eat red meat anyways."

I thought he had said "I tend not to eat rat meat." When I told him he laughed. "I don't eat rat meat, either," he said.

"When you talk about a creature," I said, "that has culture and intelligence and emotion, somewhere on the continuity with human beings but not—"

"Identical," he said.

"How far do you have to go before you give them rights?" I said.

"Maybe you should define what you mean by animal rights first."

"There are different layers of rights. There is a difference between a chicken and an orangutan that orangutans have a right not to be slaughtered. They have a right to existence—"

"Yes, but the problem I have is that I don't have an argument except from some gut feeling as to why the individual orangutan has that right to existence and the individual chicken does not. To me, that's arbitrary. That's literally a matter of taste."

"But some societies believe in cannibalism," I said.

"Exactly."

"That cannibalism is morally right."

"Right. Or that it's morally okay to stone a woman to death after she has committed adultery."

"But," I said, "I'm not sure I have an argument to prove that cannibalism is wrong—"

"Exactly."

"But the fact that I don't have an argument shouldn't stop us from saying cannibalism is wrong."

"Right. But then you are totally aware of the arbitrary nature of your decision and, if somebody else says, 'I don't buy this,' then you don't have any logical ways of convincing him."

"Maybe sometimes we need to make arbitrary decisions."

"Absolutely. And that could be based on all kinds of stuff. For instance, having read a book like yours on orangutans and saying, 'God, these animals deserve special treatment.' But, there's no compelling moral, no compelling theological, no compelling scientific argument. For me, of course, I wouldn't think of killing an orangutan unless to help it out of its misery, so, in many respects I suspect I will treat orangutans very much like humans."

"Which is a moral decision."

"Of course."

"You decide to put it out of its misery. You could say, 'No, I think nature has to take its course and the creature has to suffer.'"

"In the wild I generally take that view. I let an orangutan die. What could I have done? I wasn't sure it was going to die anyways, although I was pretty sure. But, that's when you say, 'I am an outsider; I am observing a system; I don't want to meddle with the system.'"

"This is part of the science culture, this feeling, metaphysically, that you're apart from it—"

"Yeah," he said, but drawing the word out reluctantly like he was stretching an elastic substance. "That you're separate," I continued, "that you're an observer, that you need to preserve your status as an observer—"

"Yeah," he said.

"And not a meddler."

"Right. I guess most scientists would agree with that."

"But," I said, "we started with a question that had to do with rights."

"Yes."

"And the basic one is a right to existence."

"Okay."

"That an orangutan has a right to existence that a chicken doesn't."

"I wouldn't say that. I think every creature has a right to existence, but the question is, at what price, compared to our needs, where do you then draw the line?"

"Well, if we need to eat orangutan meat, should we?"

He paused and thought and gave a halfhearted "yeah" of consideration, leaning back in the chair in his long narrow office at Duke University in North Carolina. I could hear a thunderstorm rumbling outside. "I'm uncomfortable with that. I don't know why. I have very little qualms about eating a chicken and I have great qualms about eating an orangutan. If I ask myself why that is, it's emotional. It has something to do with 'but, yes, that's a creature almost like us.' I can relate to the orangutan. The orangutan must feel pain. It's that I can't relate to a chicken as much. I don't believe in moral absolutes. Everybody will have to draw the line themselves and they will draw them in different places. There's just no rationality to these things."

The people who understand the threat to the existence of orangutans have different opinions what the extinction of the orangutan would mean. Some think it will mean complete extinction with a few survivors in zoos. Others think it will mean fragments of small groups of orangutans scattered in rain forest ghettos. One of the optimists, Gary Shapiro, explained how real he thought the possibility of extinction is.

"It is not an incredible scenario to see a majority of the populations driven to extinction within fifteen to twenty years. It's like the fireflies. You're going to find flash, flash, flash of each one as it blinks out from existence. You're going to find individuals straggling, but you're not going to find that healthy unit of reproduction. Most people don't want to go that far in their understanding. Is it going to go to extinction or not? They want a simple yes or no. With the exception of those areas like Tanjung Puting where they're going to be protected, you're going to find most of the animals becoming extinct in their natural range. On the island of Borneo, you're going to find isolated populations. And the animals in between are going to be gone."

"Let's imagine a scenario where orangutans are extinct," I said, playing the devil's advocate again. "What happens then? Who cares?"

"Yes, a rain forest without orangutans will still continue on," Shapiro said, and talked about losing some major species of trees that depend on orangutans for the distribution of seeds.

"If they go extinct, the rain forest loses some species of trees, so what?" I repeated. "Why can't we live without orangutans?"

"The orangutan is our closest primate relative and, to allow it to go extinct, would be, I think, on the same level as genocide. There are so few great apes in terms of species and there's only one Asian great ape. For Southeast Asia to lose the orangutan would be a tremendous loss. The genetics, the culture, the personal experiences, personal relationships, all that would be gone. I don't think we can just merely say, 'Well, it's just another of the thousands of species in the forest that if we lose it, so what?'"

"Isn't extinction a natural process?" I persisted.

"It is and one might say, 'Just let it go. Don't worry about it.' But I think for those of us who have studied the orangutans and gotten close to them, we see them almost as family. Anybody who has worked closely with them and has interacted with them comes to understand that the connection with human beings is very real. Raising Princess, for example, and treating her like my adopted daughter. Perhaps these are things that I create in my own mind, but, when you hold an animal like that, who is as intelligent as a young child and who demonstrates her cognitive abilities, you can't help feel that there's something close to humanness there. We know they're not humans, but, in the way they express themselves, in using tools, in solving problems, even in some of the aspects of the earliest linguistic abilities, we feel that connection to family and, for me, I would hate to see that gone. I would hate to see a species with an individual like Princess who I've gotten to know, wind up in the history books. It would be part of my life that would be gone, too. Another universe would blink out of existence."

I had similar discussions with the others about the prospects of extinction for orangutans. Rod Brindamour took a strongly radical position and said that he thought that it's better to let them die in the jungle than live in zoos, and the orangutan zookeeper Leif Cocks startled me with a similar position by saying, "Essentially I believe that keeping orangutans in captivity is an abuse of their rights." Cocks has since become a curator of a zoo in Australia and president of the Australian Orangutan Project, a nonprofit volunteer organization both raising money for orangutan conservation and doing it. He says it is a "myth that zoos can be arks to save orangutans." Unless there is an immediate effort to save the rain forest of the orangutans, he says that their numbers can't be sustained and will plummet.

Brindamour talked about the moral implications of saving orangutans. "I think as a species our survival is not ensured unless we can make sacrifices that allow for another species to survive. In Indonesia it is extremely bad luck to have no rice left in the house. If you take the last grain of rice, that is an extremely bad thing to do. And I think that's the essence of what we're talking about."

"The orangutan is the last grain of rice," I said.

"Yes. If we cannot manage ourselves to accommodate the orangutan, then we are on the verge of starvation."

"What does that last grain of rice mean to the Indonesians?" I said. "What is it that bothers them that somebody would take the last grain of rice? We'd say, 'Tomorrow we'll put more rice in the jar.'"

"To Indonesians it is saying you have not managed yourself. You are in peril. You have allowed yourself to come to the edge of peril. And that is a very disturbing admission. I don't think we have quite the same concept."

"We have overdraft insurance at the bank," I said.

"We do."

"We're putting things on credit." I said.

"You can go into debt and you're fine."

"We feel we can let ourselves go into debt on the environment and still be okay." The talk about the meaning of the last grain of rice reminded me of seeing the spirit jar in a Dayak house in the village of Pasir Panjang. The spirit jar is also the household rice container, but the last grain of rice is a moral and spiritual principle, too. It isn't just a commodity that is bought and sold. There are rituals in the household that must be observed for the care of the rice jar, because of a light that radiates from it to help the family understand the future, to guide them to what is right and avoid what is wrong. The Indonesian word for rice, *padi,* from which we get our phrase "rice paddy," also means small and is used in the phrase *ilmu padi* to mean "the humility of wisdom." The spirit jar radiates light at times, brings good luck to the house and makes predictions. If it is empty, it can't do that. The orangutan is becoming the last grain of rice in our spirit jar.

I sometimes wonder what it would be like to say good-bye to the last orangutan. I probably won't live long enough to see that happen, but I wonder what I would say. "Thanks, orangutan, for all the good times. Sorry to see you go. Maybe we will meet in the next life."

It's difficult to imagine that moment. And yet the changes to the natural world are happening quickly, and orangutans are vanishing like the ice melting at the poles. It is inevitable that the human population will grow larger and, as it grows larger, consume more and more of what is left. That makes it inevitable that the patches of rain forest necessary for the survival of the orangutan will grow smaller and smaller. That's not good for orangutans.

When you say good-bye, you think of the sweet moments. I remember a sweet moment with young orangutans in quarantine cages at the Wanariset station in Samboja, in Kalimantan. It is one of those moments that makes you feel alive and part of the world. I remember how the eyes watched us. I remember how the small leathery hands reached out to us—it was as though the hands became longer and longer as they reached out. The orangutans wanted to touch us. They felt the need to touch us. I wondered what urge in them needed to be satisfied that way. What were they thinking?

We have a sense of why they reach out. They are like us, and we know why we would do it. We also know that these minds think and feel in ways we don't. And that kind of undefined territory between us and them would be wonderful to explore. That's what you do in a relationship, explore the known and the unknown. Never to know that, never to reach out to touch them, would be to lose something in our lives. There's so much more to learn about orangutans. So much more to feel and think. Moments to seize just because they are moments. And yet so little time. I hope our minds don't grow too dark and confused in the end to do what is right.

References

Note on quotations: Quotations in this book that do not have a citation in the references come from either conversations with the author that he recorded and transcribed to get the exact wording or from e-mails to him.

3 Gary Shapiro says, "Siswi is the only orangutan I ever named at Camp Leakey. I was there the day she was born. I held her placenta in my hands and rushed it to the camp freezer for safe keeping. I have photos of it somewhere in my collection. Biruté Galdikas and Rod Brindamour were not in camp when Siswi was born on September 9, 1978, so as camp manager I made the choice of giving the newborn a name (most staff would defer to Biruté). I got Siswi's name from her mother, Siswoyo. Putting the diminutive "wi" after her mom's nickname of Sis, created Siswi. Basically Little Sis."

8 Frans de Waal, *Bonobo: The Forgotten Ape* (University of California Press, 1998), p. 4.
   ———, *Our Inner Ape: A Leading Primatologist Explains Why We Are Who We Are* (Riverhead Books, 2005), p. 32.

9 Gisela Kaplan and Leslie J. Rogers, *The Orangutans* (Perseus Publishing, 2000), p. 51.

18 See ibid., p. 30.

25   Ibid., p. 4.

Sixty thousand is a common average figure given for the estimated number of orangutans surviving in the wild. Serge Wich of
the Iowa Great Ape Trust led a group that issued a report in 2008
citing the 2004 estimated total of 60,600 orangutans in Borneo
and Sumatra and warning that there had been loss of rain forest
habitat in that period. The report said that seventy-five percent of
orangutans are vulnerable because they live outside protected park
land. The report was published in *Oryx—The International Journal of Conservation*. The 2007 UNEP report *The Last Stand of the
Orangutan* cites estimates of between 52,300 and 76,300 surviving orangutans, with between 45,000 and 69,000 in Borneo and
7,300 in Sumatra. Christian Nellemann, editor in chief. *The 2004
Orangutan Population Habitat Viability Assessment* has a partial
chart of orangutan populations that totals 44,000.

According to the *Habitat Viability Assessment*, "Serious down-
ward trends in the integrity of Indonesia's forest estate occurred
throughout the 1990s due to widespread logging and conversion for plantation agriculture. Some protected areas were, in
retrospect, left relatively unscathed, while others suffered from
devastating fires that resulted from unwise land use practices.
Since the change in government in 1998, however, conservation
in Indonesia has seen a virtual collapse, and deforestation has
been enormous regardless of the legal status of the land (Holmes
2000; Jepson et al. 2001; Robertson and van Schaik 2001). As
a result, wild orangutans are in steady decline due to logging,
habitat conversion, fires and poaching."

The same edition of the *Habitat Viability Assessment* says, "Sensitivity testing of the baseline model suggests that in the absence of
logging or hunting, only populations of 250 or more orangutans
show long-term viability. Logging decreases viability, and high

271

annual logging rates of 10–20 percent quickly drive even large populations to extinction."

25 Herman Rijksen and Erik Meijaard, *Our Vanishing Relative: The Status of Wild Orang-Utangs at the Close of the Twentieth Century* (Kluwer Academic Publishers, 1999), p. 19.

32 *The 2004 Orangutan Population Habitat Viability Assessment*, p. 116 (*2004 OPHVA*, hereafter).
Ibid., p. 18.
Ibid., p. 119. See also map, p. 157.

40 Rijksen and Meijaard, p. 117.
Ibid., pp. 118–19.

49 John MacKinnon, *In Search of the Red Ape* (Holt, Rinehart and Winston), p. 43.
Ibid., p. 52.
Ibid., p. 81.

51 In the same spirit of denial, Galdikas would tell those coming after her that it was impossible to follow the male orangutan. See Biruté Galdikas, *Reflections of Eden* (Back Bay Books, 1995), p. 355.
Anne Russon, *Reaching into Thought: The Minds of the Greats Apes* (Cambridge University Press), p. 31.
MacKinnon, p. 56.
Ibid., p. 134.

53 William Faulkner, *Go Down, Moses* (Vintage, reprint 1990), p. 199.
MacKinnon, p. 19.

54 *2004 OPHVA*, pp. 118–99.
MacKinnon, p. 19.
Ibid.

55 Ibid., p. 25.
Ibid., p. 26.

56 Ibid., pp. 42–43.

Ibid., p. 50.

Ibid., p. 50.

The connection to Digit is made by the author, not MacKinnon.

MacKinnon, pp. 51–52.

57　Ibid., p. 54.

Ibid., p. 53.

Ibid., p. 58.

Ibid., p. 70.

58　Galdikas, p. 184.

MacKinnon, p. 71.

59　Ibid., p. 148.

Ibid., p. 172.

Ibid., p. 209. Also, Kaplan and Rogers p. 15. Colin Groves pointed out to the author that there are no panthers in Sumatra. Kaplan and Rogers cite the Sumatran tiger. The panther reference came from MacKinnon.

Kaplan and Rogers, p. 15.

MacKinnon, p. 123.

Ibid., p. 197.

Ibid., p. 199.

60　Ibid., p. 198.

Ibid., p. 215.

65　Ibid., p. 64.

Ibid., p. 209.

Ibid., pp. 75–76.

Ibid., p. 75.

66　Ibid., p. 76.

70　Freifrau is a title of nobility. Willie Smits explained that the title is not quite the level of baroness. It means a free woman with special privileges, once granted by royalty.

74　Robert M. Yerkes, *Almost Human* (The Century Company, 1925), p. 55.

74 Barbara Harrisson, *Orang-Utan* (Collins, 1962), p. 29.

76 Ibid., p. 184.

Ibid., p. 122.

Ibid., p. 73.

Ibid., p. 105.

81 Jane Goodall, *Through a Window: My Thirty Years with the Chimpanzees of Gombe* (Mariner Books, 2000), p. 14.

Ibid., p. 17.

82 Ibid., p. 15.

Ibid., pp. 18–19.

83 Jane van Lawick-Goodall, *In the Shadow of Man* (Collins, 1971), pp. 240–41.

Dian Fossey, *Gorillas in the Mist* (Mariner Books, reprint 2000), p. xvi.

Ibid., p. 141.

84 Ibid., pp. 141–42.

Ibid., p. 110.

Galdikas, p. 9.

Ibid., p. 7.

85 Ibid., p. 202.

Ibid., p. 342.

Ibid., p. 16.

98 *2004 OPHVA*, p. 37.

Ibid., p. 11.

106 Kaplan and Rogers, p. 14.

113 Romans 12:1–2. This is an interpretation of that section of the Bible and not literally what it says. See also Romans 7:18 and John 17:15–16.

116 Anne Russon, in *Reaching into Thought*, p. 7.

117 Kaplan and Rogers, p. 54.

118 Julian Paul Keenan, a Harvard-trained neurologist and author of *The Face in the Mirror*, is an assistant professor in psychology

and the director of the Cognitive Neuroimaging Laboratory at Montclair State University and a researcher at the New York State Psychiatric Institute, Columbia University. He was previously on the faculty of Harvard Medical School.

Julian Keenan, in the *Globe and Mail*, December 9, 2004.

120 Anne Russon, *Orangutans: Wizards of the Rain Forest* (Key Porter Books, 1999), p. 76.

Kaplan and Rogers, p. 32 and p. 75.

121 Russon, in *Reaching into Thought*, pp. 164–65.

122 Russon and Galdikas, "Imitation in free-ranging rehabilitant orangutans," *Journal of Comparative Psychology* (June 1993), p. 16.

123 Russon, *Reaching into Thought*, pp. 164–65.

See also Kaplan and Rogers on bridge building, p. 73.

This was my experience and Biruté Galdikas interpreting the photo. Still, interpreting the difference between a smile, a grimace, baring of teeth, and laughter is difficult in a species like the orangutan. Cf. smiling in orangutans, Kaplan and Rogers, pp. 102–3.

124 Russon and Galdikas, p. 12.

Kaplan and Rogers, p. 73.

Russon, *Orangutans*, p. 85.

125 Russon, *Reaching into Thought*, p. 162. The study was conducted in June to August 1989 and 1990.

Ibid., p. 160.

126 Russon, *Orangutans*, p. 85.

Kaplan and Rogers, p. 89.

Russon, *Reaching into Thought*, p. 161; Russon and Galdikas, p. 2.

Ibid., p. 165.

126 Ibid., p. 165.

Ibid., p. 172.

128 Russon, *Orangutans*, p. 181. Kaplan and Rogers also describe an orangutan taking a bus, p. 33.

130 Russon, *Orangutans*, p. 106.

Ibid., p. 76.

131 Frans de Waal, *Primates and Philosophers: How Morality Evolved* (Princeton University Press, 2006), p. 27.

132 www.greatapeproject.org/en-US/oprojetogap/Historia

135 The known children of Princess are Prince (1987, deceased), Peta (1990), Pan (1995/96), Percy (2003), and Putri (2007).

143 Roger Fouts, *Next of Kin: My Conversations with Chimpanzees* (Bard, 1997), p. 4

Ibid., p. 101.

Kaplan and Rogers, p. 110.

Ibid., p. 112.

Gary Shapiro, PhD thesis.

Ibid.

144 Ibid.

Russon, *Orangutans*, p. 46. Kaplan and Rogers, however, say that Chantal could do 140 signs, p. 112.

Kaplan and Rogers, p. 112.

146 Shapiro.

Fouts notes that Washoe would use her eyebrows for expression, p. 68.

148 Ibid., p. 103.

Ibid., p. 81.

Ibid., p. 59.

Ibid., p. 81.

Ibid., p. 83.

149 Ibid., p. 84.

Ibid., p. 83.

150 See Kaplan and Rogers, p. 93.

Ibid., p. 94.

163 *Science* magazine, January 3, 2003.

166 Noam Chomsky, *Chomsky on Miseducation* (Rowman & Little-field Publishers, 2004), p. 16.

170 Kaplan and Rogers, p. 40.

174 Sy Montgomery talks of the impression of arrogance in Galdikas and the stories of her keeping others waiting. One time Galdikas kept a London *Times* reporter waiting four days for an interview in Pangkalan Bun. Montgomery also relates a story where an assistant said that Galdikas was angry with someone for keeping her waiting an hour. *Walking with the Great Apes: Jane Goodall, Dian Fossey, Biruté Galdikas* (A Peter Davison Book, 1991), p. 250.

182 William T. Hornaday, *The Experiences of a Hunter and Naturalist in the Malay Peninsula and Borneo* (1885, Oxford University Press reprint 1993), p. 179.

183 The author unconsciously repeated a line of William Blake, the subject of his unfinished PhD thesis on the poet.

187 The phrase "social instincts" is one Frans de Waal takes from Darwin as part of restoring the thought of Darwin about the development of morality in evolution. *Primates and Philosophers: How Morality Evolved* (Princeton University Press, 2006), p. 14. For the distinction between empathy and sympathy in human beings and apes and the moral implications of that, see de Waal, *Primates*, pp. xiii–xiv.

188 "Update on the orangutan situation at Wanariset and in Indonesia," Willie Smits, April 24, 1999, on the website of the Balikpapan Orangutan Survival Foundation on May 2002.

191 "Nyaru menteng general information," on the website of the Balikpapan Orangutan Survival Foundation, on May 8, 2002.

191 "Indonesian illegal wildlife trade threatens biodiversity," Green Nature, VOA News, Patricia Nunan, April 9, 2002, www.

greeennature.com. See also "Now an ordeal by fire," Yenni Kwok, Asiaweek, undated, www.asiaaweek.com.

191 "Orangutans edging closer to brink of extinction," Hillary Mayell, National Geographic News on the web, October 24, 2000.

192 "On Monday April 27," Willie Smits, dated April 1998, on the website of the Balikpapan Orangutan Survival Foundation, on May 2002.

193 Ibid.

194 Ibid.

195 Ibid.

"June update," Willie Smits, dated June 2000, on the website of the Balikpapan Orangutan Survival Foundation.

208 Galdikas, p. 111, p. 156.

209 Ibid., p. 33.

210 Ibid., p. 322.

217 Ibid.

218 *National Geographic*, October 1975, p. 470.

Ibid., p. 449.

Outside, May 1998.

219 Galdikas, p. 43.

220 *National Geographic*, October 1975, p. 455.

Carole Jahme, *Beauty and the Beasts* (Virago Press, 2000), p. 175.

221 *National Geographic*, June 1980, p. 830, p. 832.

222 Galdikas, p. 356.

Kaplan and Rogers, p. 143.

223 *National Geographic*, June 1980, p. 832.

Ibid., p. 845.

Galdikas, p. 147.

Ibid., p. 398.

Sy Montgomery says that Brindamour left Galdikas saying that she loved orangutans more than him. *Walking with the Great Apes*, p. 9.

224 Galdikas, p. 320.

225 Carole Jahme agrees. She thinks the incident with Sugito was felt by Galdikas as a greater betrayal than Brindamour's affair. See Jahme, *Beauty and the Beasts*, p. 175.

226 Galdikas, p. 310.
Ibid., p. 329.
Montgomery, p. 7.

229 Galdikas, p. 344.
Ibid., p. 344.

233 Ibid., p. 293.

234 Ibid., p. 43.
Ibid., p. 390.

255 Kaplan and Rogers, p. 139.

261 Rijksen and Meijaard, *Our Vanishing Relative*, p. 123.
Ibid., p. 124.
Rijksen (ibid.) thinks eating orangutans is cannibalistic.

For More Information

The Ethical Consumer as a Protector of Orangutans and the Rain Forest

Saving orangutans means primarily protecting the rain forest where they live and supporting that protection politically, legally, and morally. That has to be done largely by the Indonesians and the Malaysians within their own countries, because orangutans are only found in the wild in Borneo and Sumatra, which are mainly in the control of Indonesia. Outside Indonesia and Malaysia, saving the rain forest and orangutans depends on funding the organizations that are fighting for the rain forest and fighting for orangutans. It also means changing what we buy as consumers.

The rain forest in Borneo and Sumatra is being devastated mainly by the expansion of palm oil plantations and secondarily by the timbering and pulp and paper industries. Palm oil is used in products like chocolate, ice cream, margarine, toothpaste, soap, cereal, and cosmetics. It is also used as a cooking oil and as a biofuel with questionable value. Indonesia and Malaysia supply most of the world's palm oil, most of that being produced by Indonesia and most of it coming from Borneo, and the demand for palm oil is growing.

If you buy the products of companies using bad practices to produce palm oil, you are rewarding them for those bad practices and giving them an incentive to continue. Not all palm oil is a problem, though.

So, an ethical practice means being selective to encourage the ethical companies producing sustainable palm oil and to discourage the unethical companies. Some organizations are working toward sustainable certification for palm oil producers. One easy way to have an effect as an ethical consumer is to buy products with the certification label of the Rainforest Alliance (see www.rainforest-alliance.org) and of the Roundtable on Sustainable Palm Oil (RSPO) (see www.rspo.org).

Suggested Reading

De Waal, Frans. *Our Inner Ape: A Leading Primatologist Explains Why We Are Who We Are.* Riverhead Books, 2005.

———. *Primates and Philosophers: How Morality Evolved.* Princeton University Press, 2006.

Fouts, Roger. *Next of Kin: My Conversations with Chimpanzees.* Bard, 1997.

Galdikas, Biruté. *Reflections of Eden: My Years with the Orangutans of Borneo.* Back Bay Books, 1995.

Harrisson, Barbara. *Orang-Utan.* Collins, 1962.*

Hornaday, William T. *The Experiences of a Hunter and Naturalist in the Malay Peninsula and Borneo* (1885). Oxford University Press reprint, 1993.

Jahme, Carole. *Beauty and the Beasts.* Virago Press, 2000.

Kaplan, Gisela, and Leslie J. Rogers. *The Orangutans.* Perseus, 2000.*

*Out of print, but used copies can be tracked down on the Internet.

MacKinnon, John. *In Search of the Red Ape.* Holt, Rinehart and Winston, 1974.*

Masson, Jeffrey Moussaieff, and Susan McCarthy. *When Elephants Weep: The Emotional Lives of Animals.* Delta, 1995.

Montgomery, Sy. *Walking with the Great Apes: Jane Goodall, Dian Fossey, Biruté Galdikas.* A Peter Davison Book, 1991.

O'Hanlon, Redmond. *Into the Heart of Borneo.* Penguin, 1984.

Rijksen, Herman, and Erik Meijaard. *Our Vanishing Relative: The Status of Wild Orang-Utangs at the Close of the Twentieth Century.* Kluwer Academic Publishers, 1999.

Russon, Anne. *Orangutans: Wizards of the Rain Forest.* Key Porter Books, 1999.

Schuster, Gerd, Willie Smits, and Jay Ullal. *Thinkers of the Jungle: The Orangutan Report.* H.F Ullmann, 2008.

Van Schaik, Carel. *Among Orangutans: Red Apes and the Rise of Human Culture.* Harvard University Press, 2004.

Online

A New Leaf (the author's website)   www-a-new-leaf.com

The Australian Orangutan Project   www.orangutan.org.au

*Out of print, but used copies can be tracked down on the Internet.

The Borneo Orangutan Survival Foundation International
savetheorangutan.org

The Borneo Orangutan Survival Foundation U.K.
www.savetheorangutan.co.uk

The Great Ape Project   www.greatapeproject.org

The Leuser Foundation (Sumatra)   www.leuserfoundation.org

The Nature Conservancy in Indonesia
www.nature.org/wherewework/asiapacific/indonesia

Orang Utan Republik   www.orangutanrepublik.org/ourei

Orangutan Foundation International   www.orangutan.org

Orangutan Foundation U.K.   www.orangutan.org.uk

Orangutan Outreach   redapes.org/

The Rainforest Alliance   www.rainforest-alliance.org

Sumatran Orangutan Society   www.orangutans-sos.org

The UNEP Great Apes Survival Partnership (GRASP)
www.unep.org/grasp

The United Nations Environmental Program (UNEP)   www.unep.org

Acknowledgments

The book is finished now. Time for the credits to flash by. I am a writer and I rely on the generosity of people who open their hearts and minds to me so that I can write. I also rely on people who get me access and help me travel in a foreign country.

I wish to thank my friend Gary Shapiro and his partner, Inggriani, a caring couple. Gary read the manuscript of the book with the eye of a scientist and suggested changes. Gary, like many others, would write his own book on orangutans if he were not so busy with orangutans.

I want to thank Rosa Garriga for her support as a friend when I was cast adrift in Kalimantan, a stranger in a strange land, and likewise to Zainal Abidin Ja'afar, my lifeline in Sabah.

A special thanks to Willie Smits for challenging me so much. I should mention his own remarkable book *Thinkers of the Jungle*. It's amazing how Willie finds the time to do so much.

All the people interviewed for this book deserve special thanks for putting up with the author: Marc and Isabelle Ancrenaz, Rod Brindamour, Trish and Bruce Campbell, Leif Cocks, Nannette Driver-Ruiz, Roger Fouts, Biruté Galdikas, Benoit Goossens, Mike Griffiths, Barbara Harrisson, Leo Hulsker, Terri Hunnicutt, John MacKinnon, Ulrike Freifrau von Mengden, Lyn Myers, Lone Dröscher-Nielsen, Herman Rijksen, Yarrow Robertson, Anne Russon, Ian Singleton, Ton van Groningen, Tomin, Carel van Schaik, and Serge A. Wich. Also contributing were Raffaella Commitante, Greg Dehler, Carol Ritchie, Bill Sharp, Yvonne Wendelin, and Julian Paul Keenan.

I wish to thank the scientists and experts who took the time away from busy careers to read this book in manuscript before it was published and endorse it. Those are Leif Cocks, Gisela Kaplan, Bernard E. Rollin, Peter Fairley, Osha Gray Davidson, and Abby Ray. Also a huge thanks to Jeff Masson for his thoughtful foreword.

Also thanks to Major Jenderal TNI Hadi Waluyo, Letkol Kav. Sumedy, Direktur Jenderal Wahjudi Wardojo, Direktur Adi Susmianto, Hupudio Supardi, Aldrianto Priadjati, G. Simon Devung, Zahir Soedajat, Suhardini, Ana Pombo, Suherry, Silvia Muscardin, Selly Sita, Andriansyah Suhaery, Jeane Mandala, Mark Perry, Maria Terea Abello I Poveda, Susana Serrat, Ary Yasir Pilipus, Chandradewana Boer, Setiawati. Rujehan, the Royal Zoological Society of South Australia Inc., the Adelaide Zoological Gardens, the Fresno Chaffee Zoological Gardens, and the Jakarta Zoo.

Thanks to Mike Bruford of Wales and his son Rhys for being good traveling companions in the Kinabatangan and introducing me to the bat caves of Gomantong. Thanks to Ken MacDonald for bringing his French horn and playing it in the jungle. It was a delight to hear him play "Ride of the Valkyries" in the jungle. Thanks to my cheerful klotok captain, Nanang. I can't forget him sitting on the top of the deck of his boat, steering with his feet through an open hatch. Thanks to my other klotok captains, Mulyadi and Ahmad Sally Gunawan, Thanks to Pak Zaqui for getting me around Pangkalan Bun and upriver on the Sekonyer and to Yani, a tooth shaman and interpreter. Thanks to David Silverman of the United Kingdom, now a doctor of medicine.

My friend, colleague in the university, and fellow writer Gail

McKay helped buoy me up and encourage me along the way with her compassion and insight.

Then there is my book editor, Michaela Hamilton. Michaela has a sensitivity to animals and saw something in this book and this story that others didn't. She made publishing the book a reality. I can't say too much about what that means. There is always a chemistry between an editor and a writer, and when that chemistry is good the book shows the result, as this one did. Michaela encouraged me to take the risks to put heart into this book.

I want to thank my two children, Caitlin and Pearce, who bring so much joy into my life. Both of them added meaning to the experience of the book by traveling with me for portions of it. My son turned thirteen in a small village in the Kinabatangan. I can't forget him asking if I was getting him a birthday cake with icing in the jungle. It was also delightful to be able to share with my daughter my love of the city of Barcelona while traveling to Europe for some final interviews. While I was writing the book it helped to have them in my life to give a joyful spirit to the writing.

Finally, I want to thank my partner Wendy for her love and support. We all need that.

This book was made possible by the generosity of grants from the Canada Council, the scholarly activity fund of Thompson Rivers University, and the assisted leave and sabbatical funds of the university. That support was greatly appreciated and made the extensive travel for this book possible.

Index